DARE TO DREAM
SCARY FAST

THE ROAD TO KONA

WADE WILSON

Copyright © 2025 by Wade Wilson

All rights reserved.

No portion of this book may be reproduced in any form without written permission from the publisher or author, except as permitted by U.S. copyright law.

Bookcover designed by KJ Waters Consultancy (KJWConsultancy.com) and Jody Smyers Photography (jodysmyersphotography.com)

ISBN:
eBook: 979-8-9920522-1-3
Paperback: 979-8-9920522-0-6
Hardback: 979-8-9920522-2-0

This is for my wife, Debbie, and my three daughters, Ashley, Lia, and Amanda, the best support team any husband and father could ever have. You all made my dream possible.

Contents

Acknowledgements	IX
Foreword	XII
Part I Big Dreams Often Start Small	1
1. Chapter 1 Just an Ordinary Man with an Extraordinary Dream	2
2. Chapter 2 In the Early Years	6
3. Chapter 3 How It All Began	10
4. Chapter 4 Getting on with Life	13
5. Chapter 5 Introduction to Running	15
6. Chapter 6 My Introduction to the Sport of Triathlon	20
7. Chapter 7 Setting My Sights on Competing in a Triathlon	23

8. Chapter 8 28
   Entering My Very First Triathlon Event

9. Chapter 9 33
   Setting New Goals

10. Chapter 10 38
    Working on My Swimming Abilities

11. Chapter 11 43
    Improving My Cycling Skills

12. Chapter 12 45
    Training for My First Half Distance Triathlon

13. Chapter 13 49
    Pre race Activities

14. Chapter 14 57
    My First Half Distance Triathlon Race: Swimming Event

15. Chapter 15 60
    My First Half Distance Triathlon Race: Bike Event

16. Chapter 16 67
    My First Half Distance Triathlon Race: Run Event

17. Chapter 17 71
    My First Half Distance Triathlon Race: The Finish Line

18. Chapter 18 75
    New Goal of Racing in a Half Marathon

19. Chapter 19 77
    New Goals

20. Chapter 20 82
    Hiring a Coach

21. Chapter 21 86
    Training with a Purpose

22.	Chapter 22 A Summer of Training	100
23.	Chapter 23 The Work is Done: It is Time to Race	116
24.	Chapter 24 Race Day	124

Part II
Daring to Dream Anything is Possible — 141

25.	Chapter 25 Daring the Ultimate Dream: Year 2000	142
26.	Chapter 26 Daring the Ultimate Dream: Year 2000—Race Results	151
27.	Chapter 27 Daring the Ultimate Dream: Year 2001	156
28.	Chapter 28 Expanding My Knowledge	167
29.	Chapter 29 Daring the Ultimate Dream: Year 2002	171
30.	Chapter 30 Daring the Ultimate Dream: Planning for Year 2003	191
31.	Chapter 31 Year 2003: Training Memories	198
32.	Chapter 32 Pursuing My Dream : Year 2003—Racing	204
33.	Chapter 33 2004, The Final Push: Planning	215

34.	Chapter 34	220
	2004, The Final Push: IRONMAN® 70.3® Buffalo Springs Lake Triathlon	
35.	Chapter 35	222
	2004, The Final Push: IRONMAN® Canada	
36.	Chapter 36	236
	2004, Achieving the Impossible Dream—Traveling to Hawaii	
37.	Chapter 37	252
	Race Day	
References		268
ABOUT THE AUTHOR		269

ACKNOWLEDGEMENTS

Thanks to my amazing wife Debbie, for her endless love, support, and encouragement. She also tirelessly helped me with reviewing and editing this book. She was and still is the ultimate triathlon mate.

And to my daughter, Ashley Morgan, for her invaluable editing and critique of this book.

As well as to Coach Tim Key, for helping an entry-level triathlete achieve previously unimagined heights in the sport.

And to Mike and Marti Greer, well known for their tireless enthusiasm and promotion of the sport of triathlon. They have helped countless individuals in their quest to become triathletes. They are the epitome of what a friend is and does.

And also to my fellow triathletes, friends, and supporters, who provided an endless supply of friendship and encouragement.

Thanks to The IRONMAN Group for allowing the use of pictures containing their logo and other trademarks. "IRONMAN® and 70.3® and their respective logos, are registered trademarks of the World Triathlon Corporation in the United States and other countries."

Disclaimer: "This independent publication has not been authorized, endorsed, sponsored or licensed by, nor has content been reviewed or otherwise approved by, World Triathlon Corporation, d/b/a The IRONMAN Group`."

Lastly, thanks to my editor, Audrey Mackaman, and to KJ Waters, for her assistance with publishing and marketing.

"You do not have to be gifted or have talent far above that of the average individual to achieve extraordinary feats. What you must have is desire, a plan, motivation, grit, and undeterred tenacity and perseverance." – Wade Wilson

Foreword

Everyone has a dream they aspire to in their life. Depending on the loftiness of the dream, it may take years to achieve and untold hours of dedicated work and sacrifices. *Dare to Dream* was written to inspire those who are brave enough to pursue their dream so they may never wonder what might have been.

There are always multiple forks in the road in the pursuit of your dream. We must carefully plan for success, and even when the correct path is taken, there will be unforeseen bumps, pits, twists, and turns along the way. Flexibility and the ability to adapt to ever-changing conditions are traits I've found are incredibly important to succeed in your pursuit.

Life experiences may even point you towards a future dream of which you are not currently aware. This was true for me. Imagine that you are a severely pigeon-toed youngster tripping over your own two feet every time you run and yet you aspire to become an elite full distance triathlete. Life hands us all challenges we must learn to deal with and overcome. I was no different, as my first big dream was to become a pilot for the Air Force, only to have it dashed in the most unexpected way.

Some think once you reach a certain age pursuing big dreams is no longer a possibility, leaving you with regrets for never having tried. I am here to tell you that you are never too old to pursue that dream. My dream began to take shape in my late thirties and matured in my mid-forties.

The chase can take on a life of its own and envelop everyone around you. My wife and three daughters willingly became involved in the pursuit of my dream. We became a team of sorts, and they made all the difference in my success. No matter what your aspirations are, sacrifices of time, energy, and finances will be required during the journey. A word of caution, no dream is worthy enough to sacrifice your personal relationships with your spouse and family.

The journey of pursuing one's dream has side benefits, including adventures along the way. The unplanned and unexpected things that happen become happy memories to be enjoyed and revisited years afterwards. These can be as rewarding as the achievement of the dream itself. There will be a multitude of people you meet along the way. Some of them may even share your dream. Others will be great encouragers, and yet others will be threatened by your actions and become naysayers. The naysayers must be avoided and or ignored. Never, never let anyone negatively influence your thoughts on what you are or are not capable of.

At the outset, do not expect to know everything needed to achieve your dream. Learning along the way is as much a part of the journey as the actions required. As with the pursuit of any dream, mentors are an invaluable source of information and encouragement and are a must. Reading information written by those who have been there and done that is also necessary. There is no sense in reinventing the wheel. Expect that mistakes will be made during your journey. Failures are not indicators that you cannot achieve your dream; rather, regard them as learning experiences not to be repeated. Consider that it takes fire to make iron. The best laid plans and hard effort will not always provide the intended result. Though discouraging at times, I never let failures deter my focus on the dream. Sometimes just the smallest progress can encourage you to stay on the course.

Depending on the dream, pain and utter mental and physical exhaustion can be met along the way. In my case these were a given, something to be expected and managed based on long hours of preparation and racing experiences. Consider that after years of intense training and preparation, the achievement of your dream or goal will be determined in a single event. Many things can and do affect you during the event. Others you are competing against share your dream, but only a select few elite athletes will know the satisfaction of achieving their dream.

Mere seconds can mean success or failure. That is the world I lived in while pursuing my dream.

There are multiple references in this book to triathlon race events that are sponsored by the IRONMAN Group. The guidelines for external parties on referencing The IRONMAN Group's brands require each reference to be unabbreviated and displayed in uppercase letters. Each reference will appear as IRONMAN® and or IRONMAN® 70.3® and will state the event's name in its entirety. While this may appear repetitive it was unavoidable to fully comply with their guidelines.

PART I

BIG DREAMS OFTEN START SMALL

Chapter 1

Just an Ordinary Man with an Extraordinary Dream

I've been asked more times than I can count how my interest in the sport of triathlon began. That's a good question, considering my profession is a certified public accountant (CPA). You wouldn't expect CPAs to become world-class triathletes. The two just do not seem to mix.

The perception that most people have of a CPA is someone wearing a starched, button-down shirt and tie with thick glasses, not a driven, focused athlete. The classic joke is that an extroverted CPA will look at your shoes when speaking to you. Traits of a triathlete are on the other side of the spectrum, a Type A personality, athletic in multiple sports, and extremely determined.

I can tell you that all the hard work in getting my education, sitting for, and passing the three-day uniform exam to become a licensed CPA, and then the long hours of work and perseverance in building a career, are similar to the actions, efforts, determination, persistence, and never-say-die attitude that it takes to meet the qualifications to compete in the annual full distance IRONMAN® Triathlon World Championship race.

As a youth I was very shy and introverted. I loved experiencing new things, exploring, and participating in sports, much like any other boy, except for I never felt the need to involve others in my interests. You could have labeled me a loner.

It was not my intention to exclude others. I just didn't need anyone's approval of what I was doing.

I was competitive from the beginning. I didn't like to lose. My desire to win was never about beating others; rather, it was based on being the best I could be at whatever I tried. As a youth I had an extreme case of being pigeon-toed, so I didn't have delusions about my athletic abilities, and I knew I would likely never be the best. This did not deter me from trying though.

Despite enjoying various playground sports, I had not been pulled into trying organized sports, as my parents never encouraged the idea. One of my most cherished childhood memories was getting to play for a season on a baseball team for eleven-year-old boys. A friend of mine was a catcher on a team and asked me to pitch to him in the playground so he could practice being a catcher. Later he encouraged me to join their team. That sounded like fun. After getting the address of one of the organizers, I rode my bike a few miles to their house. I filled out the required forms and signed up. It only took a couple of practices to realize my skill level and knowledge of the sport were far behind the rest of the kids.

It was early in the season, likely in late May, when the evenings were still cool. I remember standing on the field thinking how good it felt to be on the team, wearing white uniforms with purple sleeves and a purple cap. One of my coaches was nice enough to drop by my house to pick me up for that evening's game on days when I had no other ride. I did not expect to get to play much, but it was still fun. After warm-ups, the team gathered around the coaches in the dugout, where they assigned batting order and field positions. For the first couple of games, I waited hopefully for the coaches to call my name, only to be disappointed when it wasn't. I had to watch my teammates take the field while I sat on the bench for most of the game. It felt like the loneliest place on earth.

After the first week or two, my friend encouraged me to try out for the pitcher position. I asked the coach if I could, and he let me pitch for the entire practice. The next game, the coaches were calling out names of the starting players, and to my great surprise, I was slated as the starting pitcher. That was likely the most exciting moment in my young life. I'm sure my face would have shown bright in the darkest of nights. With a smile that stretched from ear to ear, I immediately grabbed my glove and ball and headed to the pitcher's mound to warm up. I was in my own world. I remember being totally focused on the center of the catcher's mitt and trying to hit that spot with every single pitch.

When the game started, I was humming my fastball (the only pitch I knew how to throw) over home plate with great regularity, giving me loads of confidence. I loved the sound of the crowd yelling out my name after striking out batters. There is no sweeter sound to a pitcher than the pop of the ball hitting the catcher's mitt then hearing the ump yell out, "Sttttrike!"

The batters were either striking out or grounding out to the infield. I loved every minute of it. I felt ten feet tall when I returned to the dugout after each inning, absorbing the slaps on the back and encouragement from the coaches and teammates. As the evening wore on, the sunlight faded, and the bright field lights came on. To my eleven-year-old self, it felt like I was in the big league, with all eyes focused on me. I ended up pitching the entire game. After my last pitch ended the game, the coaches and my teammates rushed out to the pitcher's mound, calling out, "We won!" The coaches grabbed me and put me on their shoulders in celebration. The head coach said, "You pitched a no-hitter!" I had no idea what that meant, but I knew it was a big deal.

From that point on, I practiced pitching every day by throwing the ball at a cinderblock in my backyard fence and became a regular pitcher for the rest of the season. It was a wonderful experience. The next season I wanted to play again but no one helped with the registration details. I just gave up on the idea. It was too much for a twelve-year-old kid to work through all the ins and outs of getting signed up and getting to practices and games. That short but bright season taught me this: I loved to compete. I could succeed if I tried hard enough. It was all up to me, and me alone, to succeed in whatever it was I chose to pursue.

By now you are likely to be asking how a simple accountant could also become one of the best of the best and compete in the full distance IRONMAN® Triathlon World Championship. That is what the remainder of this book is all about.

Chapter 2

In the Early Years

Once I entered junior high, I wanted to play football after attending a meeting for those interested in playing. I knew it could bring back that feeling I'd had in my short stint in baseball.

After the meeting, I approached one of the coaches to ask what needed to be done to join the team. The guy was a huge mountain of a man. It was intimidating looking up at him. Not being mean but very matter-of-fact, he asked if I had played in the YFL Youth Football League. Again, my parents did not encourage or discourage me from playing organized sports, so I never had the opportunity and told him as much.

His next words to me were, "Well, you're pretty far behind the other kids." I read the look on his face as he was not interested in talking to me, hearing only that I was not good enough or worthy of being on the team. I do not know what he was thinking; most likely he was just telling me the reality of the situation. But as a young kid going into a sport as big as football, it was very intimidating. I was disappointed and did not pursue it any further. Looking back on it, I should have tried out for the team and let come what may. All I needed was a little encouragement from someone. Even as a twelve-year-old kid, I knew the cards were stacked against me. It was hard for me to see any possibility of succeeding in the sport, so I looked for other avenues to channel my athletic desires.

If you are a coach, be careful what you say to young, impressionable kids. What that coach did not know was that he scared off a player who would have given anything to be on the team, would have given a 110% effort. All he really needed to do was provide a little encouragement and a little more attention to teaching me the game. Had he taken the time to encourage me in that moment, he would have had an athlete dedicated to becoming the best that they could be at the sport.

With the encouragement of one of my good friends, I turned my attention to the tennis team and ended up playing for four years in junior high and a portion of high school. While I enjoyed being part of the team, I never really got into the sport, and it showed. I did not excel at it.

I was drawn to team sports, but maybe I just was not cut out for it. The athlete in me craved some action, so in college, I participated in intramural flag football and later on a city league softball team. I'd always enjoyed the competition, and on some level, I kept returning to it, wanting to be involved in competitive athletics in a more focused way.

Daring to dream big has great benefits but can also lead to disappointment. When entering college, I wanted to have a career as a pilot in the Air Force. I had hoped the culmination of that dream would have eventually led to being involved with NASA. With this in mind, I began an education path to get a degree in the sciences and entered the Air Force ROTC program. The first two semesters of college were spent pursuing this goal. Upon entering the ROTC program, I had long shoulder-length, sun-bleached hair. I decided that if I were going to be in the Air Force and be taken seriously by the campus ROTC colonel, I would need to cut my hair to look more like an Air Force cadet. The ROTC colonel was a kind man and seemed to have a genuine interest in the cadets and their future. He was very approachable, but I was still a bit intimidated by his uniform loaded with medals and patches signifying his rank and achievements.

At the end of the second semester, the ROTC colonel inquired about my aspirations within the Air Force. I explained to him my goals, and he suggested that I see a flight doctor to make sure that I would meet the rigorous physical qualifications for pilots. I made the appointment and completed an incredibly detailed questionnaire and physical examination. The doctor explained that, regretfully,

I would never be a pilot in command for the Air Force due to my multitude of allergies and a surgery on my feet during my childhood.

It was like getting punched in the stomach! My wildest dreams were dashed in a single moment, but I did not dwell on it for too long. The simple fact was that I would never be a pilot in the Air Force. There was no way around it, and I needed to quickly figure out what my future education degree plan would be.

> *"Experience is a hard teacher because she gives the test first, the lesson afterward." ——Vernon Sanders Law*

I was in college in 1977 and 1978 when the economy was not particularly great. Inflation was raging, and the job market was tight in virtually every profession. Recently, I'd taken a course that was an introduction to business school. I learned that accountants were always sought after and having an accounting degree added to a job candidate's chances of landing a job in the business world. I enjoyed mathematics, and accounting sounded like a field at which I could excel. Thus, I began the path of getting a BA degree in accounting. This is likely boring news for you, but it really did help develop the never-give-in attitude that I relied upon in my attempt to achieve my future dreams in the sport of triathlon.

I am certain that you too have experienced tragedies and triumphs in your own life. Those difficulties are one of the few guarantees that we have in this life. My future dream, seemingly impossible or improbable, was to compete with the best in the full distance IRONMAN® Triathlon World Championship in Hawaii. The hope that I have for anyone reading this book is that they too set a goal in their lives that will not only challenge them but fulfill them as well.

When I think of goals, hopes, and dreams, I am reminded of these words from Eleanor Roosevelt:

> *"The future belongs to those who believe in the beauty of their dreams."*

and

"You can never cross the ocean unless you have the courage to lose sight of the shore."

Crossing the ocean when you do not know how to sail can be a frightful excursion. Together, let us pull up the anchor, hoist the sails, and see what lies ahead.

Chapter 3

How It All Began

I doubt that you would dream of competing in the sport of triathlon if you do not enjoy swimming, cycling, and running. If you only attempt the activities at which you already excel, you cannot improve on anything. People have told me, "I could do the swim and the bike, but I hate running," or, "I could do the bike and run, but I can't swim," or a variation thereof. Communicated between the lines is: "What you are doing is not all that special. Anyone can do it." In a sense they are correct; anyone can do it if they dare to dream of it and then pursue it like their life depends on it.

From my earliest memories, I have always enjoyed the water, even before learning to swim. I was six years old when I learned. Mind you, it was just enough to keep from drowning. My grandparents on my father's side took me with them to a small rural town in central Texas to visit relatives, where we stayed at a local hotel that had a SWIMMING POOL! At the time, and at that age, I rarely had the opportunity to swim in an in-ground swimming pool. I was so excited to give it a go without an ounce of fear.

My grandparents kept watch over me so that I did not drown, encouraging me to try to swim. After many attempts, I was able to swim from one side (the short-width side) of the pool to the other. It was more beating the water into submission than swimming. I was now a swimmer and could not have been happier and was full of a sense of having achieved a great accomplishment. From that point on I was never afraid of the water, whether it was in a pool or in open water. That fearlessness served me well when swimming in triathlon events.

Like most children, learning to ride a bike was also a milestone of sorts in moving from being a toddler to a big kid. I remember thinking that if you can ride a bike, you are free to go exploring wherever and whenever you want, within reason. Nothing made me feel as free as a kid than taking off on my bike to see friends, explore the neighborhood, or pedal to the store for something.

Running came naturally, as it does with most children. What child does not enjoy running full blast wherever they are going? I was not like most children, though, as I was afflicted with a severe case of being pigeon-toed. Both of my feet turned inward from the heel to the toe, tilting slightly from the outer edge of the foot towards the inner arch. I was always wearing out shoe soles from the inside edge more quickly than the outer edge. As a result, I often tripped over my own feet, as the toe would hit the opposite ankle. It happened mostly while running.

I know what you're thinking. It is highly unlikely I'd be the one to compete in a marathon portion of a triathlon. For years, my parents took me to the shoe store to get specially designed shoes to help me correct this condition, but it was to no avail.

When I was eight, my parents sent me to a surgeon, hoping to give me some relief. I do not remember ever being afraid of the procedure. Like kids do, I just accepted it was what I needed to run and play without tripping. The surgery on both my feet involved making an L-shaped incision running from just below my toes, across the foot, and then towards the heel. To correct the condition, the doctors performed an osteotomy, which involves cutting and reshaping a bone in the afflicted area. In my case, this was in the middle joint of both feet.

After the surgery, I had casts that went from my toes to just below my knees. This immobilized my feet for ten to twelve weeks. I was fortunate I felt little pain while the casts were on, but that ended when the cast came off. At that point, I had to learn to walk all over again, and there was pain involved in doing so. It was hard to manage with both my feet healing, having no good leg (foot) to stand on. It was months before I was able to walk without pain and without effort. Of course, running was out of the question.

Thankfully, the surgery was successful, and over time my feet healed, and, I was able to resume life as a normal child, running and playing with other children. The surgery left a hard, callused bulge at the top of the arch of my right foot. This did not cause any pain but made getting shoes to fit properly exceedingly difficult, and it still does. I am describing all of this only to emphasize that you can overcome difficult circumstances and pursue your dreams.

Now let's explore what led me to the sport of triathlon.

Chapter 4

Getting on with Life

My pre-triathlon life and experiences were important layers in the road that led me to the sport. As a kid I learned how important perseverance and a never-give-up attitude were in achieving anything in life. You can be the smartest, most talented person, but if you lack grit, perseverance, and persistence to the end goal, no matter how many setbacks are encountered, you may never see your dreams come true.

My beautiful wife, Debbie, and I married after my first year of college. I had to work twenty to thirty hours a week at a local supermarket to make ends meet and pay for my education. It was a wonderful job to have, as it allowed flexible hours. This enabled me to attend classes during the day and work in the evenings. If you went to college this way, I am sure you know that going to class during the day and working afterwards does not leave you much free time. There was little time to do anything but go to class, work, and study. It was a lot to juggle. Accounting is a logical but highly technical subject, and I studied hard, never losing sight of the end goal of making it to graduation.

After four and a half years, I graduated and found a job with an accounting firm in my hometown. The firm provided income tax preparation and financial statement auditing services for clients scattered across a multi-state area requiring travel.

My education and studies were not over upon graduation. I still had to sit for and pass the CPA exam. The exam took three days, covering four major topics. I took the exam before graduation, just to see what it was like, and I did not pass any of the topics. I found out later that a grade between sixty-nine and seventy-five was not given. Seventy-five was a passing grade, and I had scored a sixty-nine on all four tests, UGH! If only I had studied beforehand. I didn't really study much for the next several tests, which were given twice a year, and thus I did not pass in the next couple of attempts. Once again, I could have just given up and gone into a private sector accounting career with some company. However, that was not my dream of becoming a CPA and working in the firm.

Realizing this was going to take more effort than just showing up for the test, I went to work studying for the exam and passed it in the next two sittings. I joined the firm in 1982 and was the twelfth employee. In 1992, I was honored to be invited to join the firm's partner group, which was another dream come true for me. All these career goals were accomplished by hard work, persistence, and perseverance.

After passing the CPA exam, my wife and I decided to start a family. Our first daughter, Ashley, was born in 1986, followed by our second daughter, Lia, born in 1988. And finally, our third daughter, Amanda, came four years later. Debbie resigned from her job after Amanda was born to start her new life as a stay-at-home mom. It was such a blessing to have her be with our children 24-7 as I was traveling with my work.

Now let's dive into where my interest in triathlon began.

> "Nothing in the world can take the place of persistence. Talent will not; nothing is more common than unsuccessful men with talent. Genius will not; unrewarded genius is almost a proverb. Education will not; the world is full of educated derelicts. The slogan 'Press On' has solved, and always will solve, the problems of the human race."
> —Calvin Coolidge

CHAPTER 5

INTRODUCTION TO RUNNING

As a child, our family lived near a park where my friends and I spent a good amount of time. I'd often see a man running laps around the park and dressed in what I thought were clothes someone on a track team would wear, which in my kid's mind made him something like an expert in running. One day I decided I would try running the three-quarter mile track he'd made look so effortless. I am not sure I made it once around the park. He had something I did not. It was not until later in life when I discovered the simple joy of lacing up a pair of running shoes and going for a run to be alone with my thoughts, enjoying the great outdoors.

I am not exactly sure at what point I started running. At the time it seemed like a good thing to do to keep myself in physical shape and to burn off the stress from my work. During college, I ran through our neighborhood covering two miles and enjoyed it. Oh my goodness, were my legs sore for the next two or three days. That was enough to discourage anyone from running, ever! At this point I knew absolutely nothing about how to train properly: what shoes to wear, what clothing was best, proper running form, heart rates, etc. What more could there possibly be to it? Just put on a pair of shorts, a t-shirt, and lace up my tennis shoes and hit the road running as quickly as I could. I had no plan or consistency in my running. I just ran when I felt like it.

Early in my accounting career, I found that one of the partners and senior auditors were both runners. On a particular work trip, I asked them if I could join them on their evening run. Of course, they said yes. I thought it would be a one-to-two-mile jog, as the partner was in his fifties. Surely, he could not run farther than that! Boy was I wrong! I thought they would never stop! Not only that, but they were also running around an eight-minute-per-mile pace, which was about a minute per mile faster than I ever ran. We ended up running around four miles. I was completely exhausted when we finished.

The next morning, we had to scale four stories of stairs to get to the office of the company we were working at. Let me tell you, it was pure torture going up and down those stairs for the next two days. Again, why would anyone in their right mind intentionally do this to themselves? It just seemed like something I wanted to do and get better at. If the partner, who was in his fifties, could do it and not hurt the next two days, then surely I could too.

During our run, I learned that there was a running club in my hometown of Lubbock, Texas. The club's name was the West Texas Running Club. It held monthly running events that varied from a 5K all the way to a half marathon of 13.1 miles. I was excited to learn about the club, as it would provide a way for me to get to know others who enjoyed the sport, but more so to have an opportunity to compete in races. I was pleasantly surprised to learn that adults had a venue to compete against other adults in the sport. I joined the club in 1994 and during the year was able to gradually build up my training so I could run continually for six miles. It felt great to be able to achieve that distance and not be too sore the next day.

I was finally ready to enter my first running club event. It was in the club's marque race held in September 1994 titled the Red Raider Homecoming 10K. I was thrilled to be competing in the event with around 300 other runners. I ran the race as fast as I could maintain, gave it everything I had, and finished with a time of 50:17. The time was good for thirteenth in my age group and eightieth overall. They gave out finishers' medals, and I was proud of it, as it symbolized the results of all my hard work in training.

At the time, my wife and I were members of a young married couple's class at the church we attended. Several of the guys in the class liked to run. One of them became a good friend and mentor. His name was Weldon. I loved to talk to him about running. I eagerly milked him for tips and details to help my new interest in the sport. He excitedly told me about his training for marathons, ultra-distance events (that is 26.2 miles), and longer running events! The most I had ever run was six miles, and I knew how tired I was from that. How on earth could someone run a marathon or longer and live to talk about it? That just seemed to be a superhuman feat, an unattainable goal. Especially for someone who was in their thirties, assuming that at thirty or more years old, a marathon would no longer be physically possible. This opened my eyes to consider elevating my running to loftier goals.

He invited me to join him early on a Sunday morning with other running club members to train at one of the city parks. They covered an eight-mile loop around a small lake. This sounded like the perfect opportunity to advance my running to the next level, and I eagerly accepted the invitation. I woke early and drove to the park. It was winter and the temperature was around freezing when I arrived to find several runners warming up. My plan was to run with them for eight miles. Mind you, that's two miles farther than I had ever run before.

Weldon was training for an ultra-distance race of fifty miles. That was beyond my comprehension. He and I were about the same age, and in the back of my mind (way at the back!) I was thinking, if he can do it, so can I. I dressed in heavy cotton gym pants and a sweatshirt. The other runners teased me about my clothing, saying I was overdressed. Well, we started the run and maintained a pace of around nine minutes per mile. That pace was around forty-five seconds per mile slower than I had normally run, and thus was comfortable for me.

At the four-mile turnaround point, I was heating up, with no way to cool down short of stripping clothing off. When we reached my usual distance, my body revolted, saying, "Hey, you, this is where you're supposed to stop!" When attempting to extend my running distance, my energy levels would significantly drop, my thighs would begin to burn, and my feet would start to ache at the point where I would normally stop. If I had been running alone, I might have stopped, but being part of a pack kept my mind off the discomfort. Exhausted when we were done, I was pleased I'd not embarrassed myself by stopping and proud I could now run nonstop for eight miles.

Weldon was a major source of inspiration and information. He taught me about training methods, how to pace myself, energy supplements to use on the run, running aids like heart rate monitors, belts to hold a water bottle, running clothing, etc. He introduced me to Road Runner Sports, which sells everything a runner needs, providing pain for my wallet, but allowing me to explore the sport with the best tools of the trade.

This was where I learned the running shoes you wore mattered. Everyone has differently shaped feet, foot width, high or low arches, etc. I tried various running shoe brands before landing on one that worked best for me. Amazingly, they were much lighter than the garden-variety shoes I was using. I also purchased clothing designed specifically for running. Again, I was amazed at how much better I felt while running in this new, lighter clothing.

As my body gradually adapted to the workouts, I looked forward to training, reaching for that often talked about runner's high. I learned about what types and brands of hydration, calories, and electrolyte replacement worked best for me and how often they should be used. I saw my life revolving more around the routine, reading and learning everything I could from running periodicals, from training tips, supplements, clothing, injury prevention, and running accessories. One of the common themes in the literature was adding cross-training to your workouts that would train your cardiovascular system without having to run every day, giving your feet, legs, hips, and knees a much-needed rest and recovery break.

It never occurred to me that there was so much to the sport. I wish I had started off learning as much as I could, with swimming and cycling as well. It would have saved me valuable time and energy unlearning bad habits I'd developed.

I readily admit to making this mistake. I mean, come on, what more could there be to running? Merely put one foot in front of the other as fast and for as long as possible. We've all been riding bicycles since childhood. Surely all that's needed to go faster is a better bike. Many of us have been swimming as long as we remember.

All that's needed to swim faster and cover greater distances is to do more of it. I was, as they say, a babe in the woods in my knowledge of endurance sports.

I read articles about the benefits of cross-training and came across an ad touting the benefits of using a stationary bicycle for this purpose and made the decision to purchase it. The resistance mechanism was a fan that was powered by pedaling. It had levers that you pulled and pushed with your arms as you pedaled, and the resistance increased the harder you worked. I could easily get my heart rate up and work up a good sweat whenever I wanted no matter the weather and without having to leave home. I also purchased a treadmill, allowing me to run when the weather was foul or if I simply did not want to run outdoors.

I soon realized these were great tools for quick workouts, but anything longer was boring and torturous. There was a time much later in my racing career when I ran a marathon on a treadmill. I was traveling for a work-related conference and stayed at a five-star hotel. My workout plan called for a long run. Not knowing the area, I elected to run on a treadmill in the hotel gym. The gym attendant kept giving me the strangest looks. As the hours passed, he kept looking at me and then at the clock. Ha, ha! There is no telling what he was thinking.

Running provided me with something to do outside of work and family activities, and I enjoyed the challenge of it. Yet I still had never heard of the sport of triathlon.

CHAPTER 6

MY INTRODUCTION TO THE SPORT OF TRIATHLON

One of the wonderful things about training with others is that you tend to share all your training experiences, methods, what did and did not work, and all sorts of topics on running. I genuinely looked forward to our Sunday morning training runs. These folks were also a major source of inspiration. Most, if not all of them, were far more experienced than I, and a major source of information. Looking back as I advanced in my running abilities, and being guys, we would turn the last two miles of the run into a mini race. I was typically last in, but it was fun, nonetheless. In the sport of running, I was a sparrow amongst eagles.

By now it was the spring of 1997, and during one of these weekly training runs, the topic turned to cross-training. I told Weldon that I had purchased the (previously described) stationary bike. After discussing it, he told me that since I enjoyed the bike, I should try the sport of triathlon. Triathlon? What in the world was that? He went on to tell me that the sport involved swimming, cycling, and running, all combined into a single event. The swim was typically the first event, followed by the cycling, and ending with a run. I vaguely remembered seeing something about the sport on a sports TV show featuring a participant crawling across the finish line after completing some insanely full distance triathlon race known as the IRONMAN® Triathlon World Championship.

I learned that there was a high-profile triathlon event held at a lake just outside of Lubbock. The name of the event was half distance IRONMAN® 70.3® Buffalo Springs Lake triathlon. To my astonishment, the event consisted of a 1.2-mile swim, a fifty-six-mile bike ride, and a 13.1-mile run. Weldon told me that the West Texas Running Club provided aid stations at each mile mark in the run course. He mentioned that he had volunteered at one of the stations in previous events. He described how the athletes looked and their condition as they came through his station located at miles two and eleven. He spoke of a friend who had competed in the race and what a high-caliber athlete he was.

I said this sounded like fun but how anyone can do such a thing seemed impossible. Here I was all proud and cocky that I could run nonstop for eight miles and at an 8:30-per-mile pace. I had just learned that people competed in events where not only was the run portion of the race five miles longer than I had ever run, but also included a lake swim of 1.2 miles and a bike race of fifty-six miles.

That news, though intriguing, effectively deflated my ego. I asked a lot of questions about the race and expressed my amazement at the mere thought that a human could do such a thing. He told me I would likely not be able to do it. I cannot say that I did not, on some level, agree with him. However, I have never been one to let anyone's opinions about what I was capable of doing deter me from trying. I feel strongly that if you listen to such talk, and adhere to it, you are giving someone else permission to dictate what you can and cannot do. NO THANKS! I will never give another that level of control over my life.

I came away from the training run with the thought that there was another athletic venue, other than just running, for me to pursue. I considered myself a decent swimmer, and who couldn't ride a bike? So why not me? During our conversations, my friend must have told me that there were two races IRONMAN® 70.3® Buffalo Springs Lake triathlon: the marque half distance race and a much shorter sprint triathlon, which consisted of a 700-yard swim, a twelve-mile bike, and a 5K run. Now that was something I could do! I had no idea how or where to start my journey into the sport of triathlon, but did I not let that deter me from setting my sights on training to enter a sprint triathlon.

Chapter 7

Setting My Sights on Competing in a Triathlon

All sorts of things can occur during the pursuit of a dream. The dream itself can start off in one direction then morph to something grander or something totally unexpected. Looking back on my journey, what started as merely competing in running events evolved to include the sport of triathlon. Who could know where else it might lead? This was what kept everything fresh and exciting. In the spring of 1997, I set my sights on finding and competing in a sprint distance (700-yard swim, twelve-mile bike, and 3.1-mile run) triathlon in the spring of 1998. This would give me close to one year to purchase a bike and train for the event. Now that I had dared to dream of competing in a sprint triathlon, I needed a new game plan. How exactly did you develop a plan to achieve a goal that you knew nothing about?

Good question! Where to start?

I knew I would need to be able to swim for 700 yards, cycle for twelve miles, and run for 3.1 miles (5K). I could already check the box for the 5K run. However, I would need a road/racing bike for the event. Did you know that swimming 700 yards is equivalent to the length of seven football fields? Umm, that is a long way to swim, isn't it? What I did not know was how I could not only complete each event, but how was I to do them all in the span of a few hours?

I must stop here and digress a little for you to appreciate all the crazy, unlikely events, twists, and turns that could and did occur in making my dream a reality.

We lived in a neighborhood with a pool. Our girls, now ages eight, six and two, loved swimming as much as I did. We spent many weekends there. I loved playing with them and their friends in the cool water. Their favorite thing to do was jumping off my shoulders, with me launching them as high in the air and as far as I could.

The girls took swim lessons with the other neighborhood kids. At the end of the summer, the pool swim coach would organize a swimming event for the kids to compete against the other pools in the area. Ashley especially enjoyed it.

The swimming instructor was also an assistant coach for the Lubbock Swim Club and encouraged Ashley, a fourth grader, to join the team, and she was eager to try it. The swim club trained the kids at the men's gym pool at Texas Tech University. It was here that I met the head coach of the club. He had been a state champion swimmer with the Lubbock school's swim team and had competed in college. He was great with the kids and was later hired as the Lubbock ISD's head swim coach. Ashley swam for him from the fourth grade through high school. To this day, he continuously produces state championship teams.

At one of the swim club racing events, I spoke with the coach, asking him if there were events I could compete in. That was not very well worded, as he said, "What? Here?" Ha ha! Like I wanted to be part of the kids' events.

Well, as luck would have it, at one of the swim meets, the organizers included an evening cookout for the families of the athletes. As part of the festivities, there was a fifty-yard freestyle swim race for the adults. Perfect! I could evaluate my swimming abilities against other adults. What I did not know was the other parents joining the competition had swum in teams in their youth and knew what they were doing. I had never competed in a swim race before and thus had never launched myself off a starting platform. Well, that was an experience! Upon diving into the water, my swimsuit almost went to my knees and water flooded my swim goggles. After coming up from the dive, I noticed the other swimmers were halfway to the finish. I swam as hard and fast as my arms and legs could take me and was sucking air when I finished. It is safe to say that I came in dead last.

Ouch! That was a bit embarrassing for me and likely for Debbie and Ashley as well. But neither ever said anything about it.

Even in defeat, what you learn will always help you grow in some way. If you are humble and attentive, you will learn something from the winners. Afterwards, I made a point of speaking with the coach to find out what I needed to do to improve. Surprisingly, he told me that the Lubbock Swim Club offered a master's division (i.e., for adults) that he coached, and I could join. Bingo!

I joined immediately and was excited to learn more. The coach put together a swim workout for each of us depending on our abilities and experience. I specifically recall that the warm-up was a mere 500-yard swim. What? That was a long way for a warm-up! I had to rest a bit at each end of the twenty-five-yard lane during the warm-up. That was eye-opening, knowing I would need to swim at least that far in a triathlon.

The coach incorporated the freestyle, back, breast, and IM strokes in our training. The whole thing was designed more for aerobics than teaching us proper swim stroke technique. It seemed like, and was, months before I could swim the 500-yard warm-up without stopping at the end of the pool to rest and catch my breath. Keep in mind that a sprint triathlon could include up to a 700-yard swim. Gradually, I became stronger and more physically fit as a swimmer. Not necessarily faster, mind you.

Somewhere along the way, I told the coach of my plans to enter a sprint triathlon, telling him that I would need to be able to complete a 700-yard swim and have enough energy left to do the remaining twelve-mile bike ride and 3.1-mile run. His response was that I would need to work on my swim form and technique. Using better form would allow me to be more efficient in the water and thus use less energy. Did he mean there was more to swimming than just pounding the water with your hands, arms, legs, and feet? Turned out there was much more.

He recommended a book on swimming that I should read, *Total Immersion*, by Terry Laughlin. That was single-handedly the best thing I had ever read, and I immediately implemented the training techniques. I will have more to say about this later.

Surely by now you're wondering about the cycling portion of a triathlon. While I was attending college, my wife and I purchased two ten-speed road bicycles each weighed in at twenty-plus pounds. Not knowing more than the basics about biking, I was sure this would be something I could use for the race. They looked like road racing bikes, each having two big gears on the front cog and ten on the back. This gave the rider twenty gears to choose from.

On occasion, we would ride from our house to my parents' place, and the round trip clocked in at around eight miles. We had fun on those rides, but to be honest, our backsides were a bit sore afterwards. How could anyone sit on those little seats for much more than an hour? This was my only experience with road bikes, so I really did not know much about shopping for a bike to race on.

At this time in our lives, I was a newly admitted partner in our firm. My wife had resigned from her job to be a full-time mom and homemaker. The side effect was that we were on a tight budget. We were using every spare nickel to pay off my debt for buying into our accounting firm. Therefore, we shopped for a used racing bike, as they could be quite expensive. Debbie searched through the internet and found one in our city and for the right price. I knew nothing about choosing one to fit my height and weight. Luckily, the seller was close to my size (i.e., 6'2" and 190 pounds). While not a perfect fit, it was close enough. The bike was a Trek 2100, made mostly of a composite of carbon fiber and metal. This made the bike exceptionally light.

The dates are a little fuzzy for the year I purchased this bike. It must have been at some point in the summer of 1997. For the first training rides I rode around twelve miles. The first few rides were much harder than I thought they would be, but I enjoyed every minute of it. Especially the downhill portions. Man, could I fly on those!

During one of my early rides, I had a flat tire at about mile four and was in a rural area. I had carried all the required flat repair tools and supplies with me. However, it is much harder to not only find the puncture, but also patch it once found. I worked unsuccessfully for twenty to thirty minutes to fix the flat.

As I was attempting to fix the flat, another cyclist pulled up to me and asked if I needed assistance. I must have had "newbie" written all over me. I told him what had happened and the little success I was having finding the puncture and patching the tube. He proceeded to pull a new tube out from his flat repair bag and put it on the rim. He then remounted the tire and inflated it using a compressed air canister. All that in less than five minutes! Wow! He then hopped on his bike and rode away.

I got to know this person better in later years. He built and maintained road bikes for folks. Most people involved with endurance sports are very nice, considerate people. That was a great lesson in riding bikes. Always carry extra tubes and compressed air canisters. Never think you can patch a damaged tube while out on rides.

My first road bike

There was no stopping me now! I was a member of a master's swim club working on my swimming ability and now had a real racing road bike. I was on my way to achieving my goal of competing in a triathlon.

Chapter 8

Entering My Very First Triathlon Event

My swimming abilities, while not great, were slowly coming around. Swimming the 500-yard warm-up at the master's swim club group was no longer much of an issue. Riding the bike for twelve miles was in the bag, and there were no issues running for 3.1 miles. By this time, I had competed in four of the annual Red Raider 10K Road Races. For the race held on October 1, 1997, I placed eighth in my age group with a time of 45:35. Much too slow, in my opinion, but I was getting faster. I was now ready to enter my very first sprint distance triathlon.

The race was held in the small city of Canyon, Texas, one hundred miles north of Lubbock. The city was home to a satellite campus for a major university. Their athletic department organized and hosted the race. We sent my registration form in advance and subsequently received information about the race. It included information on packet pick-up, course maps, distances involved, start times, etc. The race packet included a swim cap and race number panels to be mounted on the bike and pinned to the jersey.

I was incredibly nervous about all of this, having never been involved with a triathlon event. There were all sorts of questions. Where would I store the bike during the rest of the race? What should I do with my helmet and bike shoes? What were the rules? What should I do with the swim cap and goggles after the swim? What happened upon finishing the swim and then again when finishing the bike ride? Where did I put my running shoes before the run portion of the race? So many questions with so few answers.

Race day was in the spring of 1998. The swim portion started at around 9:00 a.m. If you're not familiar with Northwest Texas, the spring can be a warm, sunny day or dumping a foot of snow in a spring blizzard. Regardless, the mornings are always cold. The morning sky was sunny and clear. The temperature was crisp in the upper forties, requiring the use of warm-up clothing while preparing for the race. The cool temperature was a concern, but the swim was held in a heated indoor pool. However, it would come into play while on the bike course. There was nothing I could do about it other than endure it. I knew from my running experience not to overdress, or I would overheat during the race.

We arrived early, wanting to give myself time to observe what the other competitors did in preparation before the race. There were racks set up to mount the bikes. I noticed some competitors mounted theirs with the front of the bike facing the rack while others mounted theirs with the back of the seat resting on top the rack with the front tire facing away. Asking others, I was told that you could take your bike off quicker if it was mounted with the front tire facing away from the rack.

I watched and learned how other athletes mounted their race number panels on their bikes and how they placed their helmet, sunglasses, and bike shoes on or next to their bike. I noticed one competitor had a five-gallon plastic bucket next to their bike used to sit on while putting on their bike shoes and later their running shoes. It seemed like a clever idea at the time, but I never used this technique in future races. I mean, this was a race; who had time to sit down during the transitions?

While making all these observations, I noticed other competitors inflating their tires to the desired air pressure before the race began. Now, I had not thought about doing that. Wasn't the only time you needed to put more air in a tire when it was low? Turns out that you should start every race with the tires at or near the maximum psi. Harder tires mean less rolling resistance, thus a faster bike split time. There was so much to learn, I felt like a fish out of the water with all eyes on this newcomer rookie.

After getting my bike and running equipment set up and ready, it was time for the race to start. For this race, the swimming event was in an indoor Olympic-sized lap swimming pool. The competitors entered the water on the far end and started the race in ten- to fifteen-second intervals. The swimmers were in order according to their predicted time to complete the swim (i.e., the faster swimmers start first and so on). This was no time to be cocky, and I seeded myself towards the back of the pack, not having a promising idea of how long it would take me to complete the swim. Sure, I knew how long it took to swim 500 yards in practice, but this was a race.

We waited on deck until it was our turn to start. It seemed like forever for my turn to arrive to enter the water. Getting in the water, I was ready to start. There were three or four contestants waiting at the edge of the pool. The starter would call out your race number with a notification that you were next to start. At that point, you got ready to push off the wall. The starter would begin a countdown at around five seconds and, when done, would yell, "GO!" I was nervous and excited all at the same time. Here I was, a thirty-nine-year-old guy, a husband and father of three children, about to compete in a triathlon. How cool was that!

When it was my turn to start, I just took off at a pace that was quick for me and one I thought I could maintain. To get the 500 yards in, we had to swim fifty yards to the other end of the pool, turn, and come back on the other side of the lane, then go under the lane rope at the end of the lane, repeating the up-and-back. We did this for five lanes to get in the 500 yards. It seemed like my lungs were on fire nearing the completion of the swim. It was a huge relief to finish, and I exited the pool and ran to the bike racks. My heart was beating hard and fast. Now outside, I could feel the cold air against my wet skin and clothing as I ran to my bike, but my body was generating internal heat from the swim, so it was not a factor.

I ran to my bike as quickly as possible to prepare for the bike portion of the race. Did you know that it is exceedingly difficult to put a neoprene cycling shirt on wet skin? I did not think I would ever get that shirt on. Surely it was mere seconds, but it seemed like minutes. I just wore my cycling shorts for the swim so there was no need to change for the bike event.

Since I was at the back of the line for the swim start, most of the athletes had already left out on their bike ride. Once ready, I ran with my bike to the bike mount start line. I climbed on and took off. It was exhilarating. The cool air rushed by my wet shorts.

Pumping the pedals hard, it did not take long to warm up. I soon started to catch up to the riders ahead of me. Like the swim, my approach was to go as fast as I could for the entire ride. Trying to conserve energy, I kept telling myself, Do not forget that there is a 5K run after the bike ride.

Twelve miles is a long way to ride a bicycle, especially when you have already swum 500 yards and are pushing those bike pedals hard. The bike course was out and back on the same roadway. Within ten minutes of my starting the bike ride, the lead athletes were already coming at me in the opposite direction. It was a little disappointing, only having made it to mile four when first seeing them. Keep in mind that they did start up to fifteen minutes or more ahead of me.

At the bike course finish, there was a bike dismount line. Competitors must be off their bikes by the time they arrive at the line. I stopped right at the line, dismounted, and ran with my bike as quickly as possible to the bike racks. Once there, I had to put on my socks, running shoes, cap, and sunglasses and head out on the run course. That may sound easy, but I was a little shaky from my exertion on the swim and bike portions of the race. I had to sit on the ground atop a towel to be stable enough to get it done.

Once ready and hopping up, I took off on the run course. The run was the one event I had prior racing experience with and was more confident and prepared. Almost immediately, I began to pass other contestants. That was a good feeling. My lungs were on fire and my heart was about to burst, but I just kept pumping my legs, putting one foot in front of the other.

I have told you how most athletes are genuinely nice and considerate people. This was re-enforced while I passed other contestants. Most would say words of encouragement like, "Good job," "Nice legs," "Looking strong," and, "Keep it up." I had not expected that.

I do not remember any runners passing me, but I did start the race at the back of the pack. With one mile remaining I could see the finish line area. I was thinking to myself, Just one more mile to go, don't let up now. It was so exciting when the finish line was in sight, but even more so when crossing it. My wife and children were there cheering for me. What a special moment that was having them there to see all my effort paying off. I had dared to dream of competing in a triathlon and now I had reached that goal. What else might be possible?

I did not keep a record of my finishing time, but I'm sure I did not place in the top three of my age group. I was surprised to see my master's swim coach there competing in the race as well. Remember, he had been a state champion swimmer. He did win the fastest swim time. However, he did not place in the top three in his age group. He told me that he was the first cyclist out on the bike course, saying it was not long before a guy came screaming past. That person was Tim Key, a very experienced and elite triathlete.

One essential element in attaining your dreams is to seek out others with the same or similar interests and goals. After the race was over, I met Mike and Marti Greer, at the post-race lunch of grilled burgers and hotdogs. The Greers owned and operated the half distance IRONMAN® 70.3® Buffalo Springs Lake triathlon. Now these were folks I wanted and needed to know, as I had a desire to become more involved in the sport. After meeting and speaking with them, I learned more about their event.

My wife and I offered our service as volunteers for the event. Marti did the direct work, with Mike taking on the role of CEO, fundraiser, etc. Marti was gracious, saying something to the effect that she would appreciate the help. Based on her body language, she did not really think the offer was genuine. Little did she know! I will have more to say about the Greers as we proceed.

Did I say I was now hooked on the sport? I could not wait to race again!

Chapter 9

Setting New Goals

Pursuing and attaining a dream can mean different things to different people. Attaining the initial dream might be the end for some. For others, the dream morphs into another goal yet to be attained. That was true for me. It seemed that each time I reached a goal I was not satisfied to just relish in my achievement and let it be. It merely made me think of what else was possible if I raised the bar? Anything seemed possible at this point. I was striving to fashion my life and goals after these famous words from Henry Ford:

> *"Whether you think you can, or whether you think you can't, you are probably right."*

A thirty-nine-year-old pursuing a sport like a teenager or college aged person may seem a bit much to some. I heard the words "mid-life crisis" on more than one occasion. I did not consider myself too old to still enjoy competitive sports and I ignored those negative comments. I was on a journey of self-discovery and adamantly wanted to see where it could lead. I had never felt so alive as when I was out running, cycling, and swimming. This may have been more of a concern had there not been many men and women just like me participating in the races

I attended. In fact, my age group typically had the largest number of participants in the event. I had found a sport for which success rested solely on my shoulders.

During late spring and into the early summer of 1998, I competed in sprint and Olympic distance (one-mile swim, twenty-four-mile bike, and 6.1-mile run) triathlons, learning a lot from each event. I noticed other athletes wearing wetsuits for the swim portion of the race. I was curious to try one. It was my understanding that wetsuits provided additional buoyancy, keeping the swimmer flatter in the water, thus allowing them to swim faster. If it made you faster in the water, I needed one and made the purchase.

These suits are made specifically for triathlon competitions and fit super tight, like a second skin. They are hard to put on and likewise to take off. If you have any excess fat, these suits will reveal it.

The first time I wore the suit in a race, I found it difficult to quickly remove it after the swim. Eventually, I learned a quick way to exit the wetsuit. The suit zipper was on the back, with a long strap attached to it. To remove the suit, you had to pull down the zipper and peel the suit off your shoulders and then down to your ankles. Once at your ankles, you stepped on one side of the suit while pulling the opposite foot free, then repeated the process with the other foot. This was a good lesson that sped up my transition times from the swim to the bike event. Organization was crucial. You did not want to have to search for anything and it needed to be positioned to allow for quick access so you could get back to the race. The following are tricks I learned along the way:

- Mount the bike on the bike racks so that the front tire faces outwards.

- Clip the cycling shoes into the cleat so that all I need to do is mount the bike and slip my feet into the shoes while starting the ride.

- Place the helmet so that it cradles into the aerobars, with the straps laid out on either side of the helmet. This allows me to quickly put on and secure the helmet.

- Put sunshades in the inner bowl of the helmet. This eliminates hunting for them.

- Place a towel next to the bike.

- Place my running shoes on the towel so I can step into them without much effort.

- Put the running cap on the towel as well, along with anything else that might be needed on the run.

- Swim in my cycling shorts. Changing from a swimsuit to cycling shorts takes way too much time.

- Run in the same shorts and jersey I wore on the bike ride. Again, changing clothes from cycling to running attire wastes too much valuable time.

- Use a Bento Bag mounted on the crossbar of the bike to carry nutritional and electrolyte supplements. Everything I might need on the bike ride is easily and readily accessible.

With each race I made mental notes on what worked well and what did not. All this must seem like overkill, but it was effective in reducing my transition times. I realized the difference in the speed of the transitions from the swim-to-bike and bike-to-run had an influence on my total finishing time. These time savings were enough to change how I placed in my age group and overall. For that very reason, I continually tweaked my transitions to be as efficient as possible.

1998 was an important year in my development as a triathlete. During this period, I continued to participate in the running club events and increased the duration of my training runs. I could now run a half marathon of 13.1 miles and farther. It was tough to build up to that level, as each mile added increased the difficulty. People have asked what I thought about during runs lasting two or more hours. That is a good question. The answer depends on whether I ran with others or alone. When running with others the time passed quickly as we spoke about anything and everything but mostly about our training, what did and did not work, and upcoming races. When running alone, I spent the first couple of miles just settling into my goal pace and not starting too quickly. Afterwards I was constantly monitoring my heart rate and pace and staying properly hydrated. When not doing that, my mind drifted between issues at work and tasks on my to-do list. Mostly I just let my mind rest and enjoy the solitude and the scenery.

On one of the Sunday morning group training runs, we ran the eight-mile loop twice, something that just a brief time ago seemed impossible. From reading periodicals on running and pumping friends for information, I learned that you don't have to run a full marathon distance in training to be able to run the distance in a racing event. It sounds counterintuitive, but the last thing I wanted to do was not finish because I'd never run that far before. I also learned more about energy and electrolyte supplements to help sustain me during long course events. I tested these supplements and techniques during my training runs and found that they did help sustain my energy levels.

If you are not familiar with endurance sports, you can run, cycle, and swim for multiple hours in a single nonstop period. Your body is burning off all its readily available sugars and electrolytes stored in your blood and liver. These depleted reserves need to be replenished or you risk the dreaded "BONK." This is where the body can no longer sustain the pace you are capable of and forces you to slow down—or worse yet, even walk! Using these supplements is a bit like putting gas in your car when the fuel gauge needle is bouncing off the E. The same is true for keeping the body properly hydrated. I found that I needed to drink a minimum of one water bottle per hour or I would bonk.

After competing in my first few triathlons and a half marathon running event, I could not wait to enter another triathlon. Do you remember me mentioning the IRONMAN® 70.3® Buffalo Springs Lake triathlon race? I felt I was ready to compete in it now that I'd learned the ropes. I registered for the event scheduled for June 28, 1998.

Most dreams require you to develop new skills. Doing so will likely take study, developing a plan of action, and patience to see it through. In my experience this is where many fall short in their pursuit of a dream. People in general are impatient, wanting instant results. It rarely works that way no matter what the dream is. I knew I needed to improve my swimming, cycling, and running skills, so that was where my training was focused.

Chapter 10

Working on My Swimming Abilities

To compete in longer distance triathlons, I would need to significantly improve my swimming endurance. Realizing this, I set about learning to swim with better technique. The master's swim club coach had since moved on to coaching the Lubbock Junior High swim team. He therefore was no longer involved with the master's swim club. This was an opportune time for me to refocus my swimming from just an aerobic workout to that of training for endurance and speed.

I now need a different venue for swimming. I learned from my tri-friends that Texas Tech University allowed local city residents and alumni to join the university's recreation center, which had an Olympic-size, indoor lap swimming facility. Perfect! Even better, the facility was near my business office, and it opened early in the morning for the early bird swimmers.

You might say to yourself, "I could never swim well enough to compete in a triathlon because I have no access to a lap swimming pool." That would hamper your training for the swim. However, there are particularly good triathletes who do not swim regularly. What they do is train their muscles used for swimming in a gym setting. While you miss being in the water and learning proper swim stroke and breathing techniques, you can train this way to finish the swimming event.

Do you remember me telling you about the book the master's swim club coach gave me? The one titled *Total Immersion,* written by Terry Laughlin? This book was a fantastic resource to teach me proper swim technique. I came to realize technique is everything. You may be strong, but if you have poor technique, you will quickly run out of energy. The book introduced me to the idea that you can swim farther and faster while using less energy. I was eager to test it out.

The book explained that most people swim out of balance. To swim efficiently, the body needs to be flat in the water (i.e., parallel to the surface). This makes sense when thinking about it. If not parallel to the water, the head will be higher than the feet. Using this form, the body creates a wedge shape relative to the water's surface, meaning that a swimmer is pushing the water ahead of them instead of gliding through it. This is much the same as a jet piercing through the air with the least amount of air resistance.

Total Immersion opened my eyes on how to practice and train for swimming. It taught an assortment of drills to improve my swim form and technique. I put these drills on a computer spreadsheet, printed them, and laminated them so that I could take them to the pool. The following is an excerpt from one of those swim form drill workouts. It will give you an idea of the extent I was willing to go to improve.

SWIMMING WORKOUTS

LEGEND:

FS	Free style	SSP	Sensory skill practice
BS	Backstroke	1 S/L	One minus stroke length
BRS	Breaststroke	CU	Catch-up, alternating single arm
BFS	Butterfly stroke	S&G	3 slide & glide—3 count pauses
DH	Downhill	RA	Single arm with the right arm
RW	Reach for the wall	LA	Single arm with the left arm
WA	Weightless arm	HS	Hand-swapping or semi catch-up
BB	Belly button to wall	HR	Concentrate on hip rhythm
ASG	Advanced slide & glide		

SKILL BUILDER #1 – PERFECTLY BALANCED

WARMUP:
300 yards (mixed strokes) Notes: Swim easy

DRILLS:
Drill #1
5 to 6 minutes
25-yard repeats
10 to 20 seconds rest

Notes:
1. Keep your body straight.
2. Kick gently with legs straight.
3. Lift chin to breathe.
4. Continue drill until it feels comfortable.

Drill #2
5 to 6 minutes
25 yards Drill #1
25 yards SSP-DH
10-second rest
10-second rest

Notes:
1. Hips should feel light, legs are relaxed.
2. It should feel like you are skimming the surface.

Drill #3
5 to 6 minutes
25 yards SSP-DH
25 yards–1S/L

Notes:
1. Swim the first 25 yards without taking a breath.
2. Go slow and concentrate on the feel.
3. Bring your butt to the surface.

Drill #4
5 to 6 minutes

Notes:
1. Start face down, kicking gently.
2. Roll onto your back (one motion) then back to face
3. Hold your head still until the chin touches your shoulder.
4. Practice pressing your buoy at all points in the roll. (Your buoy is the space between your shoulders.)

Drill #5
Press down on your buoy traveling across your chest (from armpit to armpit).
25 yards Drill #4
25 yards SSP-DH
10-second rest

Drill #6
5 to 6 minutes
Repeat Drill #3

Notes: 1. Can use 50-yard repeats instead of 25-yard repeats but keep good form.

The above swim drill sets should give you a good idea of the highly targeted drills implemented and practiced in my swim workouts. Following are titles to other skill-building workouts that I routinely practiced.

- Skill Builder #2 – Making Your Body Longer
- Skill Builder #3 – Swimming on Your Side
- Skill Builder #4 – Consolidating Your Efficiency
- Skill Builder #5 – Getting the Feel for Effective Swimming
- Skill Builder #6 – Introduction to Advanced Drills and Skills

The overall goal of these drills was to make you swim in a flat position, face pointing down, rotating the body smoothly and powerfully from side to side and making the body as long as possible from the tips of the fingers to the tips of the toes. Once proficient at these techniques, you can slip smoothly and efficiently through the water.

Once I learned them all, the challenge was to do all of them in coordination while swimming. The key was to have an unbroken chain of energy that started at the kick and traveled upward through my hips and torso and ended at the tips of the outstretched arm using a twisting motion. This twisting motion is the source of the power used in swimming and it originates in the torso. This is also why you can swim for miles without tiring your arms and legs. This was particularly important, as I would need fresh legs in the bike and running events.

Once mastered, I could glide powerfully through the water in an energy efficient manner.

I practiced these form drills during the winter of 1998. The result was improved swim form, speed, and endurance. I now had the ability to cover more distance in less time using less energy than ever before. By the spring of 1998, I was swimming more efficiently and with greater distance. Swim workouts would now typically involve up to 2,000 yards of swimming. The half distance triathlon swimming event was 1.1 miles, and one mile is equivalent to 1,760 yards. This was an exciting development in my training, as I could now start to consider competing in a half distance triathlon event.

All the work I was putting into my swimming, cycling, and running skills ended up being the building blocks and foundation of becoming a better, stronger, and more confident triathlete. This concept is known as building your base.

Now that I could swim the distance required in a half distance triathlon event, it was time to work on my cycling skills.

Chapter 11

Improving My Cycling Skills

Once I purchased the Trek 2100 road bike, I could immediately ride for ten to twelve miles. I believed it was a result of the level of cardiovascular fitness I had achieved through running and swimming. However, they did not develop the muscles I needed to ride a bicycle faster and for longer distances. All I knew about developing my riding abilities was just to ride longer and faster. So that was what I did.

Riding my new racing bike was like getting my first bicycle as a kid. I felt faster than a speeding bullet on that bike. The initial rides averaged a twelve-mile-per-hour pace. This was not fast by triathlete standards, though I did not know it at the time. I always looked forward to the training rides, and each week I added an extra mile or two to the duration.

After competing in sprint triathlons, I noticed that other competitors had additional bars mounted on top of the normal handlebars. These were parallel with the bike frame. These extra bars had pads to place your forearms and had grips for your hands. Using them allowed the rider to lean forward on the bike, with their body parallel to the top rail of the bike frame. This position is known as the "aero position," as it decreases the surface area of the body exposed to the wind and thus reduces wind resistance. This position allows you to ride at a faster speed due to the reduced wind resistance. To top it off, they look cool. I purchased a set and installed them on my bicycle. Now it looked like a tri-bike.

My first few rides in the aero position proved a bit challenging. Instead of your hands grasping the handlebars outside of your body area, they are inside of it. The forearms are also stretched out in front, with elbows resting in the pads. The first few rides were uncomfortable, and I felt unstable, like I might lose control over the bike. It gradually became second nature, and it put less strain on my back and hands and allowed for longer, more comfortable rides.

My next step in triathlon was to enter and finish the IRONMAN® 70.3® Buffalo Springs Lake triathlon event. This would require the ability to complete a bicycle ride of fifty-six miles. Whew! That was over four times what I had been riding. I participated in my first sprint distance triathlon in the spring of 1998. Now a mere four months later I would attempt a half distance triathlon race totaling 70.3 miles. That, my friends, was a short amount of time to develop the swimming and running skills required. My goal and dream was to just finish the race. More time would be needed to finely hone those skills to compete at an elite level.

From the spring to the early summer of 1998, I gradually increased my training rides to the required fifty-six miles. My average speed gradually increased to sixteen to seventeen miles per hour. At that pace, it would take three hours and thirty minutes to complete a fifty-six-mile bike course. That was a sobering thought when coupled with a mile swim and thirteen-mile run in the half distance triathlon race. It was now time to start training to combine all these events together in a single race.

CHAPTER 12

TRAINING FOR MY FIRST HALF DISTANCE TRIATHLON

The half distance IRONMAN® 70.3® Buffalo Springs Lake triathlon included a 1.2-mile open water lake swim, a fifty-six-mile bike ride, and a 13.1-mile run in that order. I could complete each of the events individually but was not at all sure about doing them back-to-back with no rest between events. I wasn't sure if I was up for the task.

I later learned that in the triathlon world combined workouts were known as "bricks." An example of such a workout would be to swim for thirty minutes then run for an hour or more. Another would be to run for one and half hours then cycle for two hours. These workouts simulated the race, but not for the full distance. I was surprised to learn in preparing for a half distance triathlon event, it is not necessarily helpful to complete the full race distance in a single training session. It places too much stress on your body, which requires additional rest and recovery time. It is better to slowly build to 80% of the race day mileage so your physical conditioning is at its peak on race day.

My race preparation began in the spring of 1998. Remember my chosen profession of a CPA? My work primarily consisted of auditing the financial statements of rural utilities. This required an extensive amount of travel to remote areas, places without swimming pools or gyms. Our work was concentrated in the months of December, January, February, March, and April. We would typically travel to the location on a Sunday or Monday, working ten or more hours a day, then return home on Thursday or Friday and work at our home office until noon on Saturday. Then do it all again the next week.

This made getting in the required workouts a huge challenge. My long workouts were done over the weekend. During the work week, I rose early, around 5:30 a.m., to complete a run or swim workout. Prior to a trip, I would research if the area had a public pool facility. Often these were at a local gym or YMCA. At some locations, the local high school had lap pools. When possible, I would use those facilities in the morning or late evening. About half of the locations had a pool I could use.

My days were very busy, and it took a lot of dedication to keep with my workout schedule, but it was even more complicated when I traveled. For the morning swims, I took my business attire to the pool so that I could work out, shower, dress, and make it back to the hotel in time to pick up the staff to take them to our work location and not return to the hotel until 7:30 or 8:00 p.m. The staff would be ready to go eat but I had to get in another workout. In the evening, I'd use the hotel's workout room with weights, a treadmill, and stationary bike. If there was not one at the hotel, I looked for a local gym or just went for a run outdoors. When I finished, I would eat the take-out meal my staff kindly picked up for me while they were out at the restaurant.

With my work and training taking up so much of my time, it did not leave much time for my family. Our daughters were five, nine, and eleven at this time. As you can imagine, during my heavy travel periods, I was unable to be with them from Monday through Thursday but made it a priority to call and connect with them every night. On days at home, I worked out before they awoke and other times that did not conflict with their activities or our family time. I don't think it was ever an issue for them, as they never complained, at least not to me. My top priorities were God, family, work, and triathlon and in that order. Debbie said she functioned like a single parent while I was away, but it was not an issue for her, as she knew I was building a career and pursuing a dream. This was not exactly new for her as her father was in the Air Force and was often deployed overseas.

My career and now my sporting activities would not have been possible without her loving support.

Through January to April of 1998, my one and only goal in triathlon was to increase my endurance capabilities to the point that would enable me to complete in the event. I did not care all that much about being fast. For this first race, I just wanted to finish. How many people could say that they completed a triathlon race covering 70.3 miles? I wanted to be included in that group.

Pursuing any dream is a journey of discovery, finding out what does and doesn't work and learning from others. In this point in my training, I focused on the brick workouts. I did not have a written workout plan for each week. I was just doing what seemed appropriate and attempted to stagger the brick workouts between the ones that involved just one of the three events. It never occurred to me that there might be literature out there on the subject. I didn't know what I didn't know!

I started training in 1997, weighing in at around 190 pounds. I was losing weight but not all that much. My appetite increased significantly, so I was taking in as many calories as I was burning. By the end of April 1998, I weighed around 185 pounds on a 6'2" frame.

Now, I am sure you are asking yourself why on earth would anyone intentionally subject themselves to all this intense physical training? Moreover, why would I commit to completing an event that stretched my mind, body, and soul to the very limits? You would have a good point. My answer is not easily put into words. Given the grueling schedule I shared between work and working out, I asked myself this same question. Was this a worthy goal? Would my time be better served on another dream or goal? I will do my best to answer those questions for you.

My competitive and adventurous spirit has always led me to things that not everyone will attempt. The fact that these endurance events were hard and challenged my mind, body, and soul was one of the strongest attractions for me, wanting to know, just for myself, what I was capable of and what my limits were. I also enjoyed comingling with other competitive people who liked this type of self-discovery. This was also something completely different than my work. I like having diversity in my life and have always enjoyed expanding my horizons, experiencing the unknown, pushing myself to new heights of knowledge and experiences. We just have this one life that God has granted us. I am not going to waste one second of it regretting not trying new things.

With all the training and preparation behind me and race day quickly approaching, it was time to start making all the needed race preparations.

Chapter 13

Pre race Activities

The days leading up to race day were spent with short-duration, low-intensity workouts. It was time to let my body fully absorb and adapt to all the training I had been doing and to recover from any minor injuries. The goal of the prerace week was to have my body, mind, and spirit as ready as possible on race day. This process is known as "peaking."

I loaded up on carbohydrates two nights before the race, as it takes that long for your body to fully digest and stock the fuel stored in your blood and liver. It's like changing the oil, checking the tires, and topping off your car's gas tank before going on a long road trip. I cleaned my bike by spraying it with a hose and wiping it down with a cleaner, learning later that this was not the preferred method of caring for a road bike. Bikes should be cleaned with a degreaser and washing agents to lubricate all moving parts. Being a babe in the woods in the sport of triathlon, again, I didn't know what I didn't know. It was as if there was a huge sign hanging over my head blaring out: "ROOKIE!"

The day before the race, I went to the packet pick-up located at the host hotel. Race organizers select a local hotel that serves as the event epicenter. Athletes lodge there, the event holds meetings with the athletes, and it serves as an expo for vendors marketing their wares and products. The packet contained all the race rules and other essential information, including my swim cap and race numbers for the bike and jersey. I was not sure what to expect at this event, but when

I walked into the building, the athletes were there mingling, checking out the course maps, visiting with one another, and shopping at the expo for race supplies. The air was full of excitement and electric with pent-up energy from the athletes. Equipment and clothing vendors set up booths marketing everything from running and cycling gear, helmets, sunglasses, bikes, training equipment, and all sorts of other race needs. You could also get a relaxing massage and listen to guest speakers. Bike mechanics were on hand to help with any last-minute equipment issues. The race officials used this site to have a mandatory pre-race meeting explaining race rules, last-minute changes to the course, and other important information related to tomorrow's race. The local newspaper and radio stations covered the pre- and post-race activities. I loved every minute of it. It all provided me with a sense that I was part of something special.

I returned home to pack everything I needed. In later races I used a checklist that helped me remember everything. Here is an example of the items on the list.

For the swim:
- Goggles
- Swim cap
- Wetsuit
- Goggles defogger

For the bike:
- Bike
- Bento Bag filled with energy and electrolyte supplements
- Two or three water bottles
- Spare tubes and compressed air canisters
- Flat tire changing tools
- Pump to inflate tires to the desired psi prior to the start of the race

- Cycling shoes

- Helmet and sunglasses

For the run:
- Running socks and shoes

- Jersey

- Cap

- Energy and electrolyte supplements

- Sunscreen

- Body Glide and/or Vaseline applied to areas prone to chafing

Post-race clothing

With all the prerace planning complete, equipment packed and double-checked, it was time to rest and relax. Ideally, the day before the race is devoted solely to staying off your feet, but there always seems to be last-minute things to be done. My body felt strong and full of energy, ready to embark on this exciting new adventure. I felt like a charioteer fighting to hold back the horses.

The night before the race, I did not sleep very much. I was too excited. There were so many unknowns. What might go wrong? Would I be able to finish the race? Was I forgetting anything?

I reread the race literature again, refreshing myself about the rules, the setup, where I needed to report in the morning, etc. Competitors needed to be at the race transition area early. There was a single road that led into the lake and parking area, so traffic could be an issue. We also needed to be there early to get body marked, rack our bikes, and prepare to race. I am rarely late to anything, especially not today! I did not sleep well, and not wanting to get caught in any traffic jams at the lake, I left our home close to 4:00 a.m.

My wife, Debbie, who was a volunteer, would show up later and had a pass to park closer to the race epicenter. True to our previous offer to Mike and Marti Greer, Debbie became Marti's assistant. Whatever needed to be done or checked on in the months leading up to the race and before, during, and after the race, Debbie did it. In this manner she became as involved in the sport as I was. In that sense, this was her first half distance triathlon race as well. She was nervous, not wanting to make any mistakes, and at the same time, she was nervous about me and worried about how I would fare in the race. This day was full of unknowns for us both. In this and later races, Debbie and Marti paused just before the race to have a private prayer together requesting that the athletes have a good race experience without injuries and mishaps.

The race start was scheduled for 6:30 a.m. at sunrise, because the weather in the middle of June in West Texas can be brutally hot and windy. The city has a semi-arid climate with an elevation of 3,256 feet above sea level. The weather was forecasted to be near one hundred degrees, with strong, gusty winds from the southwest, a typical June day in Lubbock. Mornings are cool, averaging between sixty-five and seventy degrees. By midmorning, the air temperature heats up and the wind starts to blow. Oddly enough, a light covering may be needed early in the morning, even though the daytime high will be close to one hundred degrees.

The small lake is located just below the Caprock, with shores lined with homes and elm tree-covered roadways. If you are not familiar with the term Caprock, it is the geographical boundary where the flat plains drop several hundred feet in elevation into rolling ranch land. The flatlands of cotton fields fall away to canyons of thorn-covered mesquite trees, cactus, prairie grass, cattle, roadrunners, rattle snakes, and jackrabbits. The water temperature is cool due to the lake being fed by a natural underground aquifer. A perfect venue for holding a triathlon event.

The Caprock viewed from the top.

The Caprock viewed from below.

Triathlon race rules provide that a competitor can elect to use a wetsuit during the swim if the water temperature is seventy-eight degrees or below. The race announcers told us the water was exactly seventy-eight degrees, giving us the choice. I decided to wear my wetsuit, as I needed all the help I could get!

I arrived at the lake around 4:30 a.m., before anyone else, which made me laugh. I was definitely a rookie. With nothing else to do, I lay down on the bench seat of my car until the volunteers and race organizers arrived about thirty to forty-five minutes later. The first people to arrive were the race owner, organizer, and friend, Mike Greer, and the police officer who coordinated the athlete parking area.

I got out of my car to speak to them, and Mike said something to the effect of, "What are you doing here so early?"

I just said that I did not want to be late. No problems there! I waited in my car until other athletes showed up at around 5:15 a.m. It was time to unload my bike and equipment, inflate my tires to the desired psi, and then head to the transition area.

The athlete parking area was located on a mesa about 150 feet above the transition area. We had to walk our bikes and equipment down there. At the entrance, we were to stop and get our bodies marked. They marked your race number on the outside of each arm close to the shoulder and on the outside of both thighs with a magic marker. They also put your age on the back of your calf. These markings allowed the race officials, announcers, and spectators to identify the athletes. The age number on the calf was nice, as athletes could tell if someone in front of them or someone who just passed them was in their age group.

I set up my bike in the transition area that was normally a small recreational parking lot. The bike racks were pre-numbered, so each contestant had a specified spot to place their bike. With around 600 athletes, there was not a lot of space between each bike, leaving only a small area to place your towel and all your gear. Finding my spot, I mounted my bike by resting the handlebars on the railing with the front wheel under the rack. My bike was too unstable to rest it with the bike seat on top of the rack pole. I took time to set everything up to allow for a quick transition from swim-to-bike and from bike-to-run.

Once ready, I surveyed the swim course buoys that were placed about 200 yards apart. From my vantage point, I had a good visual of the swim course setup. I then knelt down to attach the provided timing chip strap around my ankle. The chip sent an electronic signal to the timing computer, identifying the contestant and the exact time the chip went across a timing mat at various points during the race.

Thirty minutes prior to the start of the race, the announcer called all athletes to the swim start area, a shallow, sandy, half-moon-shaped beach. While entering the area, contestants were directed to walk across a timing mat that read and registered their timing chip. Athletes crossed another mat at the start and end of each of the three events. This was how split times were recorded for each event and for the transition times. Great information for me to learn how I performed in my first race.

Contestants were allowed a short warm-up swim if they wanted to. I carried my gear to the start area and put on the wetsuit and cap with goggles in hand. They managed start times by color coding the swim caps to indicate the wave in which the contestants would begin the race, spaced about five minutes apart. The pros went first, followed by the twenty-nine and younger group, then the remaining age groups as their wave was called. I was in the third wave. I did a short swim warm-up just to get loose and accustomed to the water temperature, making sure my standard swim competition goggles sealed properly. Nothing is worse than getting your goggles full of water at the very start of the race. I was ready!

The twenty minutes leading up to the race start was a special time for me as I stood on the beach ready to race. This was my first half distance triathlon, and I was full of excitement and very nervous. What would the day hold for me? Would I race and finish strong, or would I fail and withdraw? I took in everything happening around me as the sun peeked above the horizon, enjoying the moment. While waiting for my wave's turn to start, I calmed my mind, body, and spirit. I had prepared well, but the day was full of unknowns. This became my routine in future races, as every race had its own unique challenges.

The start area was electric with all the pent-up energy of the 550 athletes competing in the race. I was nervous but ready to go. The first wave started as my group stood to the side waiting for our turn to start. A guy standing close by asked the surrounding contestants if anyone wanted to pray. I am a follower of Jesus Christ; I was certainly willing to join him. There were about ten of us who gathered in a circle with arms across each other's shoulders, and we bowed our heads as the prayer was recited asking God to keep us all safe and for an enjoyable experience. Perfect! Nothing left to do but get started. Looking back at my wife in the spectator area, I smiled and waved.

The race announcer told all the athletes with my color of my swim cap to get ready to start. I moved to the outer edge of the group so I would not have a huge crowd in front or behind me as I started the swim. The announcer was my good friend Marti Greer, and she provided a ten-second countdown to the sound of the starting blow horn.

Chapter 14

My First Half Distance Triathlon Race: Swimming Event

The bright red sun was just breaking the horizon, painting the sky with vivid pink and orange colors, as the horn sounded. All 150 or so swimmers in my wave hit the water. Some held back, giving themselves more room, letting those wanting to start fast go first. I was close to the middle of the pack and started the swim at a moderate but steady pace.

Once in the water, it was more chaotic than I had expected. I had a swimmer directly in front of me, with the tips of my fingers sometimes touching their toes. Someone behind me was doing the same to me. There was also a contestant on either side of me, each doing their best not to lock our arms as we swam. This crowded condition persisted for 150 yards, then we turned to the right at a rocky point jutting out from the shoreline, heading east to the first buoy. We were to keep the buoys to our left as we swam by. Race officials were nearby in boats and kayaks monitoring us in case someone was in distress or if they tried to cut the course short.

As I rounded the first corner, the blazing yellow sun peeked above the horizon and lit the path to the next swim buoy. The glare was so bad that I could not see the buoy. My only option was to follow the swimmers in front, hoping they knew where they were going. The buoy became more visible as we neared it, and I relaxed a little.

We all converged on the buoy, needing to make a ninety-degree left turn towards the next buoy. We were bumping into each other to the point where we had to stop and start again. Seeing this coming, I tried to make a wide turn to avoid the congestion. This worked and I was able to swim unabated, but it was still crowded.

Once around the buoy, the crowd dispersed so that the swimmers were yards apart. The separation grew as the race continued. I must have started a little too slow, or those that started ahead of me started too fast, as I was beginning to catch and pass other swimmers. I tried to keep my head face down and swim as efficiently and quickly as possible, turning my head only to take a breath. I looked up about every twenty to thirty strokes to locate the next buoy and stay on course.

After swimming north to the opposite side of the lake, we made a left turn, heading west. This section of the course was about a half-mile in length. All we had to do was make a straight line to the next buoy. I tried swimming for longer periods without looking for the buoys to cut some time. Wrong decision! At about midway through this section, I looked up and noticed a fishing pier about thirty yards to my right. Oops! I was at least fifty yards wide of the course. This cost me extra time, now I need to swim at an angle to get to the next buoy.

At this point, I was halfway through the swim course. My breathing was labored but not out of control. My wetsuit was sleeveless and let water in but not enough to affect my comfort or pace. My biggest concern was that my body was starting to overheat. The purpose of the wet suit is to make a swimmer more buoyant and to retain body heat, but I was overheating. I combated this by periodically stopping just long enough to pull the suit away for my neck to let some cool water wash over my body. I realized the suit was beginning to chafe my neck. I continued to swim steadily at about the same pace as we entered the final turn to the south towards the exit area. It was a huge relief to eye those final few buoys and glimpse the exit only a hundred yards away.

The finish for the swim was a submerged concrete boat ramp covered in moss and was very slick. Outdoor carpet strips had been laid on top of the ramp to keep us from slipping and falling. Volunteers on either side of the ramp grabbed our hands and arms, helping us safely exit the water. I felt victorious since I had never swum this far in open water. My time was a slow 41:07 and 467th of 548 finishers. I reminded myself this was my first half distance triathlon. My only goal was to finish.

Exiting the water, my equilibrium was out of kilter, and I was wobbly. I was breathing hard, but physically I was strong with plenty of energy to start the next leg of the race. I moved as quickly as possible to my bike. I now faced row after row of bikes, and I needed to find mine! Prior to the race, I'd picked a visual reference on the edge of the bike racks to help identify which row my bike was on. It helped but I did have to slow down in my approach to the row my bike was on. There were athletes scurrying everywhere, pulling their wetsuits off, throwing on their cycling jerseys and helmets, then running with their bikes to the bike mount and start line. It seemed like organized chaos.

It wasn't easy to put the skin-tight neoprene jersey on my wet body. I was pleasantly surprised to watch other athletes help stretch their jerseys over their backs, especially for the new triathletes like me. Once everything was ready, I grabbed my bike and quickly made my way to the bike start line. Once there, I mounted my bike and began the fifty-six-mile leg of the race. My swim-to-bike transition time was 3:34. Not horrible, but I would need to improve upon it in future races.

Swimmers as they approached the swim finish

Chapter 15

My First Half Distance Triathlon Race: Bike Event

The bike course began with a tough couple of climbs. The first climb started around a hundred yards from the start line. It was short but very steep, taking power to get up it. Most athletes were standing upright on their bikes to obtain the necessary force. Once up the incline, the path leveled out for around a quarter mile, followed by a steep decline before we crossed the dam. My weight, at close to 190 pounds, allowed me to descend quickly, reaching close to thirty-five miles per hour. With this amount of speed, I coasted on the flat one-third of a mile across the dam to start the next climb. This ascent was about a quarter mile in length and very steep. At the top of the second climb, my thighs were burning, and I was ready for hydration. This was a tough course. We'd not gone two miles yet and already there were two significant climbs. Phew, only fifty-four miles and an unknown number of climbs to go.

Leaving out on the bike course

From the end of the second climb there were two miles of flat roadway. I backed off on the power to let my legs and lungs recover from those first two intense climbs and rehydrated with a full bottle of water and ingested one of the gel packets. The supplement pack contains a gooey gel with around 110 calories that is quickly absorbed into your bloodstream, providing a quick energy boost. I just needed to rip off the top and squeeze it into my mouth.

The wind was already beginning to pick up, coming from the southwest and giving us a push as we exited the lake turning north. Adrenaline rushed through my veins as I rode faster with less effort. This part of the course only lasted for a mile and then turned ninety degrees to the east. The wind was still pushing me from a side angle, so it was still a comfortable effort at a quick pace.

At around the five-mile mark, there was an aid station. Volunteers held out water bottles and energy drinks for the riders to grab when we yelled out what we wanted. The volunteers would run alongside our bike, handing us the bottles. It was a bit chaotic, but it worked. At this point, I was down to one water bottle, so I called out, "Energy drink!" and it was delivered by an eager young man, placing it expertly in my hand as I slowed my pace. My race plan was to take in one bottle each hour. I was set with two full bottles of liquids in my bottle holders.

My labored breathing was now under control and my thighs were no longer stinging. I was eager to take on the remainder of the bike course, which took a ninety-degree turn to the south, in the direction the wind was blowing! The wind speed was now fifteen miles per hour and directly in my face, significantly slowing my pace. A headwind is not a cyclist's friend. If you stop pedaling to get a bit of rest, the wind will quickly bring you to a halt. You must keep the power ramped up but not get your heart rate too high.

After a couple of miles, the course dropped off the plains into a half-mile descent. I let my legs rest while coasting downhill to conserve energy. At the bottom, the course flattened out for a half-mile or so. Then there was yet another steep quarter-mile climb out of the canyon, back to the top of the Caprock. I tried to carry as much speed as possible into the next climb but quickly slowed when entering the steeper portion, eventually slowing to five to six miles per hour while powering my way up.

This picture is of one of the descents and climbs.

Once on top and back on flat ground, the wind battle began again, and it grew stronger. I continued south for another five miles to a turnaround point and another aid station, replenishing my water bottles and doing my best to consume about one-fourth of a bottle of liquid every fifteen minutes and an energy gel pack every forty-five minutes. All to stay as hydrated as possible and to keep my energy levels up. I was cautiously optimistic about how I felt at this stage, as I still had plenty of energy and strength in my legs. However, there were still twenty-eight miles left on the bike course and 13.1 miles to run.

The riders were excited, yelling out celebrations as we made the turnaround with the wind at our backs again. I spotted a couple of my relatives at the turn cheering me on.

This portion of the bike course doubled back upon itself for three to four miles, with the wind giving us a much-needed push. I still pedaled hard, but a tail wind reduced the constant pressure needed to keep the speed up.

At the end of this section, the course took a ninety-degree turn to the east for another few miles towards yet another curvy and steep climb, requiring greater effort. This climb was appropriately known as "the spiral staircase" and led us back to the top of the Caprock. Once on top of the Caprock, I was catching up with a female rider. When I was within fifteen feet of her, she abruptly stood upright over her pedals and began to urinate with the spray coming straight at me. I had to swerve to avoid being soaked. She briefly looked back at me with an oops expression.

With all these climbs, combined with battling the wind, my energy levels were starting to drop, and my legs were weakening. My spirits were still high, and more importantly I was having fun.

The course curved to the north for another two miles and then turned around. I was now at the farthest point from the lake. The decline back down the canyon wall on the spiral staircase was steep and curvy, requiring breaking on the sharp curves. Once at the bottom of the canyon, the course traveled west to the next aid station, where I turned to the north to yet another climb back to the top of the Caprock. This area was known as "the tree tunnel," as it was lined with large elm trees on both sides briefly providing welcome shade. Once on top, we continued for a mile then turned to the west. Mercy! The steady, hot, dry wind was strong, and while not directly in our face, it was slowing me down.

The tree tunnel.

Finally, I was headed back to the lake, having just passed the forty-mile mark. Just sixteen more miles to go! Yahoo! Unfortunately, the wind felt like a blast furnace and was against us for the remainder of the ride. Getting in the most aero position possible, I endured the hot and windy trip back.

Close to the end of the bike course, I entered the lake area, now heading east with the wind at our backs and just three miles to go. I drank another full bottle and consumed an energy pack. Hopefully, this will top off my tank before starting the run.

With two miles left, the course took a steep decline back down to the lake level, crossing the dam towards the final climb. This was the shortest but steepest climb on the course. Riders had dismounted and were walking their bikes up, only one-fourth of a mile from the bike finish line. I carried all the speed I could muster from the prior descent to start the climb. I was standing upright on my bike, giving 100% effort to make the climb.

Once on top, a 150-yard flat portion led to the final steep decline to the end of the bike portion of the race. At the bottom of the decline, there were volunteers yelling for us to slow down, as the finish line was a mere seventy-five yards away. Braking hard, I dismounted the bike as I crossed the bike finish line. I was tired with a tight sensation in my lower back, hamstrings, and my thighs were toast. I did my best to shuffle with my bike to the racks and prepare for the run. I completed the bike portion of the race in 3:34 for an average 18.2-mile-per-hour pace. My bike-to-run transition time was 2:35. My time ranked 407th out of 548 finishers. Not too bad for a challenging course and my first ever triathlon race covering 70.3 miles!

CHAPTER 16

MY FIRST HALF DISTANCE TRIATHLON RACE: RUN EVENT

After cycling for fifty-six miles, just bending over to put on socks and running shoes was a challenge. I changed into a fresh lightweight running jersey, put on my cap, loaded my jersey pockets with my energy gel packs and electrolyte tablets, and then trotted to the run start line, crossing the timing mat where aid station volunteers were handing out liquids. It was nice to see the spectators cheering us on and, of course, my wife Debbie waving and cheering for me while I started the 13.1-mile run.

It is hard to adequately describe the sensation of having cycled for a long distance then trying to run immediately thereafter. But I will do my best. The muscle groups used to propel a bicycle are different from those used to run. After spending three hours on a bike pedaling at race pace, my leg muscles were tight and stiff, not allowing me to run with a normal gait. It takes the first mile of the run for your body to transition from cycling to running. My feet shuffled and I struggled to get my legs to run with my normal gait. Triathletes coined the term "the triathlon shuffle" to describe this phase.

By this point, I had been exercising at race pace for close to four hours. My legs and my energy system were not exactly fresh. My spirits were still good, and I was determined to see this through. I just kept putting one foot in front of the other and pushed on, trying not to think about how my body felt and the miles that stretched out in front of me. My body was rebelling but my mind was the conductor telling it to gut it, you can do this.

I was a bit surprised at the two-mile mark when I saw the leader of the race flying at me from the opposite direction. What? I called out, "Great job, keep it up, you're almost done." I had eleven more miles to go, and this guy was two miles from finishing the race. How was that even possible? I had to remind myself he was fifteen years younger.

Nearing the first aid station, I was pleased to see my running mentor and friend Weldon staffing the station. He offered me liquids and encouragement. It was crazy how much seeing a familiar, encouraging face lifted my spirits, refreshing my desire to keep going. He once told me that this race was likely too much for me. On some level one of my sub-goals was to prove him wrong.

At around the two-and-a-half-mile mark, the course made a sharp left turn into the first major climb. It was a short climb of around a hundred yards with a steep grade. Many racers were walking to the top. I was trying hard to do more than just walk, but it was not much more. Scaling the hill seemed like climbing Mt. Everest with my heart, lungs, and legs reaching their maximum output. With eleven more miles to go, there was no sense in burning up my legs here.

At the top, the terrain flattened out for about a half-mile followed by a steep decline back down to the lake level. You would think that running down a steep decline would be easy, and it is when compared to running up one. However, running downhill involves putting on the brakes with each step. This puts strain on your thighs, and mine were burning upon reaching the bottom. The course then flattened out for another quarter-mile to the aid station at the mile-three marker. Whew! Ten more miles to go. There was yet another steep climb on the other side of the canyon floor. All these climbs were wearing on me, and the air temperature was quickly rising with the sun beating down on us with no shade in sight.

Once again, the course flattened out at the top of the climb. From there, the course took a sharp right turn to the west, with a gradual decline for the next few miles to the turnaround point. I was thankful for the slight downhill grade, as this made running easier, letting my legs recover from the previous steep climbs. This area of the course was known as "energy lab two," named after the portion of the 140.6-mile full distance IRONMAN® Triathlon World Championship run course in Hawaii known for its heat and still air. It was like running in an oven with no wind to help cool you down.

There was an aid station at the turnaround point where I walked just long enough to take in liquids, electrolytes, and an energy gel packet. The volunteers were handing out rags soaked in ice water. I grabbed one and put it underneath my cap. It felt so good!

The run course aid stations were staffed with friendly faces, mostly volunteers from the West Texas Running Club, many of them I had competed with in club events. Their encouragement boosted me through the rest of the race.

The turnaround point was a major milestone for me. I was halfway through the run course, having only six more miles to go. I chose not to look at it with a defeatist attitude, "Oh my, I still have six more miles to go! Can I make it?" Instead, I chose to see it as a positive. There were only six more miles to go to realize a dream! Was I tired? Was I exhausted? Had I depleted much of my energy reserves? Was I hot and ready to stop? All a resounding YES! However, that was merely a result of my efforts thus far. Nothing was going to stop me from finishing the race. I envisioned a mere six-mile run, something I'd done a multitude of times. In my mind, I had it whipped already and did my best to ignore my body's depleted condition, willing it to keep moving forward.

From the turnaround point, the course doubled back upon itself. Tackling the gradual incline we had just come down, this was the toughest part of the run course. Exhausted, hot, energy reserves bouncing off the empty line, and I had to run uphill, sapping what little energy I had. I saw the crest of the hill from a mile or so away, thinking I might never get there. Other runners were walking, trying to conserve their legs and energy. I had never liked walking any amount of time in a triathlon. I mean, this was a race! You could not walk in a race! That is not a putdown for athletes who do choose to walk. They have their own dreams and desires to fulfill. It was just not for me.

Most of you would not call what I was doing at this point running, more like a fast trot, but it was all I was physically capable of at that moment. That was what was important. Doing my best and giving it everything I had. The goal for this race was not at all about winning or finishing ahead of others. It was about assessing my limits, seeing what I was capable of in the intensity of race conditions.

At the top of the crest, a volunteer offered to spray down the athletes with a water hose. At the time it seemed like a promising idea, and I ran through the spray. The cool water felt incredible, but now my socks and shoes were soaked and made a squishing sound with every step. Ugh, that was a mistake!

From there the course dropped off back down to the canyon floor to another steep climb back up the other side. This was the last major climb in the course, and it was a doozy. Once on top, we ran back through the lake entrance and back down to lake level with three more miles to the finish line.

At the eleven-mile mark and aid station, I saw my friend Weldon again. At this point, with two miles left, I was hot, exhausted, and those remaining miles seemed like a hundred. He could see my depleted condition and was giving me cold wet rags, liquids, and offered encouraging words.

It is difficult to put into words what I was feeling both physically and mentally at this stage of the race. My body had truly little left to give. My mind was saying, enough is enough, STOP! This is where your character and will to succeed at any cost comes into play. The force of the human will has immense power. It can carry you through insurmountable obstacles. I learned about my drive at this moment of my first 70.3® race. It all came down to pushing through that last painful, exhausting step, pushing my body past anything I'd endured before. All I could do was keep moving, not really running, but not walking either.

At the twelve-mile marker, my body felt stronger, my legs lighter, and my spirits brighter. It must have been the "horse to the barn" effect, an effect I've experienced in virtually every race since. Competitors were offering each other encouragement and congratulations on being so close to the finish line. I could not see the end but could hear the announcer calling out names of the athletes as they crossed the finish line. I was getting pumped up and excited being almost done!

Chapter 17

My First Half Distance Triathlon Race: The Finish Line

Rounding the last curve, the finish line was now in sight at about 400 yards away. Spectators lined the road on each side, cheering us on. This gave me energy and strength to speed up. Now twenty-four years later, I can still clearly hear my name announced when I crossed the finish line.

The emotions tore through me. I'd completed my first half distance triathlon! It is next to impossible to convey these emotions to someone who has never been through such an experience. There is relief from stopping the physical exertion, but that is an insignificant factor. I could not stop smiling. I had accomplished something I had once believed to be next to impossible for someone my age. My run time was 2:18 and 347th overall. My total event finishing time was 6:10:21, with an overall rank of 367 out of 548 finishers.

I immediately forgot all the challenges of the race and relished my achievement. At the finish line, volunteers assessed my physical condition, then put a finisher's medal around my neck. I was shown to the refreshments stand and found the comforting shade of a tent to get out of the grueling hundred-degree day. I felt like a legitimate triathlete while swapping stories with other athletes of our race experiences. I glanced over at the med tent as I left the finish line area and knew well enough I was lucky to not be in there amongst the other athletes with IV bags, or worse, carted off in the nearby ambulance. I was physically and mentally exhausted, but not to the point of needing medical assistance.

Once recovered and feeling ready, I retrieved my bike and swim gear from the transition area. While doing so I heard several bike tires exploding. Athletes had inflated their tires to their maximum psi and the heat of the sun caused tire air pressure to rise to the point that they exploded! Then my wife and I headed to my car. As I walked by a friend, he asked about my finishing time. I proudly told him that I finished in 6:10:21. He made a snide comment about my time not being very fast. Debbie and I laughed about it later, but it stung nevertheless. Just wait! I told myself. This meant there was plenty of room for improvement.

Nearing the finish line

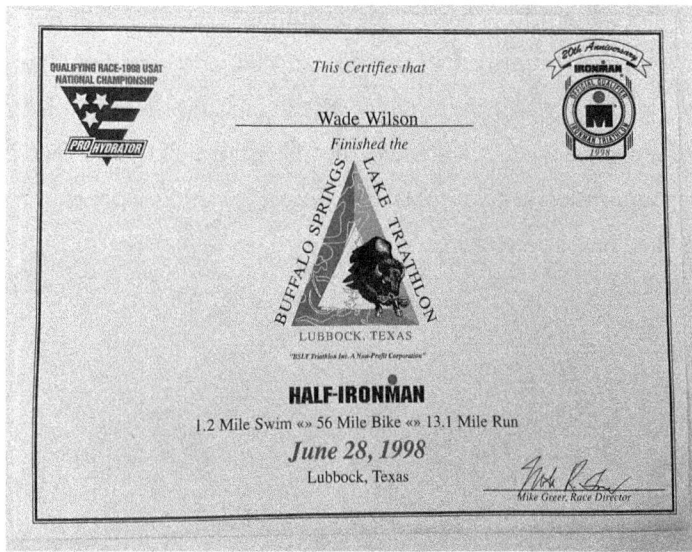

Finisher's certificate

Back home, I showered and took a two-hour power nap, having slept little the night before. Later that same evening the race organizers provided a banquet, awarding medals to the overall and top three finishers in each age group. They also awarded slots to the full distance IRONMAN® Triathlon World Championship.

As I drifted off to sleep that night, I wondered what new goal could top this. I was now a member of the small group of individuals to have completed a 70.3-mile triathlon event. I knew this was not the be-all and end-all in my pursuit of the sport, but I did not yet have any other goals in mind. That did not take long to change.

Notes from My Wife Debbie

My earliest memories of triathlon were when Wade decided he wanted a Schwinn Aerodyne stationary bike to ride indoors. He had been riding it a while when we had met friends for dinner one evening. At the restaurant Wade mentioned he would like to try a triathlon. Our friend said, "See that waiter? He is a triathlete, and you could never be that fast or be in the shape he is in." Well, that's all it took for Wade to start training, and boy did he prove him wrong. Wade became stronger and faster than the waiter.

I remember volunteering for our local running races and triathlons. All wonderful people. At the post-race awards dinner, they were awarding slots for Kona™. Wade and I looked at each other, wondering what the heck was Kona™? We ended up asking someone. It was where the full distance IRONMAN® Triathlon World Championship is held in Hawaii. Whoa! I wanted Wade to get a slot for Kona™! I had never been to Hawaii!

Chapter 18

New Goal of Racing in a Half Marathon

My fitness levels were increasing rapidly. So were my aspirations for longer and longer races. In the fall of 1998, I set my sights on running a half marathon race of 13.1 miles. My long course training runs were at that distance and more, so I had no doubts about finishing the race. The main concern was what my finishing time would be.

I entered the Buffalo Wallow Half Marathon, sponsored by the West Texas Running Club. Race day was set for November 14, 1998. The event was held at Buffalo Springs Lake, located a couple of miles east of the city. As previously described, Lubbock is set on the eastern edge of the Caprock, where the Great Plains drop off a couple of hundred feet into rolling pastures of ranch land full of grass, mesquite trees, and cactus. The small spring-fed lake sits below the Caprock, with steep descending paved roads used to reach it. On race day the weather conditions were perfect, with clear skies, no wind, low humidity, and cool temperatures. The course was difficult, with steep climbs from the lake level to the top of the Caprock and then descending back down.

All my running friends and supporters were there, making the event even more memorable. Competing with friends was one of the most enjoyable things about the sport. It was great fun with the banter and encouragement we gave each other before and during the event, then sharing our race experiences afterwards.

This race offered the perfect opportunity to practice the strategy and benefits of starting long course races at a comfortable pace, then building into the goal pace and finishing with a strong kick. I finished the race with a time of 1:44:14. Good for fifth in my age group and twenty-third overall. My average pace was 7:56 per mile, besting my goal pace of eight minutes per mile. Yahoo! I was making good progress.

With all this success of setting, meeting, and at times exceeding my goals, I was anxious to see what else I was capable of and what my limits were. This was becoming a journey of self-awareness, and I was having the time of my life.

> *"Take your victories, whatever they may be, cherish them, use them, but don't settle for them."* —Mia Hamm

Chapter 19

New Goals

It was not long before my thoughts turned to competing in a full distance triathlon event, knowing nothing about it other than it consisted of a 2.4-mile open water swim, a 112-mile bike ride, and a 26.2-mile run. Again, all back-to-back and in that order. That is a whopping 140.6-mile event with a time limit of seventeen hours. That is exactly twice the distance that I had completed at the IRONMAN® 70.3® Buffalo Springs Lake triathlon. I knew it would take some time to work toward this goal.

To even consider it, I would need to be able to run a marathon of 26.2 miles. Theoretically, I should be able to complete a marathon, having already demonstrated my endurance capabilities by finishing a half distance triathlon. However, the longest I had ever run was 13.1 miles. Knowing how my legs felt from running that distance, doubling it seemed like a lofty goal. With this in mind, I began to gradually increase my run mileage.

By late 1998, I'd increased my training mileage to eighteen miles. Entering a marathon event was within reach. I searched for and found a marathon in Dallas, Texas, titled the White Rock Marathon scheduled for January 9, 1999. Perfect! This was so exciting! Never had I dreamed of being able to complete a marathon distance race of 26.2 miles. In the weeks leading up to the race, I gradually increased my training runs to twenty miles. Increasing my ability to run longer was no easy task. Upon reaching the training mileage I was used to, my heart, lungs, legs, and feet were all ready to stop. At this point, I had to will my body to keep going. I begrudgingly complied and gradually adapted to the new demands placed upon me. It was not that long ago that six miles was all that I was capable of doing; now I was running three times that. The week before the race, I significantly decreased my run mileage, giving my body time to rest and recover before the race.

My family and I traveled to Dallas two days before the event. We stayed with my wife's parents in a nearby community, giving my family an opportunity to visit with my in-laws. Our three daughters were now thirteen, eleven, and seven years of age. They were by now used to my racing adventures and it was their new normal. The one thing I strived for was not letting my racing interfere with any of their activities nor my attendance to them.

Based on my research, the day prior to the race I needed to rest and stay off my feet, fuel up on carbohydrates, and hydrate as much as possible. This would let my muscles and connective tissues recover from any training stress and injury and give me a full tank of energy.

Race morning, I was excited and a bit nervous about this new adventure I was about to embark on. There were thousands of athletes all full of energy and wanting to get started. It was a cool, early winter morning, not much above freezing. I was dressed in a running warm-up that I ditched just before the race started. The event provided aid stations throughout the course, but I brought a belt with a water bottle holder mounted just above my hips in the small of my back. This enabled me to have a drink anytime I needed one. I also carried energy gel packets and electrolyte tablets that I planned to take every forty-five to sixty minutes, a strategy fitted and proven successful at the IRONMAN® 70.3® Buffalo Springs Lake triathlon.

I was ready!

The event had signs posted around the starting area with predicted pace per mile boldly printed on them. Athletes were to position themselves according to their abilities to allow the faster runners to start first. My goal was to run the race with an average pace of around nine minutes per mile, and I weaved my way through the crowd to the proper place. I was ready to start!

When the start gun fired, a mass of humanity took off. It was crowded at first, but everyone in my area was polite and was moving close to the same pace. I felt well-rested and strong and had to resist the urge to run faster. After all, this was a marathon. There was a long way to go.

As the miles slipped by, the runners spread out more. The day was beautiful with the perfect temperature for long-distance running. I was gliding along comfortably at around an 8:50-per-mile pace while passing through the beautiful homes of White Rock. That was a little faster than my goal of averaging a 9:00-per-mile pace. Knowing the final six miles were full of unknowns, I wanted a little cushion to play with in the final miles of the race.

I was feeling confident and strong, with all going according to my plan. That was until around the seventeen-mile mark. With nine more miles to go, I could feel my legs beginning to tire and my toes heating up, indicating the start of blisters. Oh no! Long-distance runners are aware of the term "hitting the wall." This is the point where your body is telling you it is time to stop. With my thighs and feet burning and fatigue creeping in, I was aware of this feeling. It was how I felt at the end of an eighteen-mile training run.

The problem was that I had never, as they say, run through the wall. From everything I had read about running a marathon, this was the point where the rubber met the road. You must suck it up and keep on running. The next few miles were difficult. It was time for the charioteer to start cracking the whip. Pushing through the wall is more of a mental test than a physical one. All I wanted to do was stop and rest. I tried to think about anything other than how my body felt and just keep my pace, pushing through the pain and discomfort.

Around mile twenty-two, I had come out the other end of the wall. Still very tired, with my thighs burning with each step, I felt more energized and in a better place mentally. I knew I only had four miles to go, then three, then two, then one.

Before long I rounded a street corner, and the finish line came into my view. Cheering spectators lined the street, and I was on cloud nine passing through them. Crossing the finish line was a sweet victory and symbolized the results of all my dedication, hard work, and perseverance. The best part was finishing the race with a time of 3:55:30, which was remarkably close to my goal pace of nine minutes per mile.

I found my wife and walked to the area where volunteers were handing out finisher's shirts. My legs were toast! It was painful to just step up on the curb without my thighs screaming at me. My feet and legs were very sore for the next couple of days, with my big toenails falling off, but none of it mattered. I'd achieved another milestone I thought was impossible and at the ripe old age of forty.

I felt extremely fortunate to live in a time where treatment was available to correct my pigeon-toed condition as a youth. Without it, I surely would not have been able to complete any triathlon or marathon. Rather I would have been relegated to watching others pursue their athletic dreams and wonder what might have been. A wave of heartfelt gratitude engulfs me every time I think about it.

Once back home in Lubbock, I relished my achievement before my mind turned to an even loftier goal. The one endurance event left on my to-do list was a full 140.6-mile full distance triathlon. Surely if I worked and trained long and hard enough, I could achieve this milestone as well. I did not have a particular event in mind, but I knew this was going to be my next athletic dream to pursue.

The 140.6-mile IRONMAN® Triathlon World Championship event is held during the month of October each year in Kona, Hawaii. This race is where the best of the best meet. Athletes do not just sign up for this event. They must earn a slot by finishing in the top two percent of their age group at a qualifying race. This left me out! I would need to find another full distance triathlon race to compete in. In the back of my mind, I wondered if it were possible to make the cut. Not now, that would take a lot more dedication. Did I have it in me?

The stars were aligning in my favor, as in February 1999, Debbie was working with Mike and Marti Greer on the upcoming race. They told her that she was a huge asset with her volunteer work. In appreciation, they invited us to accompany them to the 1999 IRONMAN® Triathlon World Championship. They generously offered to pick up the tab for transportation and lodging. I was traveling for work when she called to give me the awesome news. Well, heck yes, we would go! I was so excited it was hard to focus on work for the remainder of the day.

In January 1999, my tri-friends told me about a lottery process where the IRONMAN® Triathlon World Championship event invites fifty athletes who would like to join the event but were not able to earn a slot in a qualifying event. Now that sounded interesting!

In the famous words of ice hockey legend Wayne Gretzky, "You will miss 100% of the shots you don't take." With that in mind, my wife and I investigated it and decided to put my hat in the ring. We even paid an extra fifty dollars, which increased your chances of being selected. We had heard of athletes unsuccessfully entering the lottery for years. We knew that it was unlikely, but it was worth a shot. My chances were slim at best. If I won a slot, I would still have to demonstrate my ability to complete the distance of the race within the allotted time at an IRONMAN® Triathlon World Championship qualifying event. No problem there. The IRONMAN® 70.3® Buffalo Springs Lake triathlon was a qualifying event, and I planned to compete in the race in June of 1999.

Ironically, given my profession, the event announced the lottery winners on Income Tax Filing Day of April 15th. I was not overly concerned about the lottery process, and I was not expecting to be selected. I was busy trying to wrap up a busy tax season in 1999, when my wife Debbie strolled into my office with the biggest grin on her face.

She excitedly said, "You are in! You won a lottery slot for the IRONMAN® Triathlon World Championship."

It took me a few seconds to process what she had said. I had wanted to compete in a full distance triathlon event eventually but was not expecting to do so soon. Mike and Marti's invitation to accompany them to Hawaii was terrific, but now I would also get to compete in the event as part of the trip. How cool was that?

Pursuing a dream without a plan is like going fishing without bait. The enormity of what I needed to do to prepare my mind and body for a 140.6-mile triathlon event quickly sank in. The longest events I had completed to date were a half distance triathlon and a marathon. In six months, I would swim 2.4 miles, cycle 112 miles, and run 26.2 miles. Had I stepped in quicksand with my head about to submerge? I needed a new plan and quickly!

Chapter 20

Hiring a Coach

I did not have the expertise to prepare myself for a 140.6 mile triathlon race, so I contacted local pro triathlete Tim Key. Tim had competed in the IRONMAN® Triathlon World Championship and offered his services to train other athletes. He agreed to help me prepare. We both immediately got to work developing and implementing my training plan for the race on October 27, 1999.

Tim let me know he was training another gentleman from Lubbock, Dr. Todd Hegstrom, who had also won a lottery slot. Todd and I were close to the same age, so this worked out great. Tim would design and plan our daily workout schedules one month at a time. This allowed us to see what it was we would be doing every day in succeeding weeks.

Tim introduced me to new training concepts, methods, and ideas. One of our training goals was to reduce my heart rate for a given level of effort. I wasn't sure what that meant or what the benefits were. He explained by training your cardiovascular system, you could exercise harder and for longer periods of time, all the while requiring fewer heartbeats. A good analogy is a high-performance sports car. The more powerful the engine, the faster it can go with less motor revolutions, allowing the motor to work less to produce the same results as that of a less powerful motor. Now, compare that with your motor, your muscular and cardiovascular system. The more powerful and well-developed it is, the more work you can do with less stress on your motor.

Based on that concept, my training focused on strengthening my motor. I can hear you ask, "What does that look like?" Training your cardiovascular system to compete in endurance events takes long, slow, easy effort exercise. It takes time for your body to adjust to these new demands placed upon it. Changes in heart conditioning, expanding the lungs' capacity to deliver oxygen and fuel into the bloodstream, requires proper training and patience to see improvements. The goal is to teach the body to exercise at low heart rates and perceived exertion levels.

So, how do you know what your heart rate is? Do you stop and feel your pulse every so often? No, Tim introduced me to wristwatch products on the market that constantly monitor your pulse rate. These devices display your heart pulse rate on an easy-to-read screen. These watches also can serve as a clock, measure split times, track total exercise duration, and track your average heart rate during an exercise session. All that data can be downloaded into a computer program and can be used to track your training progress over time.

Coach Tim incorporated strength training into my workout plan. I had not considered including strength training in my workout routine. What could be gained? I was already swimming, cycling, and running daily. Once again, I did not know what I didn't know.

Endurance training conditions your muscles to work more efficiently for longer periods of time but does little to build muscle mass. To address this, Tim and I went to the Texas Tech University's gym where I was already swimming. He showed me various weight resistance workout routines to target the major muscle groups used in swimming, cycling, and running. We also targeted the core muscle groups, as these connect the kinetic energy chain from the foot to the shoulders and arms. Adding weight training to swimming, cycling, and running took a lot of time. When would I ever get to rest?

Training with a purpose means first evaluating your strengths and weaknesses. In the triathlon world, this process is known as determining your performance limiters. That was our next step, to determine my limiters.

We started by examining my swim stroke technique that I had been working so hard to improve. Tim observed my swim and noticed I was not keeping my body in a straight line throughout the swim stroke. I was letting my hands cross the center line of my body. This caused me to wither a bit in the water. I should be gliding smoothly in a straight line parallel to the water's surface. To correct this, I imagined swimming in the middle of a train track. Each arm was to follow the track on either side.

Another issue was that my toes were not pointed outward away from my body. Instead, my feet were pointed downward. This created drag, requiring more power to move through the water. Easy to fix, just make my feet as flat as possible by pointing my toes as far away from my body as possible.

Next, he assessed my run. Have you ever watched a group of people running? Just go to any local running club 5K race and turn your attention to the various running forms used. No two people have the same running gait. Some people shuffle their feet, some have a high leg lift, and others barely lift their feet off the ground. Some have a high heel kick, while others have little. Other runners sway their hips or lean forwards or backwards at the waist. Some have a combination of all the above.

The most efficient use of energy has the runner's posture tall and straight while leaning slightly forward. The feet come up the line of the opposite leg, giving the runner a high knee lift, followed by the kick, a high heel lift towards the runner's buttocks. Runners either land on the ball of the foot or the heel. Heel strikers are in effect putting on the brakes a little with each step. Better to land on the ball of the foot so that momentum is continuously moving forward.

Friends in the sport jokingly called me cowboy, as I had a sort of bowlegged gait. I addressed this deficiency by focusing on using good form on my long and slow running sessions. Changing your running style is not a particularly easy thing to do. I did make progress, but it took years to accomplish, as I had to retrain my muscle memory built during the past forty years.

My cycling posture also needed work. I learned that the seat height needed to be adjusted so that on the down stroke, my leg should be almost fully extended. The seat position was adjusted so I was better extended over the bike frame. This improved position reduced my body's surface area pushing against the air while moving through it. Less air resistance means cycling at faster speeds with less energy expended. I am sure that when you were a kid, you stuck your hand out the window of a car, feeling the air pressure relax as you flattened your hand. The same principle is at work when riding a bike.

Teaching an old dog new tricks is a challenge. All these changes took time to make and master. These errors in my form had been developed since I was young. That is a lot of muscle memory to overcome and is not easily changed. I like this quote regarding being patient while making changes for the better.

> *"The elevator to success is out of order. You will have to use the stairs, one step at a time." — Joe Girard*

Tim added rest into my training schedule. Training for endurance sports puts a significant amount of stress on the body. It needs downtime to recover and grow stronger. Rest days became my favorite, something to look forward to. On those days I tried to spend as much time as possible with my family. All this made sense. It is just an application of God's instruction to us to rest on the Sabbath. He knew our mind, body, and spirit needed a day of regeneration. Failure to do so can lead to injury, burnout, and other undesirable outcomes.

Tim and I spent time assessing my nutritional needs as well, as I was quickly losing weight. Simply put, I was burning more calories than I was taking in. To combat this, I added energy bar supplements, consuming these between the morning and noon meals and again between the noon and evening meals. These helped slow the weight loss and provided me with a more constant energy level. I was constantly eating throughout the day.

Armed with all this new knowledge, we could now proceed with writing my training routines.

Chapter 21

Training with a Purpose

Any dream needs to start with an end goal. Mine was simple enough. I just wanted to finish the race within the allotted time, stay healthy through it all, have the experience of a lifetime, while crossing the finish line with a smile on my face. I had seen TV broadcasts of prior World Championship races with competitors crawling across the finish line with pain and anguish painted on their faces. I did not want to finish that way.

At this point, I had a mere six months to prepare my mind, body, and soul to complete the 140.4-mile endurance race. The distance was twice as far and would take at least twice as long as I had ever gone before. If I had any chance at accomplishing this in such a short time, I had to be laser focused.

There is a science to training the body for endurance events, and there has been much research conducted on the subject. I was fascinated by everything Tim taught me. There are volumes and volumes written about each topic I am about to share, so I'll give you the condensed version. I am not trying to teach you how to train for ultra-endurance events. That would take another book unto itself. My intent is to illustrate all the study and planning that goes into equipping yourself to achieve a dream. Do you recall my saying, "Pursuing a dream without a plan of action is like going fishing without bait?"

Before we could begin developing a training regimen, we needed to determine my maximum heart rate while exercising. This information would be used to establish my goal average heart rates used during workouts.

Heart Rate

All my training plans would center on my heart rates while exercising. For those who have a history of being fit, your maximum heart rate is calculated based on a formula of 205 minus half your age. Heart rates at each level of exertion are expressed as a percentage of your maximum heart rate. Below is an example for me at age forty-one.

Maximum Heart Rate Predictor:

Base	205
Age	41
Deduction From Base	21
Maximum Heart Rate	185

Bike Training

Lactate Threshold			AT = 158 Vo2 = 166			
Zone	Low	High	RPE	Purpose	Bike Specific %	
1	103	128	6-8	Easy / Recovery - AR	65%	81%
2	128	136	9-11	Endurance - End / Over Distance - OD	81%	86%
3	136	142	12-14	Aerobic Endurance	86%	90%
4	142	150	15	Lactate Tolerance	90%	95%
L-1	150	152	15-16		95%	96%
L-2	152	153	16-17		96%	97%
L-4	153	160	17-18		97%	101%
L-5	160	167	19-20		101%	106%

Run Training

Lactate Threshold				AT = 170 Vo2 = 179		
Zone	Low	High	RPE	Purpose	Run Specific %	
1	119	139	6-8	Easy / Recovery - AR	70%	82%
2	139	150	9-11	Endurance - End / Over Distance - OD	82%	88%
3	150	156	12-14	Aerobic Endurance	88%	92%
4	156	162	15	Lactate Tolerance	92%	95%
L-1	162	163	15-16		95%	96%
L-2	163	165	16-17		96%	97%
L-4	165	172	17-18		97%	101%
L-5	172	180	19-20		101%	106%

For example, when a workout called for an easy or recovery day on the bike, my heart rates should range between 103 and 128, and my RPE (rate of perceived exertion) should be between six and eight, in other words, feel very, very easy.

Fitness Test

Before writing my training programs, we needed to determine my current fitness level. Easy enough, it should be good having just finished a marathon and a half distance triathlon event. Again, I didn't know what I didn't know. Coach Tim scheduled a fitness test for me to determine the heart rate zones for each level of perceived exertion. This test measures your running fitness level. We used it as a general test of my level of fitness for all three sports. You can conduct separate fitness tests for each sport.

A run fitness test is conducted on a treadmill and starts with a very easy speed setting of three for one minute. As each minute passes, the speed increases by 0.5. At the end of each minute, you assess your perceived effort on a scale of one to twenty. The test concludes when you reach a perceived exertion rating of 19. Below is a chart of perceived exertion ratings:

1-7	Very, very light	14	
8		15	Hard
9	Very light	16	
10		17	Very hard
11	Fairly light	18	
12		19	Very, very hard
13	Somewhat hard	20	

The heart rate is also recorded at the end of each minute. Below is an example of one of my early fitness tests:

Minute	Speed	HR	RPE	Grade
00:00.0				
1	3.0	87		
2	3.5	89		
3	4.0	100		
4	4.5	110		
5	5.0	120		
6	5.5	126		
7	6.0	133		
8	6.2	139		
9	6.4	140	10.5	
10	6.6	143		
11	6.8	143		
12	7.0	146	14	
13	7.2	149		
14	7.4	152		
15	7.6	154	15	
16	7.8	157	16	
17	8.0	159		
18	8.2	163		
19	8.4	166	17	
20	8.6	165		
21	8.8	170		
22	9.0	171	18.5	
23	9.2	174		
24:25:00	9.4	178	VT	
	Recovery = 1m45s to HR 135			

The results of this test provide evidence of my lactate threshold. Lactate is the byproduct of burning sugars for fuel while exercising. Lactate threshold is the point where your body can no longer remove lactate at the rate it is being produced. This is an especially important piece of information. If you exceed your lactate threshold for extended periods, you will be unable to sustain that level of exertion. Even worse, you will need to rest to recover from it. That is no-man's-land when racing endurance events. Better to race at efforts below the threshold so your level of exertion can be maintained.

This information is key to regulating the intensity of workouts. We repeated this test at various stages of my training to assess whether it was having the desired effect of raising my lactate threshold. Doing so would allow me to race at faster speeds for longer periods of time and with less perceived exertion with a result of improved race completion times. Coach Tim always had a cup-is-half-full attitude and was rarely critical of my fitness test or race results. They were merely indicators of where I was in my effort to become a better athlete. He never said anything that would discourage me from pursuing my dream, for which I'm eternally grateful. I did not know if my test results were good or bad. In my view, the results only indicated a baseline from which to judge future test results.

We now knew what my beginning lactate threshold was and where my strengths and weaknesses were in each of the three sports. Armed with this knowledge, we could develop training and workout plans. Your athletic performance is improved by varying stresses on the body throughout a training cycle, as opposed to doing the same thing at the same intensity day after day. I needed to divide the training period into multi-week periods with the stress changing with each new week. This concept is titled "periodization" and was the basis of my training plans for the next six months.

Normally a training cycle for a full distance triathlon would be for twelve months. I had only six months to prepare. On the plus side, all my training during the past year in preparation for the marathon and half distance triathlon would serve me well. I could pick up where month seven would normally fall. Below is a graph of what a typical training year might look like using periodization training:

Training Year						= Macrocycle
Preparation			Competition		Transition	
General Preparation	Specific Preparation	Pre-Comp	Completion		Transition	= Mesocycle
Prep	Base 1	Base 2	Build 1	Build 2	Peak	Race	Transition	
1 2 3 4 5 6 7 8	Weeks 9-42	43 44 45 46 47	48 49 50 51 52	= Microcycle

To provide you with a basic understanding of these training periods, I need to explain the goals for these training periods as follows:

Period	Duration	Goal
Preparation	3-4 Weeks	Prepare to train.
Base 1	3-4 Weeks	
Base 2	3-4 Weeks	Establish speed, force and endurance.
Base 3	3-4 Weeks	
Build 1	3-4 Weeks	Increasing intensity and "C" priority rates.
Build 2	3-4 Weeks	Improve limiters.
Peak	1-2 Weeks	Tapering and consolidation of race readiness. "B" and "C" priority races.
Race	1-3 Weeks	"A" and "B" races and maintain strengths.

The races included in my training plan are separated by their significance in my overall strategy. The "A" priority race is what the entire training plan is structured for (i.e. the IRONMAN® Triathlon World Championship). "B" priority races are important indicators of the effectiveness of my training. "C" priority races are used to obtain racing experience and can be a substitute for high-intensity training workouts. My "A" priority race goals were to finish the race within the allotted time and to have a good race experience. To achieve this, my preparation needed to focus primarily on the base periods.

The purpose of the various training periods is to establish speed, force, and endurance, followed by increasing intensity, competing in "B" and "C" level races, and improving areas that limit your performance. Surely you are asking what it looks like to train for speed, force, and endurance. The following chart should help answer those questions.

Endurance	The ability to delay the onset and reduce the effects of fatigue. It implies an aerobic level
Muscular Endurance	The ability of the muscles to maintain a relatively high force load for a prolonged time.
Anaerobic Endurance	The ability to resist fatigue at very high efforts. This is important for short races or needs for quick speeds for short periods.
Force	The ability to overcome resistance. Think swimming in rough water, cycling uphill or against the wind, and running up hill.
Speed	The ability to move efficiently, with good form which leads to increased speed.
Power	The ability to apply maximum force quickly. This is needed for fast starts, steep hills, etc.

My training focused primarily on improving my endurance and muscular endurance. I learned later that the suggested annual training time required to compete in a full distance triathlon race was between 600 and 1,200 hours. Wow! That is a lot of hours. These are spread over the available weeks to train before the race. Obviously, I could not train for a total of 1,200 hours in just six months. That volume would need to be cut in half and rely on my training hours prior to April to fill in the gap.

My training program ran in four-week cycles. The first week was light and then built in intensity and number of hours with each succeeding week. The fourth week in the cycle was a rest and recovery week. This recovery period is necessary to allow your body to recover from the stresses previously placed upon it and adapt and grow stronger. Below is an example of what my training periods looked like beginning in mid-April and ending on race day.

Total Annual Training Hours = 600

Period	Week	Beg Day	Races	Hrs	Day 1	Day 2	Day 3	Day 4	Day 5	Day 6	Day 7
Prep	1	18-Apr		10.0	1:30	1:15	1:00	1:00	:45	2:30	2:00
	2	25-Apr		10.0	1:30	1:15	1:00	1:00	:45	2:30	2:00
Base 1	1	2-May	"C"	12.0	2:00	1:30	1:30	1:00	1:00	3:00	2:00
	2	9-May		14.5	2:00	2:00	1:30	1:00	1:00	4:00	2:30
	3	16-May		16.0	2:30	2:00	2:00	1:30	1:00	4:00	3:00
	4	23-May		8.5	1:15	1:15	1:00	1:00	:30	2:00	1:30
Base 1	1	30-May		12.0	2:00	1:30	1:30	1:00	1:00	3:00	2:00
	2	6-Jun		14.5	2:00	2:00	1:30	1:00	1:00	4:00	2:30
	3	13-Jun		16.0	2:30	2:00	2:00	1:30	1:00	4:00	3:00
	4	20-Jun		8.5	1:15	1:15	1:00	1:00	:30	2:00	1:30
Base 2	1	27-Jun	"B"	12.5	2:00	1:30	1:30	1:00	1:00	3:30	2:00
	2	4-Jul		15.0	2:30	2:00	1:30	1:30	1:00	4:00	2:30
	3	11-Jul		17.0	2:30	2:30	2:00	2:00	2:00	4:00	3:00
	4	18-Jul		8.5	1:15	1:15	1:00	1:00	:30	2:00	1:30
Base 3	1	25-Jul	"B"	13.5	2:00	2:00	1:30	1:00	1:00	3:30	2:30
	2	1-Aug		16.0	2:30	2:00	2:00	1:30	1:00	4:00	3:00
	3	8-Aug		18.0	3:00	2:30	2:30	2:00	1:00	4:30	3:00
	4	15-Aug		8.5	1:15	1:15	1:00	1:00	:30	2:00	1:30
Build 1	1	22-Aug		15.5	2:30	2:00	2:00	1:30	1:00	4:00	2:30
	2	29-Aug		15.5	2:30	2:00	2:00	1:30	1:00	4:00	2:30
	3	5-Sep		15.5	2:30	2:00	2:00	1:30	1:00	4:00	2:30
	4	12-Sep		8.5	1:15	1:15	1:00	1:00	:30	2:00	1:30
Build 2	1	19-Sep		14.5	2:00	2:00	1:30	1:00	1:00	4:00	2:30
	2	26-Sep		14.5	2:00	2:00	1:30	1:00	1:00	4:00	2:30
	3	3-Oct		14.5	2:00	2:00	1:30	1:00	1:00	4:00	2:30
	4	10-Oct		8.5	1:15	1:15	1:00	1:00	:30	2:00	1:30
Peak	1	17-Oct		10.0	1:30	1:15	1:00	1:00	:45	2:30	2:00
Race		27-Oct	"A"	8.5	Easy days leading up to race day						

I am sure you noted the column for races. Races are assigned three distinct levels of focus. "A" level races are events that all your training is designed to prepare you for and thus are top priority. "B" level races are events that help assess how you are progressing with all the training. In other words, is the training achieving the desired results? For my race plan, "B" level races were half distance triathlon events. "C" level races are short in duration and performed at high intensity. These events could be a local running club 10K or a sprint distance triathlon, both done at high intensity. The "B" level races should be conducted in the build periods, but I had to pick races that I could attend. These races required extended travel, time, and money, all of which were in short supply. The "B" priority races selected were the IRONMAN® 70.3® Buffalo Springs Lake triathlon in June 1999 and the 70.3 Vineman® in July 1999. The "C" priority races were a local 5K running race and a sprint triathlon.

The details of my training plan were a lot to absorb. Following it closely would be critical to achieve my dream of completing a full distance triathlon competition. I recall telling Tim, "Just tell me what and when to do the training, and rest assured, I will get it done."

"Hustle beats talent when talent doesn't hustle." – Ross Simmonds

Strength Training

Prior to hiring a coach, I thought strength training was for body building enthusiasts, not a crucial requirement to compete in an endurance event. Turns out that the muscle groups used in swimming, cycling, and running all need to be further developed through strength training. This training should be done in the preparation period and then maintained during the remaining periods. Coming late to the party, I had to incorporate it later than the ideal time. This created additional challenges for me when budgeting my time, as it was recommended that I allow for recovery time between strength training and swim, bike, and run workouts. As such, I typically performed my strength training in the early morning hours or late in the evenings. It helped that my strength training was done only three to four times per week. I used a series of strength training workouts ranging from plans A through E. Here are examples of my strength training B, C, and D routines:

Strength Workout – B
Moderate 60 - 75% 1 Rep Max

Exercise	Week 1	Week 2	Week 3	Week 4
Squat / Leg Press	60% 2 x 12	60% 1 x 12 70% 2 x 10	60% 1 x 12 75% 2 x 10	70% 3 x 12
Dead lifts	60% 2 x 12	60% 1 x 12 70% 2 x 10	60% 1 x 12 75% 2 x 10	70% 3 x 12
Calf Raises	60% 2 x 12	60% 1 x 12 70% 2 x 10	60% 1 x 12 75% 2 x 10	70% 3 x 12
:05 Jog				
Bench Press	60% 1 x 12 70% 2 x 10	60% 1 x 12 70% 2 x 10	60% 1 x 12 75% 2 x 10	70% 3 x 12
One Arm Row	60% 1 x 12 70% 2 x 10	60% 1 x 12 70% 2 x 10	60% 1 x 12 75% 2 x 10	70% 3 x 12
Shoulder Press	60% 1 x 12 70% 2 x 10	60% 1 x 12 70% 2 x 10	60% 1 x 12 75% 2 x 10	70% 3 x 12
Cooldown / Stretch :10				

As you can see my strength training sessions included both upper and lower body muscle groups. The upper body routines focused on the muscle groups used for swimming, while the lower body routines focused on developing the muscle groups used to cycle and run. Some of these routines involved the use of free weights while others involved resistance machines. For example, a squat was done with a bar with weights on either side and attached to a metal frame. The routine involves placing the weighted bar across your shoulders and using your thigh muscles to lower the weight to a squatting position then lifting it to the starting point. Dead lifts involve the use of a weighted bar. The bar is set on the ground and is lifted using your thighs until you are in a standing position then lowered back to the ground.

Calf raises are normally conducted by standing on a supporting metal frame with your heel extended past the bar. The routine is to lower and raise your heel using your body weight for resistance. The bench press can be done using free weights or on a machine that involves using the chest and arm muscles to lift and lower a weighted bar from the chest while lying on a bench. The one arm row is conducted on a weight machine in a seated position. Weight is lifted by pulling a hand grip towards the body then lowering it. The shoulder press is also done on a machine. Using hand grips, the weight is lifted from shoulder level to a fully extended overhead position then lowered back to the starting position. The cool down/stretch of 0:10 represents ten minutes of rest and stretching tight muscles to cool your body down after the exercise session has been completed.

The following C and D strength training routines will give you an idea of the various other routines I used in my training.

Strength Workout – C
Moderate 60 - 75% 1 Rep Max

Exercise	Week 1	Week 2	Week 3	Week 4
Lunges	60% 2 x 12	60% 1 x 12 70% 2 x 10	60% 1 x 12 75% 2 x 10	70% 3 x 12
Step-Ups	60% 2 x 12	60% 1 x 12 70% 2 x 10	60% 1 x 12 75% 2 x 10	70% 3 x 12
Jump Rope	3 x 30 secs RI = 30s	3 x 45 secs RI = 30s	3 x 60 secs RI = 30s	2 x 60 secs RI = 15s
Incline Bench Press	60% 2 x 12	60% 1 x 12 70% 2 x 10	60% 1 x 12 75% 2 x 10	70% 3 x 12
Lat Pull-down	60% 2 x 12	60% 1 x 12 70% 2 x 10	60% 1 x 12 75% 2 x 10	70% 3 x 12
Front / Rear Raise	60% 2 x 12	60% 1 x 12 70% 2 x 10	60% 1 x 12 75% 2 x 10	70% 3 x 12
Triceps Extension (various)	60% 2 x 12	60% 1 x 12 70% 2 x 10	60% 1 x 12 75% 2 x 10	70% 3 x 12
Seated Hammer Curl				
Cooldown / Stretch	:10			

Strength Workout – D
Hard   75 - 85% 1 Rep Max

Exercise	Week 7	Week 8	Week 10	Week 11
AB Circuit (3-5 exercises)	3 x 20	3 x 30	3 x 35	3 x 25
DB Bench Press	75% 1 x 8 80% 2 x 6	85% 3 x 5	75% 1 x 8 80% 2 x 6	85% 3 x 5
Seated Row	75% 1 x 8 80% 2 x 6	85% 3 x 5	75% 1 x 8 80% 2 x 6	85% 3 x 5
Incline Bench Press	75% 1 x 8 80% 2 x 6	85% 3 x 5	75% 1 x 8 80% 2 x 6	85% 3 x 5
Lat Pull-down	75% 1 x 8 80% 2 x 6	85% 3 x 5	75% 1 x 8 80% 2 x 6	85% 3 x 5
Overhead Shoulder Press	75% 1 x 8 80% 2 x 6	85% 3 x 5	75% 1 x 8 80% 2 x 6	85% 3 x 5
Hammer Curl	75% 1 x 8 80% 2 x 6	85% 3 x 5	75% 1 x 8 80% 2 x 6	85% 3 x 5
Triceps Extension (various)	75% 1 x 8 80% 2 x 6	85% 3 x 5	75% 1 x 8 80% 2 x 6	85% 3 x 5
Cooldown / Stretch :10				

In the early stages of strength training the workout focus is on using light resistance with a high number of repetitions, which develops one's endurance capabilities. Remember, the goal was not to become a body builder, but rather to condition and strengthen the muscle groups used to swim, bike, and run (i.e., building a stronger motor). I knew I was making progress when lifting the weight became easier and I was not sore afterwards. Adding weight training to an already demanding schedule was a challenge, but I made it work, as it was needed if I was to achieve my dream.

Swim Training

To complete the 2.4-mile swim and have the strength and energy left to complete the cycling and running portions of the race, I needed to further develop my swimming endurance abilities to enable me to double my then current maximum distance of 1.2 miles. Following are examples of my swim training routines:

E3 - Endurance 3
Warm Up: 300 - 500 yards (mixed strokes) - Swim Easy Focus on form, rest at walls as needed to ensure proper form is maintained.

Main Set: **Focus:**
The RI on the following set should equal the time to do the set.
 	
     3 X 75 easy   Focus on reaching for the wall.
     3 X 75 easy   Focus on head position (nose pointed to the bottom).
     3 X 75 easy   Focus on tight kick (keep toes pointed out)
                                 (no scissor kicking).
     3 X 75 easy   Focus on stroke count per length and try to keep
                                 it constant or no more than 1 additional stroke.
     3 X 75 easy   Focus on body roll (should feel like you are swimming
                                 through pipe without touching the sides).

Cooldown = 100 easy Mix strokes of Breast, Back, and Free   Total **1,350**

The notation of RI equals "rest interval." In the above table, the rest interval is equal to the time it took to conduct the set of three seventy-five-yard swims.

E4 - Endurance 4
Warm Up: 300 - 500 yards (mixed strokes) - Swim Easy Focus on form, rest at walls as needed to ensure proper form is maintained.

Main Set: **Focus:**
The RI on the following set should equal the time to do the set.
 	
     2 X 100 easy   Focus on reaching for the wall.
     2 X 100 easy   Focus on head position (nose pointed to the bottom).
     2 X 100 easy   Focus on tight kick (keep toes pointed out)
                                 (no scissor kicking).
     2 X 100 easy   Focus on stroke count per length and try to keep
                                 it constant or no more than 1 additional stroke.
     2 X 100 easy   Focus on body roll (should feel like you are swimming
                                 through pipe without touching the sides).

Cooldown = 100 easy Mix strokes of Breast, Back, and Free   Total **1,600**

Run Training

My training for the run focused primarily on endurance, and therefore, my workouts had me staying in heart rate zone two. Refer to the previous discussion on heart rates. My zone two heart rates ranged between 139 and 150 beats per minute. This was a bit boring, as all my training to this point was done with the intent of increasing speed. Early in my training there were days where the workout plan was to run for two hours, never letting my heart rate exceed 120 BPM. Ugh, that reduced my exertion level to walking fast with short, intermittent, slow runs. If it helped me accomplish my goal, I was all for it. Some of my workouts were conducted at a high school track with the purpose of adding speed to my endurance base.

Workout Plan

We used all this information in forming my weekly training plans. Each week varied depending on the training period. This helped to keep the workouts fun and fresh, as no two days during the week were the same. Below is an example of what my training schedule might have looked like for the week beginning May 9, 1999.

Week Beginning 9-May		MON	TUES	WED	THU	FRI	SAT	SUN
Week 2 / Build 1	SWIM	:30 E3		:30 E4				:30 E4
	BIKE		1:15 hr Zone 2	:30 Zone 1	1 hr Zone 2		3 hr in Zone 2	
	RUN		:45 in Zone 2			:30 Zone 2		1.5 hr in Zone 2
	Brick							
	WEIGHTS	:30 ME		:30 ME		:30 ME		
	Hours	2.00	2.00	1.50	1.00	1.00	4.00	2.50

One of the things I enjoyed about training using periodization was that I did not swim every day, did not cycle every day, did not run every day, did not go to the gym every day, and that most workouts were unique. Each workout had a goal such as improving a limiter, endurance, strength, or speed. Each workout week and day reflected the training goal of the period I was in. I felt much more confident knowing I had a plan. All I needed to do was to stick to it, making me feel in control of reaching my dream. I'm so glad I hired Tim.

Chapter 22

A Summer of Training

Typical Week of Training in the Base Training Periods

Now that my training plan was in place, it was time to go to work executing it. Based on the annual hours chart, the training would be anywhere from eight and a half to eighteen hours a week. This was like having a part time job to go along with my professional career. I was happy to be out of our busy season, allowing more flexibility in my day to get my workouts in. There was still work to be done during the summer and fall months, but it was much more manageable.

Coach Tim and I decided to put the long training days on the weekends. Monday through Thursday involved training hours ranging from one to three hours in length. Friday was my rest and recovery day, involving noticeably short, extremely easy workouts. Or I could elect to not work out at all. It was up to me and how my body felt, as the goal of the day was rest and recovery. My workouts involved training in two of the three sports on the same day and were completed at various times through the day unless it was a brick workout.

My office was located only three miles from Texas Tech University, where I conducted my strength and swim training workouts. If necessary, I could also run on a treadmill or ride a stationary bike at that same location. It was a huge benefit having the facility so close to my work. On strength training days I typically went to the gym at 5:30 to 6:00 a.m., getting my workout in, showering, changing, and heading straight to the office. The same was true for swim workouts, as I could go to the university's lap pool at noon. Leaving the office, I could be at the pool, ready to swim, in ten minutes. Most weekday swims involve a total of 1,600 yards. Getting this done in around forty minutes, I then showered, changed clothes, and was back at work by 1:00 p.m., allowing me to do strength and swim training without interfering with family time.

I was determined to limit the impact my training had on my family. It was one thing to pursue a dream and quite another to do so at the expense of the relationship with my family. Again, my top priorities were God, family, career, and pursuit of my dream and in that order. Highly motivated people sometimes let their career or the pursuit of their dream creep to the top of their priority list. That is when difficulties can happen in your relationships. This was a battle that I had to constantly fight. It required relentless planning to protect that time with my precious family.

I accomplished most weekday running workouts in the same way. Rising at 5:30 a.m., I dressed for the workout and headed out the door. These training runs typically took between forty-five minutes and one hour and fifteen minutes to complete while the rest of the family slept or was getting ready for their day.

The bike was more difficult to train without interfering with family time. If riding outdoors, I had to wait until I came home from work. There was no way around it. The weekday bike training could last from one to two and a half hours. My job allowed me to get home by just after five, where I could quickly change and prep the liquids and be on the road by 5:30. Training right from our doorstep was another huge benefit, saving me the time to load my bike in a vehicle and drive to a starting location. Normally, I was back by dinner and could spend the rest of the evening with the family. Looking back on it all, I was truly fortunate to be able to get in all the required workouts without interfering too much with family time.

The weekends always involved long hours of cycling and running. To not unnecessarily interfere with family activities, I started these workouts at morning's first light. Even when training continually for up to four hours, I could still be back home by noon and be free the remainder of the day.

Typical Week of Training in the Build Training Periods

The build periods were used to add intensity to the aerobic base developed during the base periods. These workouts focused on increasing my endurance, muscular endurance, anaerobic endurance, and power. As a refresher, endurance training increases the ability to delay the onset of fatigue. Anaerobic endurance training increases the ability to resist fatigue at extremely high efforts. Power training adds the ability to apply maximum force quickly. All these attributes are enhanced by powerful muscles. Therefore, my strength training was altered to increase my muscle mass by increasing weight and shortening the number of repetitions.

During the build periods, the total number of weekly training hours decreased slightly. However, the intensity portion of the workouts increased. I am sure you are curious about what these workouts might look like. The swim workouts focused on speed. Adding speed requires swimming at the best pace that can be maintained for short intervals. An example would be to perform one-hundred-yard repeats at the best pace that can be maintained with a twenty-second rest between each repeat. These intervals might be repeated multiple times with varying yardage. Below is an example of such a workout.

SPEED		
S1 - Speed 1		
Warm Up: 300 yards (mixed strokes) - Swim Easy		
Focus on form, rest at walls as needed to ensure proper form is maintained.		
Main Set:	**Focus:**	
Don't sacrifice form for speed!!!		
4 x 50	Start at T-Pace + :06 then descend :02 per 50	RI = :30
2 x 100	@ T-pace + :10	RI = :15
2 x 75	@ T-pace	RI = :20
2 x 150	@ T-pace + :15	RI = :20
2 x 100	@ T-pace	RI = :25
Cooldown = 100 easy Mix strokes of Breast, Back, and Free Total 1,450		

The term T-pace is the best pace that I could maintain for the given distance. In other words, it was fast! The freestyle/crawl swim stroke was used for the warm-up and workout, as this is the stroke that I would use when racing. The workout cooldown allowed for a mix of the breast, back, and freestyle strokes. It was up to me which was used. I mixed them up but enjoyed using the backstroke, as it uses different muscle groups and you can constantly breathe. Prior to being coached by Tim, I merely swam continuously for a selected distance, which developed my endurance but did little to increase my speed and power.

My run workouts were altered as well by adding short bursts of speed and running up steep inclines. These workouts were done in heart rate zones four and five—in other words, at an extremely hard exertion level. My speed-focused running workouts were normally done on a track. Below is an example of such a workout.

RST-2 C	
Pace	at 10K pace or Z4-5
Workout	4 X 600, 4 X 400, 3 X 300
Rest Interval	RI = :01 walk
Notes	Complete each interval (i.e. 600, 400, 300) then do the RI before starting the next interval never skip the RI

Cycling workouts in the build period were much the same as swimming and running. Anaerobic endurance and power were improved by adding short intervals of high intensity. Below is an example of a workout designed to increase my power when cycling.

PR-1		Gear					
	Time	Front	Rear	Description	Sets		Total Time
	0:10			Warm-up			0:10
	0:35			:60 T = 5 x 20-30s (uphill accelerations)			0:40
				RI = :05 spin at 100-110 rpm			
	0:15			Cooldown			1:00

Table header: **Power**

Purpose:
> Is a form of resistance training that builds quads coupled with aerobic training.

Notes:
> It is best if you can find a good hill to do these on but you can simulate hills just by using a gear that provides the same level of exertion that a steep grade hill provides. The idea is to start slow and steadily accelerate through the interval to where at the end you are at 90% effort.

The build period workouts were designed to build anaerobic endurance and power. These workouts were hard. They placed new demands on my current fitness levels. When this is done, the body compensates by growing stronger muscularly and cardiovascularly. These attributes added to the aerobic endurance built in the base periods and were designed to improve my race day performance. Aerobic endurance conditioning continued in the build periods. We merely added build period training to it.

One of the "C" level races on my workout schedule was the New Mexico Sprint Distance State Championship event titled "Milkman." The title was in recognition of the dairy industry in the area. Being the state championship event, it drew top caliber athletes. I had just purchased a new wetsuit and was anxious to try it under race conditions. The race distances were a 0.5K swim, 20K bike, and 5K run. My race results were an 11:48 swim, 41:54 bike, and 25:09 run for a total finishing time of 1:18:51. This was good for ninth in my forty to forty-four age group and seventy-third overall. Not impressive results, but I was improving. With each race I observed what other athletes were doing during their transitions and was able to apply those techniques to speed up my transition times. I also noted what did and did not work with my hydration and nutrition plans while out on the course. It was a great test of my training and practice for the important transitions. After the race I was shocked to learn that a man in my forty to forty-four age group won the race outright. This was an exciting development, meaning that someone my age group could win the race overall. There was hope for me!

The next "B" level race in the training plan was the IRONMAN® 70.3® Buffalo Springs Lake triathlon event held on June 27, 1999. This would be my second attempt at this race. As previously described, this was a particularly challenging course. In fact, I would rate this as the toughest half distance triathlon I would ever compete in. At the time, this was a qualifying event for the IRONMAN® Triathlon World Championship, thus it drew top talent from pro, elite, and amateur competitors. Most states were represented and even a number of foreign countries. My finishing time was 5:51:07. My time at the previous year's event, and my first attempt at a half distance triathlon, was 6:10:21. If my math is correct, my time improved by just over nineteen minutes. All this focused training was having the desired results and I could not have been more pleased.

At the post-race award banquet, the race owners presented my wife Debbie with a plaque in recognition of all the work she did behind the scenes to help the race be successful. It was a great moment, and I was quite proud of her.

The second "B" priority race was the 70.3 mile Half Vineman® held on July 31, 1999, in the wine country of Northern California. Coach Tim recommended it as part of my "A" priority race preparation plan. I considered the race a long brick workout accomplished at race pace. The results determine the areas I needed to focus on in my training, also known as my limiters.

Coach Tim, our good friends Mike and Marti Greer, and I competed in the event. When our plane departed for California, the temperature in Lubbock was close to a hundred degrees. Our flight ended in Oakland, California. Boy, were we shocked by the very cool air temperature while getting off the plane! It was July and me and Debbie had not thought to pack any cool weather clothing. It was downright chilly, reminding me of the quote by Mark Twain: "The coldest winter I ever spent was one summer in San Francisco." Truer words were never spoken.

Debbie and I had never been to California. We were impressed by the city and how beautiful the scenery was on the trip to the race site of Santa Rosa. The swim was in the Russian River and the morning air temperature was in the low fifties. Not bringing a warm-up, I put on my wetsuit early just to stay warm. After setting up our bikes in the transition area, we had to wait for the athletes competing in the full distance triathlon race to make the turn in the double loop swim course before those competing in the 70.3-mile race could start. The water was significantly warmer than the air temperature. It felt good to enter the water prior to my wave's start.

It was an unusual, remarkable sight as the waves of athletes starting ahead of me began their race. All that churning of the water caused a light cloud of fog to form just above them. The flow of the river was against us during the first half of the course. I could not detect the flow, but I knew I was progressing slowly. At one point I noticed that athletes were walking in knee-deep water close to the shore. Now that seemed like cheating. Thinking more about it, they made slower progress than the swimmers, as it is not particularly easy to walk in knee-deep water. It seemed like forever before I was able to make out the buoy marking the turnaround point. Once around the buoy, we were flying, reaching the swim finish in no time. It was like going downhill on a bike.

The bike course was mostly flat with rolling terrain. The course took us through beautiful vineyards, lush with green leaves surrounded by rolling hills of grassy farmland and tree-lined roadways. It was like being on a tour of the California wine country. The scenery was amazing for someone from West Texas, where the plains are very flat, with cotton fields as far as the eye can see. I loved it and it helped keep my mind off the effort I was putting forth. The run was also through picturesque rolling hills and gorgeous terrain. I was used to running mostly on flat ground. All this up and down wore on my legs a bit.

The race finish area was at the Kendall Jackson Winery. Very cool! My race split times were a 42:43 swim, a 3:00:56 bike, and a 1:58:26 run for a total race time of 5:41:56. My IRONMAN® 70.3® Buffalo Springs Lake triathlon race time just one month ago was 5:51:07. I was thrilled to shave off another ten minutes. Coach Tim wanted me to keep my heart rates no higher than zone three and I'd accomplished that. All this focused training was having the desired effect of allowing me to go faster at lower heart rates. As previously mentioned, the IRONMAN® 70.3® Buffalo Springs Lake triathlon was an incredibly challenging course. The Half-Vineman® was not what I would call easy, but nowhere near as tough, accounting for a portion of my time improvement. No matter, I liked the direction this was taking.

Part of the joy of participating in the sport of triathlon is all the great people you meet, and friendships made along the way. Following is a post-race photo taken of me and Debbie with friends.

With three months left before the Ironman "A" priority race, I was gaining confidence that my dream was possible. Until I did a reality check. The distance was still twice as far and twice the duration of anything I had done thus far. A sobering reality after a half distance triathlon given how tired I was afterwards. This was a concern but not to the point of becoming discouraging. I just stayed focused on sticking with the training Tim had set up for me.

The plan called for another two months of build period two workouts. It was an intense period, with adding anaerobic endurance, force, speed, and power training to an already demanding workout schedule. During the final four weeks of the build period, the key workouts became bricks. Remember, bricks are combination workouts where the training combines two and up to all three of the sports in the same workout. Below is what such a workout week might look like.

Week Beginning 3-Oct		MON	TUES	WED	THU	FRI	SAT	SUN
Week 3	Build 2	SWIM						
		BIKE		2:00 hr Zone 2		1 hr Zone 3		4 hr in Zone 2	
		RUN							2.5 hr in Zone 2
		Brick	:45 swim 1:15 run at Race Pace		:30 swim 1:00 run at Race Pace		:30 swim :30 run at Race Pace		
		WEIGHTS							
		Hours	2.00	2.00	1.50	1.00	1.00	4.00	2.50

The most memorable workout was in week four of the build two period. It was a race simulation with a fifty-minute swim, followed by a ninety-mile bike ride, and ending with an eighteen-mile run. Whew, that is a lot of time and mileage. If I could do it, it meant it might be possible to accomplish my goals at the full distance triathlon race.

One of the goals of the workout was to keep my heart rates in zone three (between 136 and 142 BPM). This would also be considered my race pace while competing in the IRONMAN® Triathlon World Championship. The perceived exertion at those heart rates ranged from fairly light to somewhat hard. It seemed like I could go forever at those heart rates and was the goal of all the training, to race at efforts that could be maintained for extended periods.

This was a race simulation day. As such, I loaded up on carbohydrates with a spaghetti dinner the night before. That morning's breakfast consisted of a large bowl of oatmeal and a banana about two hours before the workout began. Lubbock's climate in early October was beginning to cool down. The day of the brick training workout was cool, with a light gray, overcast sky.

The issue with the swim was that it was to be done in open water. The only nearby option was at Buffalo Springs Lake. I did not think the lake officials wanted folks to swim outside the designated swim areas. I opted to do it anyway and, if questioned, would beg for forgiveness.

I was leery of swimming in the lake by myself and asked one of my nephews, who had access to a small aluminum fishing boat, to accompany me. He agreed to follow alongside me in the boat. Perfect!

We met at the lake, and I put on the wetsuit, slipped into the cold, murky water, and began the swim portion of the workout. I kept the effort level at a comfortable pace, cruising along with no issues for the designated forty-five minutes. Upon exiting the water, I pulled off the wetsuit and prepared myself for the ninety-mile bike ride. I wore my cycling clothing underneath the wetsuit so there was no need to change. The clothing was wet from the swim, making for a very chilly first few miles on the ride.

The area along the lake consisted of wide-open farmland full of ready-to-harvest snow-white cotton as far as the eye could see and providing an exceptional view. This was a race simulation workout, and I therefore loaded the Bento Bag with everything needed while on the bike ride, including four bottles of water and energy drinks, energy gel packets, electrolyte tablets, and even a peanut butter and jelly sandwich. Remember, this workout would last for about eight to nine hours, and I would burn between 700 to 900 calories per hour. I would need something more substantial to sustain my energy levels than gel packets alone.

Cotton Fields

The ride was uneventful and followed a chosen path that included some of the hills in the IRONMAN® 70.3® Buffalo Springs Lake triathlon course I described earlier with dramatic elevation changes. My most vivid memory occurred around the seventy-mile mark. At this point, I had been continually exercising for four hours, the halfway point in the bike course. My energy levels were dropping. The effort at the beginning seemed fairly light, but now fatigue was setting in. Ugh, my spirits were dropping as well. Not good!

To combat this, I ate the sandwich, washed down by an energy drink. Though a bit discouraged by this bout with fatigue, low energy, and a waning spirit, I was determined to get past it. The strategy was effective, as about ten to fifteen minutes later, I felt better. This was a huge mental note for race day. I needed to get ahead of the "wall" and time my meal well.

This is why the race simulation day was so important. It prepared me to deal with similar challenges that might arise during the race.

I continued the ride for the next twenty miles and was relieved when the lake came into view, signaling the end of the bike portion of the practice race. I reduced my exertion levels during the last mile in preparation for my bike-to-run transition, thus giving my legs a bit of rest and slowing my heart rate. I was now posed to run for eighteen miles. My elapsed exercise time was six hours. That was the longest I had ever continuously exercised, yet I still had the eighteen-mile run to go.

The transition from bike-to-run was much the same as I had done in prior races. The run course was a four-mile loop around the lower end of the lake. I was not able to carry all the water, energy drinks, gel packs, and electrolytes needed during the entire run, therefore I needed to get back to my vehicle at least every forty minutes to replenish items needed during the run. I used a runner's belt that secured a bottle of water located behind my back at hip level. This allowed me to drink every ten to fifteen minutes as needed. I changed into a running jersey, electing to run in the same neoprene shorts I had cycled in. Ready to go, I began to run.

As mentioned before, it takes time for your muscles to transition from cycling to running. I was using the triathlon shuffle during the first mile until my legs loosened from the long bike ride and did my best to keep my heart rate in the target zone. The run course had minor rolling hills but nothing too drastic. However, running on already tired legs, even small inclines felt like climbing Mt. Everest.

I ran in a recreational area of the lake, and people enjoying the day took notice after the first couple of loops. I imagined what they were thinking. "What is that guy doing? How many times is he going to come by?"

The first ten miles were not bad at all. Sure, I was tired, and my legs were getting heavy, but I ran at a reasonable pace while keeping heart rates in the target zone, forcing myself to not think about anything but keeping up with my hydration and energy packets. The goal was to keep fatigue at bay for as long as possible.

Starting that last loop was a huge relief. Just four more miles to go! No problem, I kept telling myself, you have run four miles hundreds of times before. That was what I was thinking to keep motivated and my mind off how my legs and body were feeling. I was not hurting anywhere, but exhaustion was creeping in as my energy levels dropped.

Completing the last mile and arriving back at the car was a big relief. I was proud of what I had just accomplished but very, very tired. I have found that after long runs it is best to take a five-minute slow walk. Doing so allows your muscles to relax. It also helps flush out built-up levels of lactate in the blood. I had not kept the time, but I estimate the workout lasted for close to nine hours.

This was the last training hurdle I had to cross. I had just swum for a mile and a half, cycled for ninety miles, and ran for eighteen miles. All combined, it was close to 110 miles. I was careful not to get too excited, as the full distance triathlon is 140.6 miles. I had an additional thirty miles to cover.

Peak Period

The final build two period started on October 10. Just two weeks of training left before the IRONMAN® Triathlon World Championship race. I was a bit anxious and excited about embarking on this new adventure. The rest and recovery week was next since I had just completed the race simulation training. Hopefully, my body would quickly recover, adapt, and grow stronger during the next few weeks.

The final peak period workouts consisted of short bursts of speed interlaced with easy endurance efforts. The training purpose at this stage was to not tear down any muscle while maintaining the fitness level I had worked so hard to attain. The goal was that my body would be as good as it could be, with fitness levels reaching their peak on race day. Peaking on race day was never a given. I could do everything possible to peak on race day and still come out flat not performing to my fullest potential. There were simply too many variables, any one of which could affect how I performed on race day. It was rare for me to hit the mark perfectly. You see this play out in any sport. One day the athlete can do no wrong and the next they underperform.

All this high volume and intense training can leave the door standing wide open for contracting some sort of bacterial or viral illness. I had to be on constant alert to avoid anyone who was showing any illness. If I got sick, it could be disastrous, ruining all my preparations. Contracting an illness during training is inevitable. The general rule of thumb is that if the symptoms stay above the neck, it is okay to continue training, otherwise take a break until you have recovered. Luckily, I had avoided this pitfall.

Notes from My Family

From My Wife Debbie

The first time Wade was able to race in Kona™ was from the lotto. I remember signing him up around Christmas, and they drew names and announced them on April 15. Tax Day! Wade is a CPA, so more stress.

When I pulled up the IRONMAN® Triathlon World Championship website on the 15th, I could not believe his name had been drawn! I went up to his office so I could tell him in person. He had six months to prepare, and in the meantime, he had to race the IRONMAN® 70.3® Buffalo Springs Lake triathlon in June as part of his qualification process.

After Wade's first full distance triathlon race, we started hauling the kids to the events all over Texas, New Mexico, California, Florida, Wisconsin, Idaho, Canada, and Hawaii. When I say hauling, I do mean hauling! The athletes in these events must be onsite on race day while it is still dark outside. Our middle daughter, Lia, was sick at every event. She would be nauseous before every race. I am guessing nerves, because by the time the race was over, she was fine.

From My Daughter Ashley

The whir of the stationary bike blades is my earliest memory of Dad training for triathlons. He would ride the bike in the evenings before dinner in the living room. I had no clue what a triathlon was then, but I knew that Dad was dead set on working hard to do one. Soon enough, he brought home a racing bike and training suits. On cold mornings, I would wake up to find him sitting on the front doorstep to cool off after a run with steam seeping from his scalp into the crisp air. It was not long before it was time for his first race. I do not remember the race exactly, but I remember all of us cheering for him as he came through the finish line. There was so much joy from the spectators and the competitors.

After that, our home, and family, became a triathlon-supporting machine. Dad continued to train even harder while Mom essentially worked as his manager. She booked the hotels, registered for races, planned spots for us to cheer him on, and volunteered at the races. Soon, we started volunteering with her. My sisters and I passed out water, waved flags, body marked, and passed out shirts at registrations. We would play and sing while waiting to cheer Dad on when he went through transitions.

At the Buffman and Squeaky race, Marti had us stand at the end of a dock to wave flags for the different age groups of the swim. We chatted in the golden dawn waiting for the starting gun and dipped our toes into the water. Once we heard the shot, we waved our flags and then ran to our next job at the swim finish line to help peel the wetsuits off the racers. I loved hanging out with my sisters and volunteering at those small races, but my favorite race to work was the IRONMAN® 70.3® Buffalo Springs Lake triathlon.

I was in high school when my dad started training for Buffalo. At times he would train at the same time as me, at the Pete Ragus Aquatic Center, and occasionally, he would be in the lane next to me. When you swim, there are rhythms that you follow in practice. I was a long-distance swimmer, and that meant that my practices consisted mostly of Coach Hayes giving me a distance to swim and time to make each lap. I would try not to go over or under because I was trying to build my endurance as well as my speed. However, my dad did pass on his competitive gene, so there would be times when I would try to beat him to the end of the lane. In a sprint, he could have easily passed me, but I like to think I could have given him a run for his money in a 500-yard race. (Ashley is too modest, she had no problems besting me in a 500-yard race—Dad.)

Mom began working for Marti, so I helped her prepare for the registration expo. I got to meet people from all around the world. We even hosted a few of them in our home. The week before the race was always hectic. Mom would be running back and forth between the expo, Dad would be training and going over the course, and Lia, Amanda, and I would be packing the swag bags and unloading t-shirts. We would spend hours at the registration hotel getting racers checked in and helping Marti, but I did not care. I loved hanging out with everyone and working as a body marker.

After volunteering for a few years, I was put in charge of the body marking volunteers. Mom and I had to be at Buffalo at three o'clock in the morning to help set up the body marking station. Close to four, I would show the volunteers how Marti wanted us to mark the racers. Then, at around five in the morning, racers would start to show up to rack their bikes and get marked. Dad would arrive not too long after with Lia and Amanda. Those dark mornings were full of energy, excitement, and the smell of permanent markers. Using giant Sharpies, we would write the racers' age on the back of their calves and their race number on their biceps. The age range of the people that I marked was astonishing. I met pre-teens competing in the sprint alongside adults well into their seventies.

You meet such a wide variety of people at this race because triathletes come from all over the world to use the IRONMAN® 70.3® Buffalo Springs Lake triathlon as a test run for the IRONMAN® Triathlon World Championship in Hawaii. More than a few athletes have told me that the hills and heat you experience in this small West Texas town will tell your body if you can manage racing in the Hawaiian climate.

For example, one of my jobs was to snatch the ankle monitors off the racers once they had crossed the finish line. The monitors would be soaking wet with sweat, which was a good thing because that meant that they had kept themselves somewhat hydrated. However, one year a man came stumbling through the finish line with people grabbing at his elbows to support him. I ran over to take off his monitor and was shocked to discover that it and his clothes were bone dry. Triathlons of this size and larger have medical tents that racers can visit for an IV after the race. That guy was immediately taken to the med tent to be evaluated and had more than one round of IVs to get him rehydrated. When Dad came through the finish line, I was relieved that his monitor was sweaty and gross.

Chapter 23

The Work is Done: It is Time to Race

Travel

The week before we departed for Hawaii, I took my bike apart and cleaned and lubricated the chain, cogs, and all other moving components. I checked the tires for any embedded glass chips, thorns, or cuts. The chain and tires were newly purchased and replaced, so there were no worries there. I did not want to take unnecessary risks with worn components. It would be devastating to put so much time and effort into preparing for the event just to have a chain fail or a tire blow out. I also replaced the handle and aerobar cork grip covers. I was not going to let chance interfere in reaching my dream.

We left for Hawaii three days before the race. Arriving early allowed me time to recover from jetlag, acclimate to the time zone, and get in last-minute training to keep my body loose and ready to race. I had purchased a heavy cardboard box designed for packing and shipping bicycles and other race gear, including my bike, pump, bike shoes, bike clothing, helmets, towels, running shoes, caps, running clothing, etc. Below is a picture of everything I put in the box.

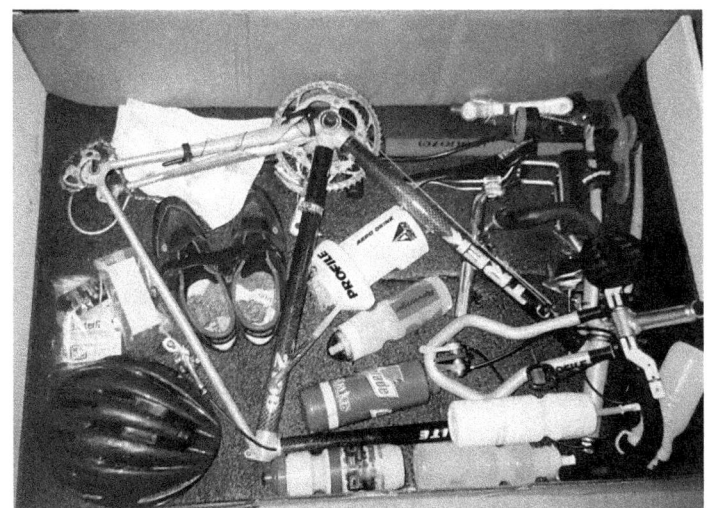
Packed bike box

Race wheels

We were traveling with Mike and Marti Greer. They went every year to represent the IRONMAN® 70.3® Buffalo Springs Lake triathlon at the annual IRONMAN Group Corporate planning sessions. I was relieved to have them with us. They knew all the do's and don'ts of race etiquette and where everything was located. Our flight to Hawaii left Lubbock at around 6:00 a.m., flying to Los Angeles for a brief layover, then on to Hawaii.

When we arrived at the small Kona airport on the big island of Hawaii, we deplaned, and at the bottom of the stairs, attendants placed leis around our necks. The air was humid and salty, and the palm trees and shrubbery were lush and green, gently swaying in the ocean breeze. We had to wait a while for airport personnel to unload our luggage and, of course, my bike box. I was so thankful when I located it. Clothing I could replace, but not my bike or race gear. It was quite a sight to see hundreds of bike boxes, with anxious triathletes combing through to locate their gear.

We did not need to rent a vehicle, as we were staying at the host hotel close to the race start area, and most of what we needed was within walking distance. We took a taxi to the hotel and found a long check-in line. We were so grateful when we were in our rooms and could relax and begin to enjoy our trip.

Prerace Activities

The event is attended by athletes from across the globe. They recommend athletes to be in Kona a few days early to acclimate to climate and the change in time zone. Hawaii is five hours behind Lubbock, so we needed a few days to get used to that big of a change. Our first morning there I awoke at around 8:30 a.m. CST. That was 3:30 a.m. in Hawaii and I could not go back to sleep. I dressed and went down to the lobby to find coffee. Imagine my surprise when I found a lobby full of people. I assumed they were all having the same issue as I.

One morning prior to the race, Debbie and I joined Mike and Marti for breakfast at the host hotel restaurant. We chose a table close to one of the hand cyclist division athletes. The Greers introduced us to him and said he had won his championship race slot at the IRONMAN® 70.3® Buffalo Springs Lake triathlon. I was amazed at the size of this guy's chest and arms. He had served in the military as a Navy Seal and was wounded, leaving him paralyzed from the waist down. These athletes were almost superhuman in their abilities to swim two miles with only their upper bodies to propel them. They then had a specialized wheelchair looking like a dragster used to complete the 112-mile bike ride. A different chair was used to complete the 26-mile run portion of the race using only their chest, shoulders, and arms to propel the wheelchairs. My hat is off to these superb athletes refusing to let their disability limit what they can achieve in life.

During the week leading up to the event, the race officials set up buoys on the swim course, providing the athletes with the opportunity to conduct practice swims. This was helpful, as we could determine where the ocean currents were, wave conditions, and be prepared for the water temperature. I had yet to compete in the ocean and wanted to get the feel of it. I was pleasantly surprised to find out how buoyant I was in saltwater. Wetsuits were not allowed, and I was eager to get in the water to get a sense of what the swimming event would be like.

Two days before the race, Marti Greer joined me for swimming practice. We arrived at the start area at around 7:00 a.m. I had not expected to see hundreds of other athletes doing the same thing. We began our swim at a very relaxed pace. It was a little challenging to site the buoys, as the wave swells were three to four feet high. I found it best to wait until a swell lifted me before looking for the buoys. This was good to know for race day.

The practice swim provided several surprises. First, I could see clearly up to a depth of fifty feet. It was like going snorkeling for free. There were bright blue-and-yellow-colored tropical fish swimming around rocks and other structures. Marti was not particularly keen on open water swimming, especially in the open ocean with all the predatory fish in it. Second, I stopped once to take a longer look at the beautifully colored fish. When Marti stopped to see why I wasn't beside her in the water, I gestured at the beautiful view. She misread my intent, thinking I had seen a larger, more menacing fish and climbed on my back. Ha ha! Sorry for giving you a heart attack, Marti.

I remember clearly when we turned to swim back to the start area, we took a moment to tread water and enjoy the experience. It was an incredible moment for two West Texans to be out in the open ocean three-quarters of a mile from the shore of a ridiculously small island in the middle of the Pacific Ocean. I was hoping the current did not sweep us away. There were plenty of other swimmers around us and folks in canoes to assist anyone in trouble so no worries. I will never forget this experience.

Below is a picture of me and Marti ready to leave for the swim practice and of the practice swim start area.

Going to the practice swim

Starting the practice swim

My bike and all my racing gear were still in the box, and after the swim practice I reassembled it. It was an anxious moment. You never know what might have happened during airport baggage handling. If something were missing, it would be a scramble to get the parts I needed to make race day. Whew, everything was intact and in good condition. Once reconstructed, I adjusted the brakes and the front and back chain derailleurs so that the gear shifting was smooth and secure.

The wheels on my race bike were lightweight and made for racing. Coach Tim loaned these to me for the race and I felt fast riding on them. Both wheels together weighed about the same as one of the wheels used on training rides. The last step in making sure my bike was in good working order was to go for a ride. Mike and Marti joined me for a nice ninety-minute, easy-effort ride. It felt good to be back on my bike. All systems were a go.

The most unexpected and tenuous event came at bike check-in. Every competitor had to have their bike inspected the day before the race. This was new to me. Inspection had not been required at other races I had competed in. No problems, I had everything in order and ready to go.

When it was my turn, the inspector did a very thorough job examining my bike. He checked every working component. After checking my bike, the inspector asked me if I knew about a crack at the top of the front wheel fork. What!? Anxiously, I replied that I did not know about it. He said the fork frame twisted more than it should and likely had an unseen crack. Thankfully, he allowed me to compete on it, saying it was up to me, but the fork may fail under heavy stress. Goodness, that was an unnerving and unexpected bit of news. My race and dream were almost over before they began. The bike had been through rigorous training rides, so I was not too concerned about it failing. Hopefully, that will be the one and only surprise.

Bike check-in.

Bike in race configuration

My prerace workout plan called for a couple of noticeably light, thirty-minute runs designed to keep my legs fresh but not totally inactive. I enjoyed these runs, and they helped burn off pent-up energy.

One of the prerace activities included a parade of the competitors separated by the countries they represented. Countries from all over the world were represented. The organizers asked me to carry the sign for the United States, and I was immensely proud and honored to do so.

Parade

Nothing was left to do the day before the race except to stay off my feet as much as possible, rest, and relax. Tomorrow will be a big day and I will need every ounce of energy I can muster. That night, I gathered my race day gear and packed the items in the bags for swim-to-bike and bike-to-run transitions and for after-race needs. We were required to turn in these bags at a designated site as we arrived at the bike transition area. This time was also used to put anti-blister coating on all areas prone to developing blisters. Lastly, I set out the banana, instant oatmeal, and energy drink I intended to eat three hours before the race.

Now it was time to get some shuteye. My wife and I set at least three different alarms to go off at around 3:30 a.m., when I will wake and eat my prerace meal, then try to go back to sleep for an hour or so. Thankfully, I was able to sleep, but I would not say it was a sound sleep. Who can sleep well the night before an attempt to fulfill a dream that they have just spent so much time and effort preparing for?

Chapter 24

Race Day

Race day had finally arrived, as all alarms sounded at 3:30 a.m. I jumped out of bed, shutting off my alarm, and got busy on my prerace checklist.

The first task was to eat my prerace meal then rest for about an hour. At around 5:00 a.m., I put on generous portions of sunscreen and placed the temporary race number tattoos on both upper arms and thighs. There was also one for our age, which I rubbed on the back of my right calf, then attached the timing chip strap to my ankle.

One last coating of anti-blister paste for my toes and ankles. Other areas needed anti-chafing treatment, and I know this is personal, but for those of you who are reading this and inspire ultra sports, these are critical areas to protect your body. I added lubricant to where my backside and saddle met. Guys can have issues with their running jersey chafing their nipples, so I applied a generous amount of lubricant in that area as well. Just imagine running for up to four hours with the jersey rubbing your skin raw with each twist of your body and arms. No thanks, this race would be hard enough without dealing with blisters or chafing. I knew it would be an exceptionally long day, and I wanted no additional irritations I could prevent.

With the transition and post-race needs bags in hand, my wife and I made our way to the race site just outside of our hotel complex.

The race area was very restrictive. Race officials were stationed everywhere to prevent non-competitors from entering restricted areas. The first order of business was handing in the transition and post-race needs bags. I then went to the bike transition to locate my bike among the thousands racked there. Locating it, I made sure the gearing was set on the intended cog and checked the pressure in each tire. Next, I loaded the Bento Bag with a peanut butter and jelly sandwich, packets of gel, energy bars, and electrolyte tablets. Lastly, I put three water and energy drink bottles in the bottle racks mounted on my bike.

Satisfied that all was in order and ready to go, I finished drinking the water bottle I had been carrying around all morning then headed to the swim start area, on the way stopping to visit with my wife. This was all nerve-racking. It is difficult to put into words all the thoughts and emotions I was experiencing before beginning such an epic adventure. So much planning and preparation had gone into this single day and event, yet there were no guarantees of success. In fact, failure was a very real possibility. There were just too many unknowns in each phase of the event, any one of which could ruin my day and chances for success.

Honestly, I cannot recall ever thinking one minute about the possibility of failure. Those were negative, discouraging thoughts and had no place in my plans to achieve my dream. I have always had a glass-half-full attitude about everything. Challenges are just bumps in the road requiring an alternate route to arrive at the desired destination.

The Swim

The swim start was the point of no return. Everything I'd done in preparation for this day had culminated at this point in time and at such a beautiful place on such a perfect day. What better setting could there be? Waiting to start the swim was a bit like waiting your turn to walk across the stage at graduation after working so hard for four years to be awarded a degree. I was a tiny bit nervous but more so excited to start this new adventure. You cannot change unforeseen events, so why spend one second worrying about it? If something happened, I would deal with it then. The opportunity to realize my dream was now at hand. Let's get this party started!

When entering the swim start area, we had to cross the timing mat. I heard the familiar beep indicating the computer had recognized and recorded my timing chip. From there I walked out onto a pier that stretched out into the bay. Competitors were busy checking their goggles and stretching. This was a crucial step, as it is extremely hard to see through foggy or water-filled goggles. I put my goggles on prior to entering the water and then tested them for leaks. I had purchased new goggles a few weeks earlier and Coach Tim taught me to put a very thin film of baby shampoo inside the lens to prevent fogging. It worked like a charm. Such a small thing could make swimming a very unpleasant experience. Again, leave nothing to chance.

Satisfied that all was ready, I jumped feet first for the four-foot drop from the pier to the water. Then I swam to what I thought would be the back quarter of the athletes. I was competing with the top two percent of all age groups and pro athletes. I was certain I would not be the fastest swimmer, and I positioned myself accordingly. It's hard to describe being shoulder to shoulder with 1,500 anxious athletes treading water, waiting for the start of an epic day of racing. I could almost feel the pent-up energy. Nothing to do now but wait for the cannon to fire to begin the race.

Finally, the starter gave us a countdown, ending with a loud boom of the start cannon. It took a few moments for the mass of humanity to get moving. It felt like trying to leave the parking area after a major event had ended. In short order we were all swimming. The conditions were very crowded at first, and it was a bit difficult to get into a stroke rhythm. Once the competitors dispersed after the first 400 to 500 yards, I settled into a pace that was comfortably hard, one I could maintain for 2.4 miles and have energy left in my tank afterwards.

As we left the starting area, I noticed scuba divers filming us from below the water. How cool is that! As I approached the first bright orange buoy, standing about six feet tall and about four feet wide, I spotted officials in kayaks monitoring our compliance with the event rules. The rolling waves were constantly lowering and lifting us as we swam, so I had to time my breaths to keep an eye on my progress, keeping the buoy to my right.

There were spectators in large boats anchored at the turnaround point about fifty yards away. In my mind's eye, I can clearly see them lined up along the edge of the boat, clapping and cheering for us. I tried to wave a couple of times while my arm swung forward for another swim stroke.

This was my first attempt at swimming 2.4 miles, so I was excited to see the finish area only fifty yards away. To my surprise the backwash from the breaking waves pushed against us. To counter this, I swam hard for about twenty strokes, catching the downhill side of one of the final few waves, and bodysurfed my way to the swim exit area.

There were volunteers at the water's edge helping to steady us as we exited the water and made the run up the boat launch ramp. My balance was a bit unsteady after being in the water for over an hour, head twisting side to side to breathe. It can mess with your inner ear. My swim finish time was 1:17:21. Not fast but respectable for my first full distance triathlon.

Swim finish

The Bike

Out of the water, I made my way as quickly as possible to the transition bag racks. I retrieved my bag with my cycling clothing, helmet, sunglasses, and cycling shoes. Then I headed to the changing tent with benches to sit on while you prepared yourself for the bike event. Once ready, I ran out to retrieve my bike, crossed the timing mat, and headed out on the course. A race volunteer had retrieved my bike and was waiting for me to mount and take off. That was a nice touch.

As planned, I spent the first miles consuming an energy bar and drinking a full bottle of water. I had already been exercising for one and a half hours with nothing to eat or drink. Replacing lost hydration and calories was critical. Getting behind on hydration and nutritional needs early in the race was not acceptable and could become a big limiting factor later in the race if deferred. It has been said that if you wait to eat and drink until you are hungry and thirsty, you have waited too long. The only thought I had at this point was to stay ahead of my body's needs.

Once I had rehydrated and consumed calories, it was time to focus on tackling the bike course. But not before conducting a quick check of the brakes and chain derailleurs. Everything was functioning properly. I then got into the aero position and gradually accelerated until my heart rate reached the level that I planned to maintain throughout the bike race. According to the race day plan provided by Coach Tim, I would strive to keep my average heart rate at or below 145 BPM. I was wearing my heart rate monitor watch, which allowed me to constantly monitor my heart rate. If it creeped up, I slowed down and sped up if it got too slow. I would achieve my best average pace by keeping my heart rate in the aerobic zones. I took note of my speed, but only out of curiosity. Keeping my heart rate in the desired zone would give me the best chance at realizing my dream.

Athletes tend to push too hard in the initial stages of the bike race. It is easy for me to understand why. At the beginning, all systems are go and you are energized and feel strong. Why not go faster while you feel like it? The problem with doing this is that you cannot maintain that level of exertion for the remainder of the race. It will also put performance in the run portion of the race in jeopardy. Competing in full distance triathlon events is as much mental as physical. To be successful, you must continually battle your own mind, guarding against going too fast early when you are strong and feel good and when pushing yourself onward when you are discouraged and bone tired.

People may think it odd that I took a small camera on the bike ride. I had never done this before and may never again. I wanted to capture what I might see in the next 112 miles. I did take a couple of pictures but never stopped while doing so. Unfortunately, I used a waterproof camera and was too unsteady while trying to take a few pictures while riding my bike and they did not turn out very well. Otherwise, I would have shared them with you. I never tried this in future races, as there was no time for it when trying to perform at my best.

The first fifty-six miles were uneventful. It's amazing how busy you can be just making sure you stay on the race plan while on the bike course. My plan called for me to drink one-fourth of a bottle of liquid every fifteen minutes, taking in calories and electrolytes every forty-five to sixty minutes. That and constantly monitoring my heart rate to ensure I did not let it creep up above the planned maximum rate. Thankfully, the winds were light that day, which enabled me to maintain a good pace.

The bike course was out and back, and we returned using the Queen K Highway we'd started on. It was newly paved and smooth as glass. That may not sound all that important, but I can assure you after you have been on a road bike for more than a few hours, your backside feels every bump in the road. The course hugged the shoreline a good portion of the route. This was every rider's dream, especially for a landlubber to have this beautiful ocean view instead of the endless sea of cotton fields to which I was accustomed.

About a hundred yards past each aid station, the volunteers staffing them had set up an area for the athletes to dispose of used water bottles. It had a ten-foot-wide bull's-eye target painted on a sheet of plywood with the middle circle cut out. There was a large tub on the other side used to catch the bottles as they flew through the bull's-eye hole. It was a fun distraction for riders to toss used bottles at the target and hear the volunteers cheer if it went through the center hole.

The only significant climb came close to the turnaround at the small town of Hawi. Only fifty-six miles to go. After the turn, it was downhill for the next five miles, with the wind pushing us from behind. I was ready for this break after the ascent pushing against the wind. The course was notorious for extreme crosswinds at various areas on the course. These could be hard enough to push lighter riders off the road. Luckily, the wind was light that day.

As expected, the trip back to Kona was more difficult. The wind had picked up and the temperature was higher. Fatigue also began to set in. Being a lottery winner versus a qualified competitor meant most of the athletes had left me behind. I was not alone, but the riders had thinned out.

My spirits picked up as I neared the bike finish in Kona. It was encouraging to see all the spectators lining the roadway, and of course my beautiful wife and friends, Mike and Marti. My bike finishing time was 6:24:34, for an average speed of 17.5 mph. This is slow by IRONMAN® Triathlon World Championship standards, but I was pleased with my time, mostly because I had kept to my race plan. I felt good. Make no mistake, I was tiring, but I fed off the energy in Kona with the knowledge I had completed the swim and bike courses and still had fuel left in my tank to run the remaining marathon.

The possibility of realizing my dream was now much closer. All my preparation and planning were paying off and I had not yet made any significant mistakes.

Bike racks

Bike start

While on the bike course

The Run

While in the bike-to-run transition tent, I took extra time to apply lubrication to my toes, heels, ankles, the area where my arms connect with my torso, and of course on my nipples. This was also a suitable time to consume more calories, liquids, and electrolytes. I put on my socks and running shoes, electing to run in the same clothing I wore on the bike. There were plenty of unknowns ahead of me, so spending a little extra time in the bike-to-run transition seemed like time well spent.

It was such a nice feeling and experience to have all the spectators lining the streets encouraging and cheering for us when leaving out on the run. The run course left Kona along the coastline for three to four miles then turned around heading back into Kona. I am sure this was more for the spectators than for the athletes, as it gave them more opportunities to see competitors.

There was one spot known as the "hot corner," where spectators could watch the cyclists and runners when leaving and returning. They could also see the runners again as they returned around mile seven before leaving town for the final leg of the run course. It was also a good spot to watch the runners finish the race. Of course, Mike and Marti already knew about this spot. They and Debbie had their spot already staked out. It energized me seeing them as I went by leaving out on the longest leg of the run.

After passing the turn taking us back to Kona, I noticed that my heart rate was significantly higher than Tim and I had planned. Time to slow down. Ugh, but I was feeling so good! I still had twenty miles and at least three hours to go. Blowing up here would be a disaster. I slowed my pace so I could finish strong and in decent shape.

Coming back into Kona at mile seven was exhilarating. Spectators lined the streets, with the Greers and my wife on the hot corner cheering for me. This was at about the eight-hour mark in the race. As I made the turn towards the hot corner, I saw the winner of the race coming from the opposite direction. He was just a couple of hundred yards from the finish line. Here I was nineteen miles behind him.

Marti ran with me for a short distance to see how I was feeling. At that point I was doing better than I expected. From this point forward was where the real work and test lay. As I was leaving Kona for the remaining nineteen miles of the run, the air temperature was warming, and it was humid. That alone made for tough running conditions. At around mile seventeen we entered an area known as the "energy lab." The air there was still and hot. It was like running in an oven with no breeze to cool you down.

The sun was setting, surrounding me in reds and golds. I had started the race at sunrise and was still going hard at sundown. My friends, that is a long time to be continuously exercising. This is where I encountered the wall. My energy levels and spirits were significantly down, and I was getting a headache. I could either double down on my effort or give in and walk the remaining miles with my tail tucked firmly between my legs. I wasn't in any pain, though I was extremely fatigued, both physically and mentally. Before leaving the energy lab area, I walked for a minute to use the restroom, rehydrate, and consume another energy gel and electrolyte tablet. Since my head was aching, and leaving nothing to chance, I also took a pain reliever stored in a sandwich bag ready for this eventuality. Through sheer will power I continued to run.

After recovering and pushing through the wall, I ran out of the misery of the energy lab back on the Queen K Highway for the final seven miles left in the race the sun had set and it was pitch-black. Volunteers handed out glow sticks to help racers light their path. I must give a special thanks to the run aid station volunteers from this point to the last mile marker. They were so encouraging and helpful. We must have looked like the walking dead. Athletes were in fact walking by now, having already given all they had to give. I was not yet to that point. I had to dig deep to keep running as I passed other athletes while nearing the race finish.

At the twenty-four-mile mark, I reached the crest of an ascent and could see the lights of Kona below. A stunning view after such a long, dark path I'd been running. This also meant only two miles were left! I was too close to the finish. I knew nothing could stop me from finishing and a burst of exhilaration coursed through my tired bones. At the hot corner again, I saw the Greers and Debbie with the biggest smiles on their faces cheering me on to the finish line. I could not have wished for any better sight.

There is no way I could ever adequately express in mere words the happiness, relief, and satisfaction I was experiencing as I made the turn towards the finish line only a hundred yards away. Even after twelve and half hours, the stands were still full of spectators cheering for every athlete finishing the event like they had won the race. Most spectators knew one of the athletes and the effort and sacrifices made just to be there.

While crossing the finish line, I jumped up to tap the brightly lit billboard. I will never forget hearing the announcer calling out my name, saying, "Wade Wilson from Lubbock, Texas, you are an Ironman."

I finished with a run time of 4:39:09 and a total race time of 12:33:17. Good for 128th in my age group and 1,081 overall. Not too bad for being just a lottery slot competitor. I did not give my placement any thought. My goal was to finish my first full distance triathlon event within the seventeen-hour time allotment and to have the experience of a lifetime. Only a brief time ago I didn't even know what a triathlon was, let alone contemplating competing in and finishing one.

Some have downplayed this accomplishment. To those I offer the following quote from Theodore Roosevelt.

> "It is not the critic who counts; not the man who points out how the strong man stumbles, or where the doer of deeds could have done them better. The credit belongs to the man who is actually in the arena, whose face is marred by dust and sweat and blood; who strives valiantly; who errs, who comes short again and again, because there is no effort without error and shortcoming; but who does actually strive to do the deeds; who knows great enthusiasms, the great devotions; who spends himself in a worthy cause; who at the best knows in the end the triumph of high achievement, and who at the worst, if he fails, at least fails while daring greatly, so that his place shall never be with those cold and timid souls who neither know victory nor defeat."

The hot corner

Race Finish

Finisher's photo

Finisher's plaque

Finisher's medal

Post-Race

The volunteers took diligent care of me after crossing the finish line. They hung a finisher's medal around my neck and made sure I was okay physically. I had used every ounce of my physical and mental energy and was functioning only on endorphins. Otherwise, I was in decent shape. I retrieved my finish line needs bag and changed into fresh clothing. From there, I ate much-needed food the event had set out for us. Upon completing a full distance triathlon, your body is yearning for some solid food after eating only energy bars and gel packs for the last twelve hours and burning through over 10,000 calories. The problem is that your digestive system is not ready for much volume so it's better to keep the intake on the light side. After eating a slice of cheese pizza and some fruit and hydrating, I searched for and found Debbie. After congratulatory hugs, I asked her about my fellow competitor from Lubbock, Dr. Todd Hegstrom. Had he finished the race as well? She did not know.

I wanted to watch other competitors finish, so Debbie and I found a place in the bleachers. It was moving to see other athletes forever more sealing their place of those having completed the full distance IRONMAN® Triathlon World Championship. After watching for a brief time, the day's trials started taking their effect on me. The endorphins were wearing off and my energy levels plummeted.

I needed to lie down and rest, and we headed back to our hotel room. From our room we could hear the cheers as the announcer called out each finisher's name as they completed the race. After cleaning up, we went to bed. Both of us were exhausted. Yes, Debbie was very tired too. It is tough being a spouse of a triathlete. They are out there all day cheering, taking pictures, worrying, and enduring the tropical sun and heat.

The next morning, I received congratulatory phone calls. It was great to talk to Coach Tim, sharing my race experiences, giving him credit for helping me achieve my goal of finishing the race within the allotted time, doing so in decent shape, and having had the time of my life. Tim played a huge role in my success, and I will be forever grateful for his help.

He confirmed that Todd had finished the race only minutes behind me. This was surprising news, as he was a much more experienced and accomplished athlete than I. He became nauseated during the swim, which stayed with him for a good portion of the bike section. How awful for him to have had to deal with that while trying to race. You never know what unexpected mishaps can occur during a full distance triathlon race that can affect the rest of the race. My hat is off to Todd for dealing with it and persevering. Later Todd called me. His first words to me were, "You're an animal!" Thinking of it still brings a smile to my face.

The next day we were to pick up the bags with our race gear clothing and equipment after lunch. I was surprised they had let the bags sit out in the hot sun all morning long. Walking into the area, there was an awful stench. It smelt like a sewer. I grabbed my gear and headed back to the room, then washed everything in the bathtub and hung them out on the balcony railing to dry. Everyone else was doing the same, as the hotel looked like a laundry mat with all the towels, clothing, and bags hanging out on the balcony rails.

We spent a good portion of the day hanging out at the hotel pool. It was a great place to share our race experiences with all the other athletes. It seemed like everyone just wanted to sit at the pool's edge with their feet in the water. Later that morning, Debbie and I visited the IRONMAN® store to pick up mementos from the race. I selected a few things, including a black jacket with IRONMAN® emblems and logos embroidered on it. One of my favorite things purchased was a sweater with "IRONMAN® Triathlon World Championship 1999" printed on the front. On the back were the words "2.4-mile swim, 112-mile bike, 26.2-mile run and brag for the rest of your life." We also purchased a bottle of champagne with an IRONMAN® label. Later that evening we went to the awards banquet, an exciting and humbling conclusion to this epic event. From there it was time to pack my bike and equipment and get ready for the trip home the next day.

Back in Lubbock, my experience was not over. The local newspaper contacted me and Todd for interviews. Soon afterwards the paper featured both of us on the front page of the sports section with a great article about our race experience. That was completely unexpected. Later a newspaper from a nearby town—where I was born and had family members still living—contacted me for an interview. They too ran an article about my race experience. All this notoriety generated interest in local civic clubs, with invitations to be a guest speaker. I prepared a presentation with pictures, information about the race, and my race experiences. I was so proud and honored to share with them my dream and all that I had experienced in Hawaii. It was like reliving the whole experience. I could see the wonder and excitement in the eyes and faces of the audience as I spoke of what each segment of the race entailed, the trials and challenges of the day, what I ate and drank during the day, and the exhilaration and sense of accomplishment I felt when crossing the finish line. The room was in complete silence as they sat spellbound while listening to me.

At one of these events, I invited Dr. Todd Hegstrom and his wife; Coach Tim and his wife and parents; and Mike and Marti Greer. At the end of the presentation, I gave an triathlon coach of the Year plaque to Tim, a triathlete's friends plaque to the Greers, and a large bouquet of red roses to my spouse Debbie. Attendees told me it was the best and most inspirational presentation the club had ever had.

Rotary club presentation guest

Now it was time to rest, relax, and bask in knowledge that I had achieved the unthinkable. After an "A" priority race, a well-designed training schedule calls for well-deserved and needed downtime. This period is not total rest and consists of other aerobic activities that you might enjoy, such as hiking or snow skiing. I used this time to ponder all that I had just experienced and to consider what was next. I mean, what could be better than competing in and completing the IRONMAN® Triathlon World Championship? Well, that was an easy one. I now desired to become one of the best-of-the-best top two percent in my age group and win a coveted slot to compete in the Super Bowl of triathlons. Time to talk to Coach Tim.

I decided to save the IRONMAN® bottle of champagne from Hawaii. The only time it would be opened was if, and when, I qualified to race in a future IRONMAN® Triathlon World Championship.

PART II

DARING TO DREAM ANYTHING IS POSSIBLE

CHAPTER 25

DARING THE ULTIMATE DREAM: YEAR 2000

The rigors of all the intense training in 1999, coupled with the IRONMAN® Triathlon World Championship event, had taken a toll on my body. Coach Tim explained that it was time for a much-needed rest. Given a proper rest and recovery period, I should emerge all the stronger.

Aerobic activities in December 1999 and January 2000 were random, left up to me as to what they might be. I kept running, cycling, and swimming workouts short and in heart rate zones one and two. My goals were loosely to stay active yet still allow healing and recovery while maintaining a base level of fitness. This was also a perfect time to plan for the coming year. My training in the coming year would focus on making improvements in areas that limited my performance. In other words, we needed to reassess my limiters.

Determining Limiters

Using the periodization training technique I outlined earlier, Coach Tim designed my training and racing plan for the year 2000. No full distance triathlon events were included in the plan. Instead, he planned half distance events as the focus "A" priority races. I would attend the IRONMAN® 70.3® Buffalo Springs Lake triathlon and Half Vineman® events along with other "B" and "C" level priority races.

We first needed to identify my performance limiters. This information would be used to formulate specific training schedules to improve my abilities in those areas. What were my limiters? That was easy; it was everything! Making this determination involved comparing my full distance triathlon performance in each of the three events against those of athletes in my age group who earned qualifying slots at qualifying races.

My IRONMAN® Triathlon World Championship finishing time was 12:33:17. The slowest qualifying time in the forty-to-forty-four age group averaged around ten hours and thirty minutes. Oh my! My goal was to shave off two hours from my time. That was a whopping 17% improvement. That barrier needed to be broken down even further into the individual events. My race splits were 1:17:21 for the swim, 6:24:34 for the bike, and 4:39:04 for the run. To earn a qualifying slot, my time would need to be in the vicinity of 1:05:00 for the swim, 5:25:00 for the bike, and 4:00:00 for the run. You can do the math, but this indicated the most significant improvement was in the cycling portion of the race.

Looking at it from another point of view, I needed to make a 16% improvement on the swim, a 16% improvement on the bike, and a 14% improvement on the run. From this perspective, it showed that each of the events were equal limiters. I had my work cut out for me.

Before creating workouts we needed to determine what in each of the areas was creating the limitation. With so many factors at play, we looked at form, aerobic conditioning, strength, equipment, race day strategy, race day hydration and nutrition, and transition times. It was likely a combination of all the things mentioned. My 2000 training schedule equally addressed all these limiting factors.

Building Strength

I began preparing in February 2000 with a focus on resistance training. I did this in the gym weight room, with Coach Tim designing the workouts. The goal was to build the slow twitch muscle fibers.

Everyone has both slow and fast twitch muscle fibers, just as everyone has different body types such as tall, short, lean, muscular, etc. Those with predominantly slow twitch muscle fibers are naturally geared for endurance, while those with predominately fast twitch muscle fibers are geared more for quick acceleration over short distances. Slow twitch muscle fibers are long and better suited for aerobic exercise. Fast twitch muscle fibers are short and used for quick acceleration. Obviously, slow twitch is needed for competing in triathlon events. My resistance training needed to focus primarily on developing and enhancing the long slow twitch muscles.

Genetics may provide you with more fast than slow twitch muscle fiber types. This does not mean your slow twitch muscle fibers cannot be developed and your fast twitch fibers can't be retrained to act more like slow twitch muscles. Fortunately, with a tall and lean body type, I fell into the category of having predominately slow twitch muscle fibers.

Developing and enhancing slow twitch muscles requires using light weights with multiple repetitions. Repetitions are conducted using a slow lift and slow release. This method is at odds with most of the gym-goers wanting to build big, powerful muscles using heavy weights with few reps. Then there I was taking my sweet time with light weights, lifting and releasing very slowly for twenty or more repetitions. I bet the ripped body builders were thinking to themselves, "What a wimp." I had to swallow my pride and stick with the plan. I had to remind myself most of them had never competed in full distance triathlon event.

The motion of these workouts required taking two seconds to conduct the lift, as did the releasing motion. Two seconds does not sound like much, but it seemed terribly slow. Using this method develops both the contracting and releasing muscle groups. The reasoning behind this strategy is simple. Think about what you do during an endurance event. You perform the same lifting and releasing motions thousands of times over the course of the race. From another point of view, how many times can you arm curl five pounds versus doing the same with thirty pounds? Triathletes need to be able to make these smaller efforts thousands of times. The longer you can maintain the lighter effort, the longer you can perform without fatigue.

I kept up this phase of resistance training through each of the three base training periods. As the training year progressed, and upon entering the build training periods, weight training would progress into heavier weights with fewer repetitions to build a more powerful muscle mass required for bike and run course climbs or when short bursts of speed were needed. More powerful muscles also made the easy effort workouts seem even more so. Back to the analogy of a race car and how it can go a hundred miles per hour so effortlessly—that was what we were trying to achieve with my athletic performance, making being fast look and feel easy.

Aerobic Base

Beginning in February and lasting through April, I focused on building and improving my aerobic base as well. Think of the aerobic base as the first level of a pyramid. That base level is the supporting foundation of everything that will be placed upon it. Therefore, it must be solid, strong, and able to withstand all the stress the upper levels place on top of it.

Building a solid base of aerobic fitness is not something that happens quickly. In fact, it takes seasons of carefully crafted training. My body slowly adapts its cardiovascular, muscular, and circulatory systems to enable it to meet the demands I put on it in training, allowing me to be ready for race day. Endurance athletes must be patient with the process, while strictly adhering to their training plans. When you move on to more intense training too quickly, your aerobic fitness isn't up to par on race day. This results in a less-than-desirable performance, or worse, a DNF (did not finish).

Make no mistake, I was firmly lacking patience. But with Tim's coaching, I recognized he knew more than I did, and I was fully committed to sticking with the plan, if nothing more than to see if it resulted in the desired effects. I was willing to accept the advice of someone who had been there and done that. My part in all this was to stick with the plan and have faith in the process.

The base one, two, and three periods were filled mostly with workouts designed to build base aerobic fitness. Thus, the rate of perceived exertion (RPE) ranged anywhere from very, very light to fairly light, with heart rates ranging from 110 to 120 beats per minute. For the impatient athlete bent on becoming faster, this was all very boring training. That would be me. Coach Tim was aware of my perceptions, telling me to be patient, that all this easy effort training was necessary if I wanted to achieve the end goal. That was enough for me to perform the scheduled workouts as designed. The following chart is an example of the number of training hours scheduled in the preparation and base one period.

Period	Week	Beg Day	Races	Hrs	1	2	3	4	5	6	7
Prep	1	18-Apr		10.0	1:30	1:15	1:00	1:00	:45	2:30	2:00
	2	25-Apr		10.0	1:30	1:15	1:00	1:00	:45	2:30	2:00
Base1	1	2-May		12.0	2:00	1:30	1:30	1:00	1:00	3:00	2:00
	2	9-May		14.5	2:00	2:00	1:30	1:00	1:00	4:00	2:30
	3	16-May		16.0	2:30	2:00	2:00	1:30	1:00	4:00	3:00
	4	23-May		8.5	1:15	1:15	1:00	1:00	:30	2:00	1:30

My weekly and daily training hours could still be long, but the RPE and heart rates would be low. All this long, easy effort training gradually built my base aerobic fitness. Over time, I learned to look forward to and enjoy the workouts. I could head out on a nice easy run, ride, or swim and just enjoy the time with no pressure to perform.

Even during these easy effort workouts, my heart rate tended to gradually climb without increasing the effort. This is known as "cardiac creep," which is very annoying, I might add. The more solid the aerobic base, the longer it takes for cardiac creep to set in. No two days of training were the same. One day cardiac creep may barely show up. On other days it happened very quickly. Other contributing factors, such as inadequate sleep, stress, and diet can affect this creep. Deficiencies in any of these can affect how you feel during a workout.

These base period workouts presented a terrific opportunity to train with friends. That was, as long as they kept the workout in the designated RPE and heart rate zones. This meant I had to pick workout partners with a lower aerobic base to reduce the pressure on my heart rate.

This was an issue when training with other accomplished triathletes and runners. Especially if they were men. Men by nature want to compete against one another. Often these easy training runs and rides turn into mini races towards the end of a training session. Knowing this, I often invited women to join me for long training rides. Women are more laid back than men and rarely turn the ride into a race. Make no mistake, women are formidable, well-conditioned athletes and can push as hard as most men, and I found this out on more than one occasion, limping home with my tail tucked between my legs.

Swimming Limiters

The base periods presented a suitable time for me to improve my performance limiters, especially those related to base aerobic fitness and form. The ability to move efficiently with good form leads to improved endurance and speed. I had previously identified and improved on the more glaring form deficiencies in 1999. The spring of 2000 presented the perfect time to explore my weaknesses more thoroughly.

Base period swim workouts included form drills along with developing my aerobic base. Using proper form while swimming was always front and foremost in my mind. It is virtually impossible to increase speed without using good form. My high school tennis coach once told the team, "Practice does not make perfect. Perfect practice makes perfect." This concept particularly applies to the sport of swimming. Just watch elite swimmers. They seem to move so smoothly and effortlessly in the water. They literally glide. This is the result of using perfect form. The same can be witnessed with elite cyclists and runners. Later in the training year, I conducted swim speed drills using all-out effort for twenty-five-, fifty-, or hundred-yard repeats with a long rest period between each repeat. The following chart is an example of a swim speed drill.

SPEED		
S1 - Speed 1		
Warm Up: 300 yards (mixed strokes) - Swim Easy		
Focus on form, rest at walls as needed to ensure proper form is maintained.		
Main Set:	**Focus:**	
Don't sacrifice form for speed!!!		
4 x 50	Start at T-Pace + :06 then descend :02 per 50	RI = :30
2 x 100	@ T-pace + :10	RI = :15
2 x 75	@ T-pace	RI = :20
2 x 150	@ T-pace + :15	RI = :20
2 x 100	@ T-pace	RI = :25
Cooldown = 100 easy Mix strokes of Breast, Back, and Free Total 1,450		

Cycling Limiters

Many cyclists are mashers, meaning that all the power delivered to the pedal is on the down portion of the stroke. Using this form requires more effort to go at the same speed and thus is not an efficient use of energy.

Good cycling form is more than just using an aerodynamic posture. With each pedal stroke, cyclists should apply force to the pedals as evenly and smoothly as possible to gain as much forward momentum as possible without increasing the effort. Doing so provides added speed while conserving energy. One technique I learned was to envision standing on a barrel using your legs and feet to roll it. Applying this method, the pedal stroke starts just before the foot reaches the top portion of the circular path of the stroke. The stroke then continues to push parallel to the ground until the pedal enters the bottom portion of the stroke. The motion here should be like that of scraping mud off the bottom of your shoe. The complete motion should feel like you are rolling a barrel with your legs and feet. The goal is to deliver power to the pedals as uniformly as possible throughout the pedal stroke.

This technique can be practiced by unclipping one of the shoes from the pedal, letting that foot hang free, and using the opposite foot still clipped to pedal to propel the bike. This drill gives you immediate feedback on your power through the entire pedal stroke. If not uniformly applied, you will feel a slip typically in the lower portion of the stroke. If the form is correct, it should feel smooth and uniform.

I practiced this using a mid-level to a big gear and switching legs every tenth stroke. I repeated this drill throughout a cycling workout. This allows good form to become ingrained in your muscle memory so that it is used without thinking about it. Remember, perfect practice makes perfect.

Like swimming, the base periods present a suitable time to work on speed. Proper form equates to increased efficiency and thus increased speed. Speed can also be enhanced by conditioning the body to move at faster paces. This is best done with short-interval speed drills. These drills are repetitive and typically last for less than five minutes, with complete rest and recovery between repeats, starting the drill at an easy pace then building into an all-out effort. Following is an example of such a drill:

PR-1	Power					
		Gear				
	Time	Front	Rear	Description	Sets	Total Time
	0:10			Warm-up		0:10
	0:35			:60 T = 5 x 20-30s (uphill accelerations)		0:40
				RI = :05 spin at 100-110 rpm		
	0:15			Cooldown		1:00

<u>Purpose:</u>
    Is a form of resistance training that builds quads coupled with aerobic training.

<u>Notes:</u>
    It is best if you can find a good hill to do these on but you can simulate hills just by using a gear that provides the same level of exertion that a steep grade hill provides. The idea is to start slow and steadily accelerate through the interval to where at the end you are at 90% effort.

Running Limiters

Coach Tim designed a program for his trainees to improve their running skills and abilities. This group of athletes typically met at a local high school track at 6:00 a.m. The venue provided him with a better opportunity to observe us while conducting highly targeted and measured drills. As with any workout, these involved a slow warm-up run, followed by stretches. Once ready, we would begin the workout designed for that session. The end goal of the workouts was to improve our running form and speed.

One of these speed drills was to run one hundred yards on the football field, starting slowly and gradually adding speed and finishing the last twenty to thirty yards using all-out effort, followed by a ten- to twenty-second rest period. We repeated this drill a number of times. This strategy helps your body learn to run quickly without undue risk of injury while training. We also used them to conduct high knee lifts and butt kick drills, all done with the goal of improving our running form. The use of good form always equates to running faster with the same use of energy—in short, learning to run more efficiently.

After completing the form drills, we moved from using the football field to the oval track. A typical workout would be to run the straight portions of the track then walk the curved portions. As with the speed drills, we gradually increased our pace through the straights then walked the curves for the rest and recovery period. We repeated this drill for a number of laps around the track. This was followed by running 400- to 800-yard intervals at a quick pace with ample rest between repeats.

The workout typically ended with us running one mile (i.e., four loops around the track) at our best pace. Like racing, we started off at a quick but comfortable pace, then built upon it with the last hundred yards being at our best. These speed drills provided great feedback on how well we were progressing. It was very encouraging to see my one-mile times gradually improving. Hopefully, I will be able to apply this newfound run speed on race day and improve my finishing times.

Chapter 26

Daring the Ultimate Dream: Year 2000—Race Results

The only "B" priority running event on my schedule for the year 2000 was the Cowtown Marathon located in Fort Worth, Texas, on February 12, 2000. This event was in the middle of my base one training period and I was not as aerobically prepared as I would have liked. No matter, as I considered it a long aerobic base training day, a day to practice race pace and keeping heart rates in the desired ranges, along with hydration and nutritional needs. In short, this was not a race I was trying to perform at my best. The goal was to conduct a long aerobic training run and gain racing experience.

Race day was perfect with cool temperatures, sunny with no wind. The only issue was our arriving late to the race because traffic was at a standstill. When we finally arrived and parked our vehicle, I realized the race had already begun. In panic mode, I ran to the start area and found no one else was there. It was a strange sensation not seeing any other competitors. I just started the run at the planned pace, being careful to keep my heart rate in the desired zone. The problem was that I did not know the run course path and when I arrived at the one-mile marker, race volunteers were already picking up the mile markers, cones, making the challenge even greater,

Not knowing the course, I followed a path I assumed was correct. After running close to a half mile in the wrong direction, a race volunteer in a vehicle pulled up to me, telling me I was heading in the wrong direction and pointing me to the correct path. I reversed direction and picked up the pace to catch the others. I was very relieved when seeing the runners at the back of the pack. Catching up to them at around the two-and-a-half-mile point, I could now relax and settle back into the intended race pace and heart rates.

Having started the race at least ten minutes late, my race time would not accurately reflect my time to run 26.2 miles. Still, I enjoyed running with all the other competitors on such a gorgeous day. I finished the race with a time of 4:12:29. Good for 357th out of 888 total competitors. Not too bad for a late start.

The scheduled "B" priority triathlon events were half distance triathlon races. I had spent the last six months building upon my base aerobic fitness, improving form, and performing speed drills. It was time to see if all this training would result in improved finishing times.

The 2000 IRONMAN® 70.3® Buffalo Springs Lake triathlon race would be an important test. The race was held on June 25, 2000. The conditions were typical of past events, hot and windy. I used the same racing strategy as that used in the 1999 event. The following chart compares the race results to that of the prior year races.

	Swim	T-1	Bike	T-2	Run	Total
2000	0:43:03	0:02:25	2:52:35	0:01:52	2:08:06	5:49:59
1999	0:54:11	0:02:01	2:43:57	0:02:01	2:08:18	5:51:07
1998	0:41:07	0:03:34	3:04:46	0:02:35	2:18:19	6:10:21
Change	-0:11:08	0:00:24	0:08:38	-0:00:09	-0:00:12	-0:01:08

The race results were a bit disappointing. Only a one-minute improvement over the prior year. Prior to the race, Mike and Marti Greer mentioned that I should consider upgrading my bike to newer and better equipment. Wasn't one triathlon bike as good as the next? Once again, I didn't know what I didn't know. They introduced me to a bike mechanic they had hired to assist athletes at the event to help resolve issues with their bikes before the race. This gentleman knew what he was doing. He mentioned my bike was a bit outdated and that an upgrade could be beneficial. He explained that he could build a bike made of fiber carbon that was uniquely designed to fit my body dimensions. Furthermore, new light-weight race wheels could help improve my bike event times.

All this sounded great and like something that I needed. The only issue was the price. These bikes and racing wheels were expensive and not on the family budget. Achieving a dream often requires monetary sacrifices as well as time and energy. I knew this was yet another steppingstone in the quest of the ultimate dream and pulled the trigger, ordering the equipment.

He took measurements of my body dimensions, enabling the bike frame to be uniquely fitted to my body. After he made the measurements, I was told that my body dimensions were not typical of that of most elite cyclists. As I remember it, the length of my torso in proportion to my leg length did not fit the norms for elite cyclists. Now that was a bit of disappointing news. I am sure he was just being honest with me and not wanting me to set my hopes too high. It came across like he was saying, "You are not physically capable of being one of the best." I have learned not to let the comments of others, or for that matter cold hard facts, deter me from exploring my goals. I had this one God-given body type and there was nothing I could do to change that. What I could do was develop my body to reach its maximum potential, whatever that may be, and see where it led me. This spurred me on to try even harder.

> *"Stay away from those people who try to disparage your ambitions. Small minds will always do that, but great minds will give you a feeling that you can become great too."* — Mark Twain

Our good friends, Mike and Marti Greer, were competing in the 2000 IRONMAN® Triathlon World Championship race under a special provision. Debbie and I wanted to support them as they had me in the previous year's event, so we made the trip to Hawaii to cheer them on. To make the trip even better, my new bike would be shipped there. It was like Christmas in October when I opened the box with the new bike and racing wheels. The bike fit me like a well-tailored suit. The race wheels were so light, with both together weighing as much as one of the wheels used to train on. I felt so comfortable and fast while riding it. Surely this new bike would help decrease my bike event times. Triathletes grow very fond of our bikes, as we spend hours upon hours riding and training on them. We even give them a name. I chose Scary Fast, as that was how I felt when riding it.

The next race was the Half Vineman® triathlon that I had competed in the prior year, and it was a fresh opportunity to try out my new equipment and determine if my training was paying off. Following are the race results compared to the prior year's race results:

	Swim	T-1	Bike	T-2	Run	Total
2000	0:39:48		2:53:18		1:54:52	5:28:00
1999	0:42:43		3:00:56		1:58:26	5:41:56
Change	-0:02:55		-0:07:38		-0:03:34	-0:13:56

Now this was more like what I was hoping for! I reduced my finishing time by almost fourteen minutes for a 4% improvement. The swim time improved 7%, the bike time improved by 4%, and the run time by 2%. Judging from these results, the swim and bike training were having the biggest impact on overall race results.

Judging the run race results is a bit trickier, as it is the last event in the race. By the time you begin the run portion, you have been racing at a high RPE for over three and a half hours. Energy reserves are dropping significantly by that time, and you may have made mistakes in your race pace, hydration, nutrition, any of which could dramatically affect the run portion of the race.

Overall, I was happy with the race results, especially as Coach Tim wanted me to keep my heart rates in a specified range during the bike and run portions. Those ranges were lower than what I had experienced in past races. Coupled with improved race times indicated that my athletic form and aerobic base were improving. Coach Tim's expertise was paying off now, as I was able to race at faster speeds with the same or less energy being utilized.

Coach Tim and I had discussed that it could take years of focused training to have a chance at achieving my ultimate dream. I knew gains would come in small increments. My improvements in 2000, while not particularly grand in the scheme of things, were exactly what I'd hoped for. I was committed to the process and had to have patience.

"The road to success and the road to failure are almost exactly the same."
—*Colin R. Davis*

"Develop success from failures. Discouragement and failure are two of the surest stepping stones to success." —Dale Carnegie

Chapter 27

Daring the Ultimate Dream: Year 2001

The year 2001 was my third year of being involved with the sport of triathlon. I had already achieved dreams of completing a marathon, half, and full distance - triathlon events. Most folks could and should be satisfied with these achievements. I could not settle until I knew what I was truly capable of if I continued my training. What were my limits? Was I able to reach the pinnacle of triathlon, being considered one of the best of the best and qualifying to compete on a world stage? It was exciting to think about. I had a great trainer who was showing me the path. The rest was up to me to push through any issues and make it happen.

> *"Sometimes life is about risking everything for a dream no one can see but you." –unknown.*

As with the previous year, the training plan began with a preparation period where the workouts were not heavily structured. Workout efforts were low on the RPE scale and short in duration. Beginning in early winter, my training plan progressed into the base training periods, where once again Coach Tim and I assessed limiters and focused on strengthening my aerobic base. The early base training periods presented a suitable time to determine the "A," "B," and "C" priority races for the coming year. We scheduled a full slate of racing at various events. Each would serve a purpose in the overall training plan. Short-distance races took the place of intense short brick workouts. Duathlons and Olympic triathlons served as long-distance brick workouts conducted at race pace. half distance triathlon events were race preparation long brick workouts. Hopefully 2001 would show if achieving my ultimate dream was possible. We determined that my race schedule would be as follows:

Level	Date	Event	Location
C	1/21/2001	Frost Your Fanny Duathlon Run 3.1 miles, bike 18.6 miles, run 3.1 miles	Dallas, TX
C	5/12/2001	Tom Landry Sprint Triathlon Swim 437 yards, bike 15 miles, run 3 miles	Dallas, TX
B	6/24/2001	IRONMAN® 70.3® Buffalo Springs Lake Triathlon Swim 1.2 miles, bike 56 miles, run 13.1 miles	Lubbock, TX
A	7/29/2001	IRONMAN® USA Lake Placid Triathlon Swim 2.4 miles, bike 112 miles, run 26.2 miles	Lake Placid, NY
C	8/12/2001	Wool Capital Olympic Triathlon Swim .93 miles, bike 24 miles, run 6.2 miles	San Angelo, TX
C	9/16/2001	Texas Tech Sprint Triathlon Swim .5 miles, bike 12.4 miles, run 3.1 miles	Lubbock, TX
C	11/25/2001	Atlanta Marathon Run 26.2 miles	Atlanta, GA

I was excited to tackle the challenge. I had faith that my structured training and new bike would improve my race performance. I was cautious not to expect too much, still being in the initial stages of my development as a triathlete. The first race of the year was the Frost Your Fanny Duathlon held in late January in Dallas, Texas. The comical name of the race was derived from the fact that the race was held in mid-winter when morning air temperatures were typically close to freezing. That may not sound too bad to run in but add the effect of the wind chill while riding twenty-plus miles per hour on a bike and it can be downright cold, thus the name.

I did not have any performance expectations, as this was my first (and only) duathlon. It was a high-profile race for duathletes and I was curious how I would stack up against those in my age group. It was odd to me to start a race with a 5K run, followed by a twenty-mile bike ride, then finish the race with another 5K run with no swim involved. One of the competitors in my age group was a gentleman from my hometown and he held an elite status in the sport. Secretly I wanted to know how I measured up. I was surprised and excited to learn that I had finished sixth out of thirty-three in my age group and a mere three minutes behind the gentleman I spoke of who had won our age group.

The next race on my schedule was the Tom Landry Sprint Triathlon held in late spring in Dallas, Texas. I gave the race everything I had, with my heart rate being off the charts at the end of the race. I was elated when my name was called out during the award ceremony as the first-place finisher in my age group. That was a first and you could not wipe the smile off my face.

These race results were good, having performed well at both events, but I did not spend time dwelling on either; there were bigger fish to fry.

The IRONMAN® 70.3® Buffalo Springs Lake triathlon would be the first significant test to determine if I were making any advances. I considered this a "B" priority race, and I had worked hard at improving my bike and run limiters. Race day conditions were similar to that of previous races, being hot, dry, and windy. As with any race, I had a plan for the day. My plan was to take in more liquids given the hot, windy, and dry conditions, to attack the hills and rest and recover on the descent, and to keep my heart rate average in the 145 range and run at a comfortably hard pace.

I executed my race plan flawlessly and was excited by my performance on such a challenging course and in the harsh weather conditions. Following are the 2001 race results compared to that of previous years:

	Swim	T-1	Bike	T-2	Run	Total
2001	0:38:02	0:02:32	2:50:20	0:01:59	1:53:24	5:25:04
2000	0:43:03	0:02:25	2:52:35	0:01:52	2:08:06	5:49:59
1999	0:54:11	0:02:01	2:43:57	0:02:01	2:08:18	5:51:07
Change	-0:05:01	0:00:07	-0:02:15	0:00:07	-0:14:42	-0:24:55

Wow! My finishing time improved close to twenty-five minutes over the prior year, equating to a 7% improvement. Most of my gains came from swimming and running. These were the kinds of results I had worked so hard for.

The next big test would come on July 29, 2001, at IRONMAN® USA Lake Placid triathlon held in Lake Placid, New York. IRONMAN® triathlon events are typically held in resort areas. As such, they provide a wonderful opportunity to combine the annual family vacation with triathlon events. What better way to share my sport with my family and prevent it from unduly interfering with family time? Lake Placid is a beautiful area with lush mountains, green forests, and sparkling clear water lakes and rivers and was also the site of the 1980 Winter Olympics. The race had the athletes crossing the Olympic circle at the finish line. How cool is that!

We left our home in Texas a week before the race, giving us ample time to see the sites in and around Lake Placid. We especially enjoyed the Olympic training village. Olympic athletes were there using the facilities to train for the next winter Olympics. It was interesting to see how they trained in the summer for the winter games. Among these were the acrobatic snow ski jumpers twisting and turning in the air then landing in a pool of water. Jets of air were blasted into the water as they landed to soften the impact.

We also were able to watch athletes practice the alpine ski jump. All they had to land on were rubber mats. I have no idea what would have happened if they crash-landed. We stood at an observation station just below the bottom of the ramp and watched as jumpers flew by at high speeds. There were observers nearby relaying wind speed and direction to the jumpers as they readied themselves for the jump. Watching the alpine ski jumpers reminded me of a keynote speaker talking about how he had competed in the Olympic event in past games. He described himself as laughing while he descended the ramp and took off flying through the air. He said it helped him relax while going through the jump. I would have been too terrified to be laughing. And they call doing full distance IRONMAN® triathlon events crazy!

We stayed at the host hotel, which was more like a ski lodge. It was within walking distance of most everything we needed. The kids loved exploring the village shops and dining at the cozy Black Bear log cabin-style restaurant. They had an exciting time at the ice-skating arena, as we did not have any of those in Lubbock, Texas. As with other IRONMAN® full distance triathlon events, I dedicated the day before to rest and relaxation. I needed to stay off my feet the entire day and rest. Debbie took the opportunity to give me some time alone by taking the kids to an amusement park located about an hour's drive towards Albany, New York.

My eldest daughter Ashley said, "My favorite memory was of the Olympic Village and the nature around us. I loved the dense trees, mountains, and the gray fog that covered it all. My favorite thing was walking my sisters down to the Black Bear, where we had breakfast each morning. It was a homey log cabin kind of place. Down the road a little was the ski shop where we bought my snowboard. Unfortunately, I don't remember the finish line. I just remember loving the rain and chill. However, I do remember not being envious of swimming in that lake. Dad, and all the other racers, looked half-frozen coming out of the water. Especially, their bare feet."

I was concerned about the safety of my bike while away from the room, so I secured it to the steel bed frame using a steel cable with a keyed lock. This was a bit overly cautious on my part but consider the amount of time invested in training for this "A" priority race along with the considerable financial investment made in the bike and the trip itself. I just could not risk having my bike stolen and ruining this event. Bike check-in was scheduled for that day, and I was preparing all the transition and special needs bags until my time arrived. I soon realized that my wife had the key to the lock securing my bike. Oops! In a rush, I had no other option than to cut the cable, but with what?

The hotel staff took me into the maintenance room in the dimly lit basement of the facility. It looked like a seventeenth-century junk room with a dirt floor and timbered walls. I eventually found a hand-powered metal hacksaw and was able to cut through the cable, freeing my bike. Whew! That was unexpected! Thankfully, no further surprises occurred the remainder of the day. I spent the evening going through my prerace routine of preparing for the race.

Debbie and the kids returned after a fun-filled day at the amusement park, and we all shared our adventures, then turned in early to get as much sleep as possible.

Early the next morning, we rousted three sleepy girls, I ate my prerace meal, and we prepared to go to the race site. Once there, I went to the bike racks to check tire pressures, testing to see that each wheel spun freely, loaded the Bento Bag, and placed water and energy bottles on my bike. The announcers called all competitors to the swim start area. I donned my wetsuit, checked the seal of my goggles, then entered the chilly water and made my way to the area to start the race. Once there, I treaded water until the start cannon sounded. Treading water in a wetsuit takes truly little effort, as they make you more buoyant.

Like in Hawaii, 2,500 athletes began swimming and it was very crowded for the first ten minutes. The athletes gradually dispersed. During this race, I did not have trouble sighting the buoys, as there was a submerged metal cable at a depth of about ten feet that ran the length of the out-and-back course. Lake Placid was a chilly sixty-seven degrees with the morning air temperature at fifty-four degrees, and the water was noticeably clear, with the cable easily visible. All we had to do was follow the cable. This was great, as there was no need to periodically look up in search of the next buoy.

I finished the swim in good condition then retrieved my swim-to-bike transition bag and headed to the changing tent. Once ready, I rushed out of the tent to find my bike and ran with it to the bike mount area. I mounted the bike and headed out onto the course.

The bike course path took us through various small towns and forested roadways with steep mountains on each side. It was incredibly beautiful, especially after the terrain in Lubbock with flat, arid landscape with limited trees. There were long climbs and descents. The path was a double loop course, bringing the athletes back to the start area before heading back out on the second loop, giving me multiple chances to see my cheering family.

The course descended as I entered the second loop and speeds were fast. Course officials had warned us of a small hump at the end of a flat portion of the course before entering another descent. They said it was common to become airborne briefly while going over the hump. Sure enough, that was exactly what I experienced, an unexpected thrill flying through the air going twenty-plus miles per hour.

The second loop of the course felt much harder than the first, slowing my pace. I am sure it was a result of my pushing too hard during the first loop. At one point on the bike course, I was passing by a massive, sheer rock wall rising hundreds of feet above the roadway. I could hear spectators cheering but I could not see them anywhere. I soon realized the sound was coming from high above me on the face of the rock wall. Rock climbers had scaled the cliff wall to rest on a rock shelf where they were perched, cheering for the riders.

Finally, I finished the bike event, racked my bike, grabbed the transition bag, then headed to the changing tent, taking time to put extra lubrication on my toes, ankles, under my arms, and on my nipples to avoid chafing. I donned my running shoes and exited the tent, crossing the timing mat to start the running event.

The run course was mostly flat with gentle inclines curving through forested roads next to a sparkling mountain river with stunning views. The air temperature was cool, making for good running conditions. I ran as smoothly and comfortably as you can after having swum 2.4 miles and cycling 112 miles. That is, until I reached the eighteen-mile mark, where my energy levels plummeted, at which point I just focused on getting to each mile marker. I dared not think about the remaining six miles to cover and the fifty additional minutes needed to do so. That would have been too discouraging when my body, mind, and soul had little left to give.

Every triathlete knows that the final six miles of a 146-mile triathlon race is a huge mental challenge to ignore what your body is telling you and just keep moving. I had to draw upon a few strategies I had learned from prior racing experiences, such as focusing only on making it to the next mile marker, staying as hydrated as possible, keep consuming calories, and finding visual distractions to draw my attention away from my burning thighs and feet and a feeling of complete exhaustion. Finding visual distractions was easy, as we were surrounded by majestic forests and beautiful streams and rivers. I also encouraged the runners going in the opposite direction, as they had many more miles left to cover than I.

As I neared the finish line, light rain began to fall. I finished just before the heavy rain sat in. Upon crossing the finish line, volunteers hung a finisher's medal around my neck as medical volunteers assessed my condition. It was so cool to finish the race and cross the Olympic circle. I had the sense of somehow being connected to the Olympic athletes having competed there in years past. A volunteer handed finishers space blankets to help keep us warm as we made our way to the food tents. I was impressed with the effectiveness of the lightweight metallic sheath at keeping in my body heat. Initially, I was cold, but the space blanket had me quickly overheating after using it for only minutes.

Full distance triathlon events provide a food court of sorts for the athletes in the finish line area. It consists of hot chicken broth, pizza, pasta salads, fruits, and an assortment of other foods and drinks that help replenish a spent body without causing gastric distress. I grabbed a small plate of the available food and made my way to the spectators' area, where I found my wife and children. They greeted me warmly and congratulated me.

By this point, the rain was coming down more heavily, so we retrieved my bike and headed to the hotel for a hot, soothing shower and much-needed rest. My family was physically and emotionally spent as well, since they had been up since 4:45 a.m. and had watched the event over the eleven hours that I was on the course. Our kids were ages fourteen, eleven, and nine. It was a lot to ask of them to support me for such a prolonged period of time. They were proud of me, but all looked as tired as we were, all ready to call it day. I doubt our kids fully understood the dedication and commitment I had made to the sport, as they have watched me train and race for most of their short lives. I felt sorry for the athletes still out on the course in the chilly rain. It must have been miserable for them.

When I returned home, we examined my results. Was all the planning, training, and racing having the desired effect of advancing me towards my ultimate dream? Below is a chart comparing my split times at IRONMAN® USA Lake Placid triathlon with that of the 1999 IRONMAN® Triathlon World Championship.

	Swim	T-1	Bike	T-2	Run	Total
2001	1:13:07	0:01:56	5:41:33	0:03:38	4:17:32	11:22:30
1999	1:17:21	0:06:25	6:24:34	0:06:29	4:39:09	12:33:17
Change	-0:04:14	-0:04:29	-0:43:01	-0:02:51	-0:21:37	-1:10:47

I was elated at my considerable progress, with all events reflecting gains. The swim time improved by 5%, the bike time improved by 11%, and the run time improved by over 9%. There was no doubt my training plan proved to be effective in all three events.

There was still work to be done in pursuing my ultimate dream. I still needed to shave another fifty minutes off the total time to have any chance at earning a slot for the IRONMAN® Triathlon World Championship event. I placed thirty-third out of 243 in my age group and would need to be in the top six or seven to earn a slot. Knowing what it took just to achieve these results, I wondered if attaining my dream was even possible.

The remainder of 2001 would bring me two additional "C" level races. My finishing time improved with each event. The last scheduled race of the season was a Thanksgiving Day marathon in Atlanta, Georgia. The course was previously used for the marathon event in the 1996 summer Olympic Games. Another impressive venue for amateur athletes.

My wife and I traveled to Georgia two days early and stayed with friends who were also triathletes. Race day conditions were perfect with sunny skies, light winds, and cool temperatures. The plan was to maintain an average pace of eight or less minutes per mile. To achieve this goal, the initial pace would need to be comfortably hard, becoming somewhat hard by mile eighteen, and very hard by mile twenty-two. Hydration, nutrition, and electrolyte intake throughout the race would need to be near perfect to achieve this goal.

All went according to plan. My initial pace was slightly below the average goal pace, but I was running very comfortably. As racing sometimes goes, I was in a zone, feeling comfortable while running a 7:45-minute-per-mile pace. I was surprised at how easy those first thirteen miles felt. It was like I was gliding on air. All systems were operating to perfection. I recall holding conversations with other runners with no effort at all and checking my heart rate monitor as each mile passed, noting that my heart rate was within the planned zones and that I was holding a sub-eight-minute-per-mile pace. In the back of my mind I was thinking, All I have to do is continue like this and a sub-3:30 time was in the bag.

At the same time, I was careful to stay with my hydration and nutrition plan, as a misstep on either could prove disastrous. As planned and expected, the RPE needed to maintain the goal pace began to creep up beginning at mile seventeen, becoming somewhat hard through mile twenty-two. At that point, with only four miles to go, the RPE became very hard. My energy levels were waning, but my spirits were high. At this point I had to concentrate on maintaining good running form. I could sense the finish line was near and longed to hear the announcers and crowd at the finish line area. I just concentrated on putting one foot in front of the other and maintaining an 8:00-per-mile pace. Since I was below the average per mile goal pace, I luckily had room to play with.

At mile twenty-two, there was a one-mile climb aptly named "Cardiac Hill." Mercy, that was tough! While entering the first portion of the climb, my thighs began to burn in protest of the demands I was placing on them and my breathing became labored. I focused on nothing more than the top of the climb and continued at the best pace I could maintain without blowing up. It drained my body of what little strength and energy I had left.

My legs and lungs leaped for joy while rounding the top of the climb with the remaining three miles being flat or even at a slight decline. I could now just cruise to the finish line. It is impossible to adequately relay the feelings I had when seeing the end approaching after such a long and grueling event. There was an overwhelming joy of knowing that I was almost done, along with an intense sense of pride in myself that I had accomplished a lofty goal. One I had trained so rigorously for. The emotions involved have more than once brought me to tears. I entered that last mile joyfully knowing that I would achieve my goal. I finished the race with a time of 3:29:01 and received a special engraved medal for those finishing under 3:30:00. This was an improvement over previous marathons by twenty-six minutes and at a full one-minute-per-mile faster pace. Things were looking up. The prospect of realizing my ultimate dream seemed closer than ever.

Georgia Marathon Medal

Chapter 28

Expanding My Knowledge

I once heard a keynote speaker address the keys to success in business, and the things they said have stayed with me. The speaker said that reading one hour every day on topics of your business interest would result in becoming a recognized expert in your chosen field within seven years. One hour of reading every day is a lot when every minute of every day is already filled to the brim.

I never found the time to follow this advice to the letter, but I did make a point to read professional journals, research materials from standard-setting bodies, and information on my industry. Surely even this amount of reading was more than what my peers were doing. Unless I needed to resolve an issue at hand, this reading did not seem to have an immediate impact of separating myself from others in my field as a certified public accountant practicing as a financial statement auditor and income tax preparer for rural utility companies. The impact began to reveal itself over a span of years. I was eventually recognized by my peers as a specialist in these fields and was routinely asked to speak at training seminars.

If this was an effective business strategy for separating myself from my peers, why not in the sport of triathlon? My coach gave me great information on the theories and strategies behind effective training methods. I realized being in the sport for over three years, it was time for me to take my knowledge to a higher level. To this point, everything I had learned had been from Coach Tim, watching and talking with others, reading periodicals, and from trial and error—no doubt all valuable sources of knowledge, but ones that could only carry me so far.

I began to search for books on the topic. I found several that piqued my interest. By far the most complete and beautifully written book I found was *The Triathlete's Training Bible*, by Joel Friel. This book was like finding a pot of gold at the end of a rainbow. It was a wealth of information on every topic a triathlete could ever need. I have since read it multiple times. It became a reference manual used anytime I needed to advance my knowledge in certain areas. Over the years its pages have become worn and tattered, looking like the old, loyal friend that it is.

As good and useful as it was, it never hurt to read from other sources and perspectives. I read books on training based on heart rates, and one of my favorites became *Going Long*, by IRONMAN® Triathlon World Championship legend Dave Scott. As previously mentioned, the book *Total Immersion*, by Terry Laughlin, proved invaluable in learning to swim with proper form.

Reading all these books provided me with a much deeper understanding of the training methods used by Coach Tim. My workouts came to life with timing and purpose. Knowing the purpose in the plan of my workouts made it much easier to push myself. Training using the periodization method now made more sense. All this newfound knowledge provided me with a greater sense of my potential in attempting to achieve my ultimate dream.

From these books I learned about other key areas of proper training for endurance athletes. Sleep is instrumental in maximizing performance. While asleep, the body repairs the damage training does to tissues. It is also when the body builds new muscle and capillaries, strengthens the skeletal systems, and makes other adjustments needed to meet the demands placed upon it during training workouts. This process is known as "super compensation." If an endurance athlete is cutting corners in their sleep, they are effectively putting limits on the benefits received from all the work they have put into their training.

The same thing can be said of effectively managing nutritional needs. Certain foods provide the building blocks required by the body to perform the super compensation adjustments in building a stronger, aerobically capable body. Inferior quality food will result in less-than-desirable results. Using automobiles as an analogy, you would never put low-grade fuel and oil in a high-performance race car. Why would you do that to yourself as a high-performance athlete?

I was learning the importance of all my inputs. It made no sense to waste the long hours of training just to sabotage it with poor food choices and lack of adequate sleep. Being a bit of a maverick and enjoying junk food, this was a constant struggle for me. Doing my best to follow the 80/20 rule, I did what should be done 80% of the time and what I wanted the other 20%. This allowed me to indulge every now and then. All work and no play can lead to lack of resolve to stay with the plan. At least that was true for me.

Anyone attempting to achieve an athletic dream will tell you that the process is as much mental as physical. No matter the subject, you should do things that keep the dream continuously in front of you. I put this into practice in a multitude of ways—like putting a picture or visual reference on my vanity mirror, placing it where I could see it multiple times a day as a constant reminder of my dream. I read the previously mentioned books on the subject as another way to keep my mind focused on my ultimate goal. I kept a diary on my daily workouts, and it provided a side benefit as a record that I could review for reasons why a workout was good or bad, such as the time of day, weather conditions, and general fatigue levels. I would give this to Coach Tim as a means of providing him with direct feedback on the effectiveness of his training plans that allowed him to make adjustments to the plan as needed.

What I am about to tell you may sound very corny, but it helped me keep the goal in focus. There is a song written by Kenny Chesney titled "How Forever Feels." The lyrics to the chorus are: "I want to know how forever feels." This song was widely played on the radio while I was training. It is a fun, lively tune that I enjoyed singing along to. I changed the lyrics to make it about my goal of qualifying to compete in the Super Bowl of full distance triathlons. I sang the chorus as: "I want to know how Kona™ feels." I changed the words to the verses as well to reflect my training. Another thing I picked up from listening to inspirational speakers was to tell others of your goals and dreams. This creates self-imposed motivation for you to continue to stay the course and not abandon it. I conveyed my ultimate dream to anyone who seemed the least bit interested in hearing about it. I did this more for my benefit than theirs.

Chapter 29

Daring the Ultimate Dream: Year 2002

The year 2002 marked the beginning of the third year in my quest of earning a slot in the IRONMAN® Triathlon World Championship. I spent November 2001 through January 2002 in the preparation training period with no racing on the schedule. I focused my workouts on preserving my aerobic base. The goal for 2002 was to shave additional time off my full distance triathlon times.

2001 ended with significant improvements in all three events. I hoped the same would occur in 2002, inching ever closer to attaining my goal of becoming one of the best-of-the-best long-course triathletes and to compete in the Kona IRONMAN® Triathlon World Championship race. I still needed to reduce my full distance triathlon finishing time by fifty minutes. As with any sport, gains become harder to realize the better you get. My aerobic base was now solid and strong. It was now time to include two full distance triathlon events in a single year's training plan. They would need to be spaced at least three months apart to give my body ample time to recover and super compensate from the first event.

Three years may seem like a long time for one to stay focused while pursuing a dream, and I agree that it is. However, I knew from Coach Tim and my research that it could take up to seven years of focused, highly structured training for my body to achieve my ultimate endurance physical conditioning. This was my third year of being mentored by Coach Tim, and I understood that I was in the middle of the process and I was making progress. If I stopped, I would forever wonder what might have been if I had stayed the course to its ultimate end. I have never been a quitter, and I am not about to start now. It helped that I was having the time of my life during the process. Each new racing year brought with it the promise of reaching new heights of achievement and kept me motivated.

Obviously, there were times of discouragement, including poor workout and race performance, naysayers, and recurring bouts of plantar fasciitis and Achilles tendonitis. I have come to realize that poor workout and race performances can have many causes. Some were under my control and others not. There was always a reason for inferior performance, and it was my job to reason this out and not make the same mistake in the future. Naysayers were simply ignored. Issues with training injuries were a bigger problem, and they could be painful and last for extended periods, interfering with my training plans.

With each occurrence I would implement treatments such as placing arch supports in my shoes, wearing a boot in the evenings that stretched the affected tendons, icing the affected areas, using pain relieving creams and medications, or simply extended rest periods with no running, which I hated. In every case the pain would seem to disappear over a period of a few days. The point of providing you with this information is that you will encounter setbacks and discouraging events during the pursuit of any dream. What matters is how you react. Your options are to give up or find a solution to the issue. Find the positives and do whatever it takes to keep focused on the end goal.

In early 2002, Coach Tim and I decided on the following race schedule:

Level	Date	Event	Location
B	5/12/2002	IRONMAN® 70.3® Gulf Coast Triathlon Swim 1.2 miles, bike 56 miles, run 13.1 miles	Panama City, FL
C	7/28/2002	Storrie Lake Olympic Triathlon Swim .93 miles, bike 24 miles, run 6.2 miles	Storrie Lake Park, NM
C	8/12/2002	Wool Capital Olympic Triathlon Swim .93 miles, bike 24 miles, run 6.2 miles	San Angelo, TX
A	9/15/2002	IRONMAN® Wisconsin Triathlon Swim 2.4 miles, bike 112 miles, run 26.2 miles	Madison, Wisconsin
B	11/1/2002	The Great Floridian Triathlon® Swim 2.4 miles, bike 112 miles, run 26.2 miles	Clermont, FL

I also participated in local running club running and sprint distance triathlon events. These were considered hard effort races, taking the place of workouts meant to build strength and anaerobic capabilities. People have said to me that these short races must seem easy for me. On the contrary, even though short, my efforts on the RPE scale were extremely hard, as I put forth a 110% effort, which placed my heart rate in the red zone for the event.

IRONMAN® 70.3® Gulf Coast Triathlon

My racing plans considered the IRONMAN® 70.3® Gulf Coast triathlon as a "B" level race. The race was held on May 12, 2002, at Panama City, Florida. Debbie and the girls were excited to be going to Florida. After checking them out of school for four days and getting assignments from teachers, we were ready to go. We packed up the kids and drove 1,117 miles from Lubbock, Texas, to Panama City. Once on the road we did all we could to get the girls to work on their schoolwork assignments, but they didn't have much desire to do so. We had to remind them there would be no pool or beach time until they completed their schoolwork. That motivated them to get it done during the two-day road trip to Florida. Once it was complete, we allowed them to watch movies on the portable mini-TV/VCR we carried for the longer trips.

Debbie and I discussed the race, making sure we knew what each segment entailed, where the best spectator locations would be for them to see me enter and exit the swim, the bike, and beginning and end. We planned out locations, maximizing their opportunities to take photos and cheer for me. These areas are commonly known as hot corners. Debbie outlined the backpack full of snacks, electronic games, and books she had packed to keep the girls occupied during the long stretches of time while I was on the course.

It took longer to drive across Texas than from Louisiana to Florida. This road trip was unusually long, and once we crossed the state boundary into Florida, we elected to drive on a highway that ran parallel to the beach. While scenic, it slowed our progress, as we had to pass through many small towns and other traffic lights. Once we arrived everyone was ready to check out the pool and play on the beach.

We rented a condominium on the beach, sharing it with another couple and their family from Georgia, who were fellow triathletes. Panama City is a beautiful Gulf Coast beach community with lovely white sand beaches for as far as the eye can see. We had a wonderful time hanging out with our friends and enjoying playing in the sand and surf with the kids and basking in the gulf coast sun. We were only there for a few days and as such we did not have time to explore all the area had to offer. We did take the opportunity to enjoy the succulent fresh seafood at local restaurants.

I was excited to race there since I had never raced at sea level or on an entirely flat course.

The race was never far from my mind, and we spent time with short, easy practice swims, rides, and runs just to stay loose and ready to race. I went through my normal prerace routine the evening before and morning of the race. Race day conditions could not have been more perfect, with clear, sunny skies, no wind, and cool air temperatures. The sea conditions for the swim were light waves and crisp water. I finished the swim in thirty-six minutes and seventeen seconds. This was an improvement of one minute and forty-six seconds over the previous year's IRONMAN® 70.3® Buffalo Springs Lake triathlon time, despite the change from lake to open ocean.

The double-loop bike course was flat and thus fast. I was flying through it. At one point I came up on an emergency vehicle that was moving slower than the cyclists. Several of us piled up behind it. The driver soon let us pass. With just a couple of miles left, I came upon one of our friends we were staying with as she was starting a portion of the course that doubles back on itself. I slowed down to speak with her. A competitor that had been just behind me for a good portion of the race went by us, saying, "Don't stop now, we're almost done." Enough chatting, this was a race!

I finished the bike course with a time of 2:28.01. Wow! That was fast, with me averaging 22.7 miles per hour and was a twenty-two-minute improvement over the prior year's time. This was not really a fair comparison since the IRONMAN® 70.3® Buffalo Springs Lake triathlon course was hot, windy, and full of steep climbs. I was still happy with my progress.

The run course was out and back on the same roadway that ran parallel to the beach. The scenery was impressive, with views of palm trees and the waves crashing into the white sandy beach. I ran comfortably for the first six miles, with the air temperature quickly rising along with the humidity. On no! Heat and high humidity are not a good combination, as I tend to overheat with no way to cool down short of walking. The conditions took their toll around mile eight, and the last five miles were tough. I did my best to keep a good pace without letting my heart rate get out of control. I was fighting my heart rate to keep it from creeping into the anaerobic zones, which is no-man's-land while racing. Throwing caution to the wind, I focused on keeping a good, steady pace for the last three miles. I finished the run course with a time of 1:54:34, which was one minute and ten seconds slower than the prior year IRONMAN® 70.3® Buffalo Springs Lake triathlon time. Ugh! Attributing the slower time to the heat, coupled with high humidity, I made a mental note of this for future tropical climate races, as there may be similar conditions in Kona.

My race finishing time was 5:03:00, placing me seventeenth in my forty to forty-four age group and 126th overall. The difference between first place in my age group and my time was a mere seventeen minutes. All the time and effort I was putting forth into training was paying off. Following is a comparison of this race with that of the IRONMAN® 70.3® Buffalo Springs Lake triathlon:

	Swim	T-1	Bike	T-2	Run	Total
2002	0:36:16	0:02:59	2:28:01	0:01:49	1:54:34	5:03:00
2001	0:38:02	0:02:32	2:50:20	0:01:59	1:53:24	5:25:04
Change	-0:01:46	0:00:27	-0:22:19	-0:00:10	-0:01:10	-0:22:04

The morning after the race we all packed the car, bid our friends farewell, and headed home. This time we took the interstate in lieu of the Beach Boulevard to speed up our return trip. Once on the road, exhaustion set in, with the girls napping, watching movies, playing games, and enjoying all the scenery along the way.

Storrie Lake Olympic Triathlon

Storrie Lake State Park is located four miles north of Las Vegas, New Mexico, in the Sangre de Cristo Mountains. Its elevation is 6,600 feet above sea level and offers great opportunities for fishing, camping, and other recreational activities.

The lake is surrounded by pine-forested mountains and is a beautiful setting to hold a race in late July.

My family wanted to camp at the lake and so we took our tent, camping gear, and fishing poles. This was another short trip allowing me to compete in regional triathlon events. We arrived two days before the event so that we could camp out with the kids and enjoy the lake area. I took the kids fishing but we did not have much luck catching anything. Debbie and I tried to make each of these racing trips a new adventure for our girls. They needed to look forward to them as much as I did. Debbie normally would take them on sightseeing adventures while I prepared to race.

Mike and Marti Greer joined us at the lake, staying in their RV. They joined us the evening before the race for a cookout featuring hotdogs, hamburgers, and s'mores. I enjoyed combining triathlon events with family and friends. We had the best time hanging out with the group outside and enjoying the scenery. The family was not involved as volunteers. They could just relax and enjoy watching the race and cheer for me.

Camping at Storrie Lake with my family and Mike and Marti Greer

Wetsuits were allowed and I used mine. The swim was in the clear, cool-water mountain lake. This was not a particularly good swim for me, as I veered off course several times and had to spend precious time making my way back to the main group. This was my fault, as I tried to have a faster swim time by keeping my head down without checking to see that I was on a straight path to the next buoy. Well, that idea and experiment backfired!

The first leg of the out-and-back bike course was mostly uphill, making the return downhill leg amazingly fast. The most memorable part of the race was getting a flat on my front tire when I was just a couple of miles from the bike finish line. I elected to limp in on a flat tire in lieu of stopping and taking the time to change the tube. This was a challenge in and of itself, as bikes become very unstable on a flat tire.

The run course was on dirt paths that hugged the shoreline of the lake. During the beginning of the race, I noticed three tall, very lean Black men at the race start who looked like collegiate track stars. I saw them still making their way up the hill on the first leg of the bike course while on my way back down the hill. I knew that I had better have a good cushion of time on them starting the run. I was no slouch, as I could run a seven-minute-per-mile pace. With about three miles left in the run, I could hear fast-moving steps coming up from behind me. It did not take long before all three of them blew by me. They must have had a pace of five minutes per mile or less. I said, "Excellent job," to them as they passed by me. They were making me look like I was walking, and I told them so. They were genuinely nice and complimentary, saying, "You're running well too." Not from my perspective! Of course, they were twenty years my junior.

I did not keep a record of mine or Mike and Marti's race results but it's safe to say I did not place in the top three of my age group due to my poor swim time and having a flat during the bike ride. This event was more about having fun with family and friends while competing and continuing to develop my racing skills than attempting to earn a podium spot.

Post-race activities included attending the awards ceremony followed by breaking camp and a trip into Las Vegas with the Greers for burgers and beer. We then endured the three-hour car ride back to Lubbock. Those post-race car rides were always uncomfortable, as my legs and hips were typically sore and tight after a day of hard racing.

Wool Capital Olympic Triathlon

The Wool Capital Olympic Triathlon is held in San Angelo, Texas, known for its hot, semi-arid climate, and held the distinction of being the state Olympic distance championship race. The swimming portion of the event took place in a narrow, very slow-moving river feeding the lake. The bike path was through the surrounding ranch land full of prairie grass, thorny cactus, and bushy mesquite trees. The run course was on dirt roads and walking paths.

The race site was in a park that allowed camping. The kids wanted to camp, so we took a tent and camping gear with us. The day before the race, we took the kids fishing in the feeder river within walking distance of our camp. It was a nice, relaxing afternoon, and we caught black mouth bass, sunfish, catfish, and a turtle.

One of the kids left their fishing pole unattended, and a fish took the bait, dragging the pole into the water. Debbie jumped up, stepping into the water to catch the pole, not realizing the depth of the water was about at her height. There she was, holding the fishing pole in one hand, with her head just out of the water. She was laughing and asking for help to get out. I told her to reach the pole over so that I could grab it, using it to help pull her to the riverbank, explaining that I could not get in the water to help while wearing the shoes I planned to race in the next day. I will never live that one down. That story has become a legend. We still laugh about it every time we tell it.

Following is a comparison of the 2001 and 2002 Wool Capital Olympic triathlon.

	Swim	T-1	Bike	T-2	Run	Total
2002	0:28:41	0:00:53	1:04:40	0:00:44	0:45:25	2:20:26
2001	0:30:09		1:08:26		0:47:22	2:25:56
Change	-0:01:28		-0:03:46		-0:01:57	-0:05:30

My finishing time was good enough for first place in my age group and fourteenth overall. I was now routinely placing in the top three in my forty to forty-four age group in most regional sprint and Olympic distance triathlons and in running races of all distances. With each new achievement I felt myself edging ever closer to my goal of earning a slot to compete in the full distance IRONMAN® Triathlon World Championship in Kona.

When competing in IRONMAN ® triathlon qualifying events, the top competitors in each age group are typically the best triathletes from their regions. This meant I would be competing with others typically winning their age group at races within their region to earn a slot to the World Championship. The top twenty to thirty athletes in each age group were accustomed to placing in the top three at their regional races. That was a tough group to compete against and made my goal that much more difficult to realize.

I was inching ever closer to realizing my dream of competing in Kona at the IRONMAN ® Triathlon World Championship. My aerobic base was now maturing, which allowed further development of my power and speed. I would need it when rising to the top of the best worldwide athletes in my age group.

IRONMAN ® Wisconsin Triathlon

The "A" priority race for 2002 was IRONMAN ® Wisconsin triathlon on September 15th when the air temperature averaged seventy-four degrees for highs and lows at fifty-four degrees. The weather was perfect for an IRONMAN ® full distance triathlon event, with cool temperatures in the mornings lasting until noon then gradually rising during the remainder of the day. The sky was sunny and bright. Wisconsin has 15,000 lakes and seventeen million acres of forest land covered in maple, beech, birch, and oak trees. The trees begin to change colors in mid-September, and I could see all the vibrant red, yellow, and gold colors beginning to emerge. I love being outdoors and could not wait to ride and run through this area and witness its beauty.

The race starting point was in the capital city of Madison. The swim event was in a manmade reservoir located next to the host hotel near downtown Madison with the state capitol building nearby. The bike course wove its way around the surrounding countryside. The run course was mostly flat and at one point going through the field of the Madison University football stadium.

This was a short trip, with us arriving just two days before the bike check-in and leaving two days after the event. We did have time to tour sites in the capital city. We spent the day before the event relaxing at the pool with our kids and friends from Georgia. Goofing around at the pool, a couple of us made a friendly wager on who could make the most somersaults in the four-foot portion of the pool. I won but darn near drown, as I was dizzy and unable to stand up afterwards.

We spent time exploring the state capitol building and being in the historical rooms where legislators conducted their meetings and hearings. Unbeknown to me, my youngest daughter did get her ears pierced during the time I was out on the racecourse. She proudly showed them off to me after the race. These fun events and activities made for great memories and stories to tell friends and family and are just as important to me as racing. Pursuing my dream would mean so much less without having my family there to support me and enjoy these side adventures along the way.

As always, I did a practice swim to become familiar with the swim start area setup and water temperature. The swim start area at Lake Monona was compact, causing me to be concerned over how 2,500 athletes were going to fit in such a confined area. The water was a comfortable seventy degrees and wetsuits would be allowed. The area was not conducive to having short rides and runs, and I elected to rest and relax instead, staying off my feet as much as possible. The prerace evening was spent making race preparations and checking in my bike and transition bags.

As was normally the case, the night before the race, my sleep was restless, with multiple alarms going off at around 4:00 a.m., at which time I ate the planned meal of oatmeal, bagel with cream cheese, coffee, and orange juice. After eating, I attempted to sleep for another thirty minutes before heading to the bike racks.

Once there, I checked tire pressures, gear, and brake settings, loading the Bento Bag with nutritional needs and placing water and energy drink bottles on my bike. With 2,500 bikes in a small, confined space, I wanted to make sure I knew how to find my bike easily. Knowing exactly where it was enabled me to run to it without wasting time searching for it. Some folks tied a balloon to their bike, making it easy to find. The most memorable thing about the bike transition area was that it was located on the top uncovered parking garage of the host hotel. When exiting the swim and running to the bikes, we had to run up three levels of a helix to reach them.

Satisfied that everything with the bike was in order, I made my way down the helix to the swim start area. Once there, I put on my wetsuit, swim cap, and goggles, crossed the timing mat to register my timing chip, and went on to the swim start entrance area. I then waited with 2,500 other anxious athletes for the announcer's call for everyone to enter the water prior to the start of the race.

The swim start area was small and thus had all 2,500 of us remarkably close to one another. Seeing how crowded the swim start was, I positioned myself closer to the front to start fast and to quickly create separation of myself from other competitors.

It was the strangest sensation when the start cannon fired, as all 2,500 competitors began swimming at the same time. All IRONMAN ® full distance triathlon event swim starts are congested, but this was on a whole different level, literally being shoulder to shoulder and fingertips to toes with the surrounding competitors. There was no way to pass anyone. There simply was not sufficient space. During the first 400 yards, I had the sensation of being pulled forward by the vacuum left by swimmers in front. The effort required to stay with the pack was very minimal. It was much like drafting behind a pack of cyclists.

The tight conditions were not a huge issue for me, as all major triathlon events had some degree of congestion during the first 500 yards. What was a concern was the risk of being kicked in the face or locking arms with other swimmers. I kept my leading arm in front of my head long enough to block the feet of the swimmer in front of me. Doing so proved beneficial, as there were multiple occasions it protected me from being kicked. Many years later and during my final IRONMAN ® full distance triathlon race, I did take an elbow to the bridge of my nose, hearing a loud crack with a subsequent bloody nose. That hurt and the next morning I woke up with a swollen nose and black eye. There have been multiple times at past races that Debbie and the girls had mentioned athletes being pulled from the water with busted lips and missing teeth from mishaps during the swim.

We did eventually begin to spread out for the two-lap swim course, although there were swimmers near me for the entire event. I was able to find others swimming slightly stronger than I, and I positioned myself directly behind them. The lead swimmer created a slight vacuum in the water that helped pull the tailing swimmer along behind them. No, that is not cheating; it's just a good race strategy. I finished the swim with a time of 1:12:59, just an eight-second improvement over the prior year's IRONMAN ® full distance triathlon event, and I attributed this lack of improvement to the crowded conditions. Throughout the swim, I was never able to get into my own rhythm.

During the swim in any long-course race, my primary focus was maintaining proper swim stroke form and staying directly in line with the next course buoy. This was going to be a long day of racing, so keeping a strong, steady pace without going anaerobic was also foremost in my thoughts. I was able to judge my effort by how often I needed to take a breath. If I was able to take a breath every other arm stroke, I knew my level of effort was right. If I needed to take a breath on every arm stroke, it was time to slow down. I was constantly jockeying for position among the swimmers, always trying to find a slightly faster swimmer and stay just inches from their feet and benefit from the pull they created. The 2.4 miles of the event is a long way to swim, and I was always amazed at how quickly the time went by.

Exiting the swim, I ran to the wetsuit strippers. These are volunteers who unzip the back zipper of the suit and pull it down to your waist. It was easy to then pull it down to my ankles and step out of it.

With my wetsuit in hand, I ran to the swim-to-bike transition bags, retrieving my cycling gear, then on to the changing tent. I always wore my cycling shorts and jersey underneath the wetsuit during the swim. Doing so allowed a very quick swim-to-bike transition. All I needed to do was to store the wetsuit in the transition bag, then run to my bike, where my helmet and sunshades were positioned on the bike, ready to be picked up and put on.

Next, I had to run up three levels of the parking helix to get to the bikes, which was very strange. I positioned my cycling shoes beside my bike, so it was easy to step into them then run with the bike to the bike mount area. Mounting the bike and crossing the bike start timing mat, I began the event. We started the ride by descending the helix, literally going in circles until reaching the bottom and going past the cheering spectators and out onto the double loop bike course.

The bike course headed south then west before arriving at the hilly two-loop portion of the course and weaving its way through the farmlands of Wisconsin.

Each IRONMAN ® full distance triathlon qualifying race is held in locations that are vastly different than other races and each has their own unique challenges. For example, the IRONMAN ® USA Lake Placid triathlon in Lake Placid, New York, is held in a mountainous terrain with steep climbs and cooler temperatures. The IRONMAN ® Wisconsin triathlon features flatter terrain, but the air temperature is hotter.

Altitude was another huge factor for me. I always performed better in low altitude. Madison sits at 873 feet above sea level, so that worked in my favor. Humidity can also be quite different from one location to the next. The average relative humidity in Madison in mid-September is eighty-one percent. That would be okay for me as long as it did not get too hot.

The variances between locations may or may not play to the athlete's strengths and weaknesses. This race had already presented one of its challenges with the congested swim event. The bike course was windier than I was expecting, and windy conditions never bode well for a fast bike split. Being from hot and windy West Texas, these were conditions that I was accustomed to riding in, but it still made the ride more difficult.

At every race I intentionally tried to pay attention to the countryside that we passed through during the bike and run events. I had never been to Wisconsin before and wanted to soak in as much of this pristine environment and its unique beauty.

In the small town of Verona, we were met by cheering spectators as we started the second loop and now headed back to the Monona Terrace host hotel. The bike course finished with an ascent up the helix. Finishing a 112-mile bike ride with a climb was tough, but we all had to do it. My bike course finishing time was 5:39:54, an improvement of one minute and thirty-nine seconds over the 2001 IRONMAN ® USA Lake Placid triathlon event. Ugh, I would need more than that to reach my dream of being invited to race in Kona.

Racking my bike, I ran to the bike-to-run transition bags and changing tent. I do not remember why, but I took twice the normal amount of time in the tent preparing for the run. Drawing ever nearer to achieving my Kona™ dream, this would need to change, as I gave up close to four minutes over the 2001 IRONMAN ® USA Lake Placid triathlon bike-to-run transition split.

> *"Success does not consist of never making mistakes but in never making the same one a second time."* –George Bernard Shaw

Exiting the transition tent, I crossed the run start timing mat. I then once again ran down the helix to start the run course. As always, it was so nice and refreshing to see my family smiling and cheering me on. Just the sight of them lifted my spirits.

The two-loop run course was spectator-friendly, taking us through the streets of downtown Madison. It was fun to run through the University of Wisconsin's football stadium, home of the Badgers. It gave me a small sense of what it must be like for the football team athletes, surrounded by a stadium full of people cheering for them. From there, we headed towards the UW Lakeshore Nature Reserve, where the path ran next to the University Bay area. The run course concluded back towards downtown, where the streets were lined with cheering crowds, and then around the capitol building and on to the finish line. I finished the run course with a time of 4:08:58, improving the 2001 Ironman USA run time by thirteen minutes and thirty-four seconds. Now that was more like it!

The following chart is a comparison of the split times of the 2002 IRONMAN® Wisconsin triathlon to those of the 2001 IRONMAN® USA Lake Placid triathlon.

	Swim	T-1	Bike	T-2	Run	Total
2002	1:12:59	0:01:56	5:39:54	0:07:27	4:03:58	11:12:43
2001	1:13:07	0:01:56	5:41:33	0:03:38	4:17:32	11:22:30
Change	-0:00:08	0:00:00	-0:01:39	0:03:49	-0:13:34	-0:09:47

Any amount of progress was better than none or, worse yet, losing time over that of prior races. Instead of being disappointed with the slight improvement of nine minutes, I preferred to consider it as being nine minutes closer to attaining my goal. I still needed to improve my finishing time by another forty minutes before that could be possible. Coach Tim and I would need to use these results to refine my training plans to gain the needed additional speed.

Finishing IRONMAN® Wisconsin triathlon. It was a special moment to see my daughter Lia holding the banner for me as I crossed the finish line. I loved that the race invited family members to hold the banner for their beloved racers.

The Great Floridian Triathlon

Coach Tim decided it was time to include two full distance triathlon events in my annual training plan, and thus we used the Great Floridian Triathlon as the next long-course race and as a "B" priority event. The location was about sixty miles due west of Orlando in Clermont, Florida, and was held on November 1, 2002.

This race was not among the IRONMAN® Triathlon World Championship qualifying races, so there was no chance of winning a slot at the race. I selected this one just to see if my training during the year would yield improvements in my full distance triathlon race times. The results would then be used to identify areas that required additional improvements (i.e., my limiters). Athletes created the Great Floridian Triathlon for competitors of all abilities, and it has always been known as the people's race. Though not an IRONMAN® Triathlon World Championship qualifying event, it still typically draws up to 800 athletes from all fifty states and from thirty or more foreign countries.

The swim consisted of a two-loop, triangular-shaped course in Lake Minneola, starting at Waterfront Park. The bike course meandered its way through the back roads north of Clermont then through the rolling hills typical of the Florida peninsula, with elevation changes of slightly less than 300 feet. The run was a four-loop course that hugged the Lake Minneola shoreline, had little more than one hundred feet in elevation changes, and ended in Minneola, Florida.

I was looking forward to the race, having performed well in Florida earlier in the year at the IRONMAN® 70.3® Gulf Coast triathlon. As previously discussed, each race location presented their own challenges and opportunities. I have always had my best performances at locations that featured low altitude, cool temperatures, and flat terrains. This race had all of those attributes, and I was excited to see how I might perform here.

We did not consider this a vacation/race trip. Rather, let us get there, race, and get back home as soon as possible with just me and Debbie going. I do not think the kids were very happy about being left behind and I hated leaving them at home. My mom (Granny) thankfully volunteered to stay with them at our house so as to not unduly disrupt their routine. During her stay, Mom rearranged our refrigerator contents and that really annoyed my youngest daughter Amanda.

I traveled a lot, so they were used to me not being home, but Debbie was always there with them while I was gone. Not so for this trip. Not having them with us felt like something important was missing.

We booked a plane trip to Orlando, Florida, arriving two days before the race, giving me little time to acclimate to the local environment, temperature, and humidity. In the fall, the average high temperature in Clermont was seventy-nine degrees Fahrenheit, with an average humidity ranging from around 70%. Sounds like my kind of weather to race in.

Going through all my normal prerace routines, checklists, and preparations, I was ready to go the morning of the event. The weather was perfect, a cool morning and the high temperature forecasted to be in the upper seventies, with little to no wind and bright, sunny skies.

While the competitors prepared to enter the water, the race announcer mentioned that there were alligators in the lake but not to worry, as they seldom bothered humans. Umm, that was a new wrinkle in the things to think about! No worries, I did not need to be the fastest swimmer, just faster than those the alligators were after.

The lake was very shallow for the first hundred yards, and I found it faster to walk through the water than swim. My swim time was significantly faster than normal, and I'm sure this was a contributing factor.

Finishing the swim, I exited the water, found my swim-to-bike transition bag, and headed to the transition tent to ready myself for the bike competition. I took a couple minutes too long to prepare for the long day on the bike. When competing for the top positions, races can be won or lost in the transitions. Most high-profile races provide the competitor's transition times and how you place among other competitors.

Once out on the bike course, my plan was to conserve as much energy as possible while on the bike in hopes of having a good run time, yet still competing well on the bike. The biggest mistake most competitors make is putting too much effort on the bike course. It's an easy trap to fall into, as you have all this energy and strength during the first half of the bike race and hate watching other riders pass you by.

My solution was to set a heart rate range I wanted to maintain while on the bike. My plan was to stay within that range and not worry about the bike speed. I knew that following this plan would allow me to conserve strength and energy while on the bike course and to have the best run split as possible. I had provided Debbie with the times that I expected to finish each individual segment of the race. I was ahead of my predicted time for completing the bike course and whistled at her to get her attention as I flew by. She was not expecting or prepared for me to be there so soon and was upset that she missed taking my photo.

The most vivid memory I have while on the bike course was of the later portions of the race. There was a point at which there were no other competitors in sight. Normally there are always other riders around and in sight at any point in the race. I was shocked at how lonely I felt out there all by myself. It didn't even feel like I was in a race. Panicking for a bit, thinking I had somehow gotten off course and had no idea of exactly where I was, I opted to just maintain my pace, hoping to see an aid station, mile marker, or other indication I was still on the bike course. It was a huge relief when I came upon an aid station.

The four-loop run course was great for spectators, family, and friends, as they were able to see the competitors four separate times during the run. The only issue was that I could see miles ahead as we rounded the circular lake. It seemed like, and it was, an exceedingly long way around. I prefer seeing at most just a mile or two in front of me so I can concentrate on making it to the mile markers one at a time.

While crossing the checkpoint for the last loop of the course, with six miles left in the race, an aid station volunteer was encouraging me, saying, "You're in the top fifty." What? I had no idea I was doing that well. That bit of exciting news renewed my energy and will to push on.

My finishing time was 10:53:14. I placed third out of eighty-eight in my age group and thirty-eighth out of 529 overall. I found Debbie and relayed all that I had experienced during the race and that I had finally broken the eleven-hour barrier. While telling her all this, I was overcome with emotion to the point of tearing up. Thinking about it as I write has the same effect on me.

After racing hard all day I had to disassemble my bike and pack it and all my racing gear for the trip home early the next morning. That, my friends, that was pure torture. I did not know the race results until we arrived home and Coach Tim called to congratulate me. I was very disappointed that we did not stay for the awards banquet, as I would have been on the podium.

Third place award

Below are the results of the race compared to that of the IRONMAN® Wisconsin triathlon event held just two months prior.

	Swim	T-1	Bike	T-2	Run	Total
FL	0:54:34	0:04:01	5:43:33	0:04:18	4:06:48	10:53:14
Wis	1:12:59	0:01:56	5:39:54	0:07:27	4:03:58	11:12:43
Change	-0:18:25	0:02:05	0:03:39	-:0:03:09	0:02:50	-:0:19:29

The most exciting thing was that I was now on the cusp of joining that small group of elite long-course best-of-the-best triathletes, needing to cut only ten to fifteen minutes off my time to have a chance of earning a qualifying slot to the IRONMAN® Triathlon World Championship.

Unexpected Pleasures

After the 2002 triathlon racing season was over, I was going through our mail and found an envelope from the USA Triathlon organization and opened it. To my great surprise there was an award certificate. The organization had bestowed me with an Honorable Mention, All-American status for my achievements during the 2002 racing season. I was beaming with joy at having received the recognition certificate.

Recognition award

Chapter 30

Daring the Ultimate Dream: Planning for Year 2003

The five Ps of performance: Proper Preparation Prevents Poor Performance.

> "Give me six hours to chop down a tree and I will spend the first four sharpening the axe." –Abraham Lincoln

Now starting the fourth year of the quest for my dream, you might say, "Give up. If it hasn't happened by now, chances are good that it never will." Believe me, I heard that said on multiple occasions. It's a good thing I have never let the opinions of others alter my thoughts on what I could achieve.

> "There are two types of people who will tell you that you cannot make a difference in this world: those who are afraid to try and those who are afraid you will succeed."
> –Ray Goforth

I had now been pursuing my dream for the last three years To be honest, I had begun to question if I had reached my physical peak and if I was as good as I was going to be. I spoke with my triathlete friends and others about my desire to earn a qualifying slot to the World Championship. One of them said that maybe it was time to stop talking about it and just enjoy the sport. I interpreted that to mean, "You have taken this as far as you likely can and need to accept that you will never earn a slot." On some level I thought they may be right.

I had invested so much of my time, energy, and soul into exploring my capabilities in the sport and I was still improving. My quest had taken on a life of its own. It was now a part of who I was. When traveling to various work locations, my team would question me about the sport and my racing experience. I never brought it up, but if they asked, I would be happy to tell them about it. They also witnessed me rising early to run, go to the gym, or swim and do so again after work. I later learned that some complained about it to others in our firm. I never understood that, as I never imposed what I was doing on any of them and in fact several of them would periodically join me in my before- or after-work running workouts. I did my best to ignore the negative chatter.

Managing a portion of our firm's client base and staff could be very stressful, making sure jobs stayed on schedule and were completed in a timely manner. My workouts before and after work became a way to relieve stress. However, I would say that keeping up with my scheduled workouts was another source of stress. Skipping workouts meant losing fitness and thus slower race times.

I just loved competing in the races and the friendships made and had no desire to stop. My family had accepted that this was what I did and who I was. To them I was husband and Dad, the CPA and triathlete. They never complained so I saw no reason to stop racing and abandon my dream. If I thought for one second that what I was doing was in some way harming my professional career or relationship with my family, I would have quit racing in a heartbeat.

Although slowly, I was making progress, and that was enough to keep my sights set on the goal. I was constantly reading and re-reading the books previously mentioned. I knew it took time to develop the broad aerobic base required to compete at the highest levels of full distance triathlons. This was comforting knowledge and allowed me to just stay with the process and let it come in time. The key to success was to keep refining the plan to address failures and limiters. With my family's blessing, I continued on my path and fine-tuned the process for another year.

My 2002 race results and All-American status award by the USA Triathlon organization had instilled in me a new confidence. I was eager to build on that success during the next racing season. I decided that the year would be dedicated to training, with fewer key races. Following are the key events I would be competing in:

Level	Date	Event	Location
A	6/29/2003	IRONMAN® Coeur d'Alene Triathlon Swim 2.4 miles, bike 112 miles, run 26.2 miles	Coeur d'Alene, ID
B	10/18/2003	Rim-to-Rim 50K trail run	Palo Duro Canyon, TX

As in prior years, my training plan included other running club races and regional sprint and Olympic distance triathlons. These were merely considered hard effort running and brick workouts. In the majority of these events, I won or placed in the top three in my age group.

This limited race schedule allowed me to focus the winter, spring, and early summer months on training for those events. The areas limiting the achievement of my dream were cycling and running. Both were improving, but I would need to take them to a higher level.

> *"By failing to prepare, you are preparing to fail."* – Benjamin Franklin

> *"If you keep on doing what you have always done, you will keep on getting what you have always gotten."* –the definition of insanity

Refining the Plan: Building Strength

Strength training in the preparation period continued as in prior years and focused on the muscle groups used in swimming, cycling, and running. We added rope jumping, lunges, and dead lifts to the routine. These resistance exercises would further develop and strengthen muscles used for cycling and running.

No amount of training for force, speed, muscular endurance, power, and anaerobic endurance would be effective without a solid and wide aerobic foundation. Therefore, the first three base periods focused on making sure that foundation was solid as a rock. Workouts were focused on endurance, form, force, and muscular endurance.

Refining the Plan: The Swim

I was not the best swimmer but certainly not the worst, and I was never more than five to ten minutes behind the lead age group swimmers. I was at a point where every minute gained counted. The build period workouts would need to focus on muscular endurance. This is the ability to maintain high force loads for a prolonged period. Translating this into a swim workout meant swimming long intervals at the best pace that I could maintain throughout the interval. Following is what such a workout might look like:

E16 - Endurance 16		
Warm Up: 300 - 500 yards (mixed strokes) - **Swim Easy**		
Focus on form, rest at walls as needed to ensure proper form is maintained.		
Main Set: **Focus:**		
Focus on one element of form for each set.		
Try to maintain a constant SPL		
1 X 1500	T-pace/100 + :15	RI = 1 min
1 X 2000	T-pace/100 + :15	RI = 1 min
Cooldown = 200 easy Mix strokes of Breast, Back, and Free Total 4,200		

Hopefully, these workouts will help shave precious minutes off my swim time.

Refining the Plan: The Bike

Do you recall my telling you about the individual who designed and built my bike? That he told me that I simply did not have the body type that God bestowed on most top cyclists, thus cycling would not likely be my best event? Discouraging news for sure, yet another reason to never let anyone tell you what you are capable of. Point in case was my placing eighth in my age group in the bike portion of the 2002 IRONMAN® 70.3® Gulf Coast triathlon event. Good as that was, improvement was still needed if I was going to achieve my goal.

My cycling form was good but needed further refinement. I needed something to help me make the leap to the next level. To this end I acquired a Racermate Computrainer. This equipment is a device the bike is mounted on with the back tire firmly pressed against a roller for resistance. It has a control unit mounted on the bike handlebars and linked to a computer. Using the control unit, the rider can control the resistance, use programmed courses, etc. It even has various IRONMAN® triathlon race bike course programs to select from to give the rider the experience of riding on a course that they plan to race on.

The important thing about this equipment is that you can see, in real-time feedback, how efficient your pedal stroke is. The computer screen reflects a uniform circle if good form is used, with the circle contorting when poor form is used. This was a perfect way to tell if I was in fact using good form. If not, I could instantly see it on the computer monitor and make small adjustments to my pedal stroke form until the circle became uniform. This was not as easy as it sounds. It took time and constant effort for these slight changes in my form to become engrained in my muscle memory.

As with swimming, developing muscular endurance would be the focus of my bike training during the base and build periods. I needed to conduct power and anaerobic endurance workouts to improve my abilities to apply maximum force quickly and to resist fatigue at high efforts. Muscular endurance workouts consisted of long bike rides at a pace that put my heart rate at around 136 BPM with the RPE being somewhat hard.

Refining the Plan: The Run

Running continued to be a limiter in achieving my dream. Although I was realizing improvements in run-only events, the marathon portion of IRONMAN® full distance triathlon events needed to be improved upon. My overall aerobic base was solid, so more attention needed to be placed on taking my ability to maintain high force loads for a prolonged time to a higher level. I could accomplish this by using muscular endurance workouts.

Since the marathon is the last event of a full distance triathlon race, after a 2.4-mile swim and a 112-mile bike, energy reserves are low, and fatigue is setting in even before the run event starts. Part of the issue with my run times not improving as much as expected could very well be my overall race strategy, race day nutrition, and hydration management. It could be that I was pushing too hard on the swim and bike, not leaving enough energy reserves for the run. My race day nutrition and hydration plan would also need to be examined and refined. These refinements would need to be evaluated for their effectiveness on long bike training rides and brick workouts.

Refining the Plan: Combination Workouts

Triathletes tend to race the way they train. Given this thought, the race is comprised of three events, so you should include training that involves all three events done in succession. These workouts include a swim, followed by a bike ride, then a run. Including more brick workouts was needed if I expected to race well. Now that my aerobic base was fully developed, I could better manage the load by adding more of these workouts in the training plan. Including more brick workouts can take the form of combining two or more events into a single workout. The issue was having access to a swimming venue that was conducive to running and cycling after swimming. I could accommodate both from the Texas Tech University's aquatic center. A friend and fellow triathlete who lived at Buffalo Springs Lake also provided the opportunity to include open water swims in the brick workouts.

The 2003 training plan would include more of these combination/brick workouts than in years past. During the base period, these workouts would be conducted in heart rate zones one and two and could be from two to six hours in length. During the build periods, the intensity of the workouts increased and included rides conducted on rolling hills.

To further develop muscular endurance, workouts would need to be sixty to ninety minutes in duration and conducted at the planned race pace. This pace is merely the result of exercising at the maximum average heart rate you plan to use at an "A" priority IRONMAN® full distance triathlon event. I planned to race with my average heart rate no higher than 145 BPM. Therefore, that was the rate I used during the training. My bike pace/speed would be the result of training in these heart rate zones. Improved muscular endurance translates into faster bike speeds. The sprint and Olympic distance triathlon events I competed in were considered combination/brick workouts conducted under race conditions and at high intensities.

Chapter 31

Year 2003: Training Memories

As you might expect, my training for four years and for up to twenty hours a week resulted in very memorable moments. Training and racing in local and regional racing events were fun. I especially looked forward to the long rides and runs, which I often included in conjunction with short-distance races.

Many of my long training rides were done with triathlete friends. We would start at first light and would typically complete the planned ride by noon. It was more difficult to conduct long runs with friends, as not everyone wanted to run eighteen to twenty miles in a single training workout. My mate and Sherpa, Debbie, would accompany me on the long run workouts. She would drive our vehicle and park one mile ahead of me. When arriving at the vehicle, I would yell out what I needed, and she would hand me a water bottle or an energy gel packet as I ran by. This was great practice for race day conditions, and I cannot thank her enough for her willingness to be a part of pursuing my dream. We were, and still are, a triathlon team. Following are funny and crazy things that happened on these rides and runs.

The Parade

My friend, Shanna Armstrong, her father, Debbie, and I all traveled to Las Vegas, New Mexico, for Shanna and me to compete in an Olympic distance triathlon.

We arrived a couple of days early to conduct a long ride in the mountains surrounding Las Vegas. We stayed at the country home of a friend of Shanna's family. Our plan was to conduct a training ride for up to seventy miles and compete in the race the next day.

The day of the training ride was a crisp, picture-perfect morning with sunny, clear blue skies. What more could you ask for? We would be spending the day riding in fresh mountain-pine-scented air and beautiful blue-green-forested roads and valleys. We began riding together, but as time went by, I, being the stronger rider, pulled ahead of her during the steeper climbs. Once at the top, I circled back to pick her up, and we would then continue on our way.

There were small mountain communities on our route. By small I mean 400 or fewer in population, with rustic-looking, weather-worn houses and cabins on overgrown lots. When arriving at one of these towns, we encountered a parade on the only road going through town. Traffic was blocked and we decided to ride alongside the parade, otherwise we would have to wait for it to pass before continuing.

Here we were riding exotic-looking race bikes, dressed in bright neon-colored neoprene cycling clothes, wearing helmets and sunglasses. We looked like part of the parade. They looked bewildered, likely not recognizing us as part of their small community. Where had we come from? They were not sure if we were intruders or part of the parade. I still laugh about the expression on everyone's faces. Once past the parade, we continued with our ride, happy to have made it through without any incidents.

Bees

As previously mentioned, my mate and Sherpa, Debbie, would accompany me on my runs of eighteen or more miles. My plan was to have her hand me water, sports drinks, and energy gel packets at the end of every mile. In short, she was my aid station volunteer. I typically conducted these long runs along the roadways surrounding the Canyon Lakes Park in my hometown. It was perfectly suited for these runs, as there was little traffic on the roads. The terrain included rolling hills along the lakeside, with sparsely spaced elm and mesquite trees lining the roadway.

The only issue with running at this location was that there were very few restrooms at the park. At one point in the run, I was about at my limit and urgently needed to relieve myself. I was in an area where the elm and mesquite trees were sparsely scattered and exceedingly small. I finally located a suitable tree about thirty yards off the roadway and quickly ran to it.

I had just begun relieving myself when a cloud of buzzing, angry bees came out of the tree just above my head.

This was no time for modesty, and without a moment's hesitation, I ran away without taking the time to pull up my running shorts. Debbie was parked on the street and witnessed it all, wondering what I was doing. Luckily, the bees did not pursue me, with my pride suffering the only damage from the event. That and now-damp running shorts.

Wasp

I typically conducted my long bike training workouts on weekends and was often joined by two of my good friends and fellow triathletes. We would leave one of our homes and head east out of Lubbock, dropping off the Caprock into the ranch lands below. The ranches were filled with dry buffalo grass, thorny mesquite trees, cactus, and wildflowers. We had the best time riding together and talking about everything under the sun.

On one ride we were going through a valley on a rural county road with barbed wire fences lining rugged ranch land on either side. I was about a hundred yards ahead of my friends and hunched over in the aero position when I noticed a small dot hovering over the road at about the height of my head. Cycling jerseys fit skintight, but when in the aero position, there is a small open gap just above your sternum that is no larger than a quarter. In mere seconds that tiny dot materialized into a flying wasp, and it went straight into that tiny gap in my jersey. The wasp immediately started stinging me.

Both the wasp and I were shocked, and it repeatedly stung me. I hit the brakes hard, quickly coming to a stop, but did not have time to unclip my shoes from the pedals and fell over with my feet still clipped in, all the while grabbing at my chest to crush the wasp and prevent it from continuing to sting me.

My friends quickly arrived at my side, excitedly asking if I was having a heart attack. Nope, just getting stung by a wasp that was still in my jersey. I quickly pulled off my jersey, freeing the insect. I had four or five stings that were already beginning to turn red and form welts. I suffer from a host of allergies and my biggest concern was having a severe allergic reaction to the stings. Thankfully, that did not occur, and we went on with our ride.

Racing Mishaps

While participating in a regional Olympic distance triathlon I was making the transition from the bike to the running event hastily putting on my running shoes and ran out of the bike rack area to start the running event. I had only run a short distance when I heard Debbie yelling out my name trying to get my attention. I stopped briefly to see what she wanted. She said you still have your cycling helmet on! Oops! That was embarrassing. I ran back to my bike to exchange my helmet for my running cap and headed back out onto the course with a sheepish grin on my face.

Creative Workouts

On occasions my training plans called for a long brick/combination workout. To break up my usual routine, I enjoyed competing in area running club races and sprint distance triathlons. These events combined a competition followed by a long ride before and after the event. On one such occasion, there was a sprint triathlon event held in a town located twenty miles west of Lubbock. This was a fun race, with many of my friends competing as well.

Debbie and I drove to the event, and she dropped me off with about ten miles before arriving at the location so I could ride the remaining distance to the race site as a warm-up. It was my intention to participate in the race and then ride my bike the thirty miles back home. After the race was over, we ate grilled burgers served at the race during the awards banquet where I was awarded first place in my age group. I relayed my intentions to ride home to friends, three of whom decided to join me.

One of them was just getting started in the sport. The other two were accomplished, seasoned triathletes. One of them lived in a small lakeside community about fifteen miles east of Lubbock. The other three of us decided to ride with him to his home and then ride the twenty miles back to Lubbock.

I enjoyed racing and riding back home with these friends. I would equate it with going to happy hour after work with friends, only instead of having drinks we competed in a sprint triathlon race then rode ninety miles afterward. The ride back to Lubbock was on farm-to-market roads through endless miles of nothing but flat cotton fields. Most of our conversation was about our training, what our family activities were, what our upcoming races were, and all sorts of miscellaneous topics. There was not much vehicle traffic on the road other than local farmers in their pickup trucks.

Leaving the race site and nearing Lubbock, the novice rider decided he had had enough, opting not to ride the additional forty miles. Upon arriving in Lubbock, we rode on one of the major intercity roadways to escort the novice rider to his home. That wasn't a very safe thing to do, and motorists did not like having us in their way. That made me nervous, and I never did it again. From there we left Lubbock and the remaining three of us rode on to Slaton, Texas, twenty miles east of Lubbock and about seven miles north of my friend's house. To get to his house, we would have to twice descend and climb the Caprock. Those climbs are tough enough but seemed exceedingly hard after racing then riding the fifty miles to this point. On the return to Lubbock, I and the last remaining rider would have to make the climb back up the Caprock. The other rider decided that he did not want to do that and left the remaining two of us to continue our ride.

Once at my friend's home, I refreshed my liquids and began the solo twenty-plus-mile journey back to my home. Now alone for the remaining twenty-mile ride home I had over an hour to just settle in and press on to complete the ride. I truly enjoyed time alone on the bike. It was a chance to just be by myself and let my mind rest with no interruption of any kind. At this point, I was tired and had to concentrate on holding my pace. It was very similar to the last twenty miles in a 112-mile full distance triathlon ride. My legs were spent, and my lower back was beginning to ache. I periodically stood upright on the pedals to twist my torso, stretch my hamstrings, and lower back muscles. Similar to running, I kept my thoughts on what was going on around me, monitoring my heart rate and anything else that distracted me from the overall distance and time I had left to ride. Sometimes I thought about work-related issues but mostly I tried to keep a razor-sharp focus on what I was doing. Overall, my ride before and after the race was close to one hundred miles.

These were the types of efforts I was hoping would help break up the monotony of my training routine and prepare me for the "A" priority race. It was nearing the time to compete in the "A" and "B" priority races that I had selected. Hopefully, I will have good race results and inch ever closer to earning a highly coveted slot to the IRONMAN® Triathlon World Championship in Kona.

CHAPTER 32

PURSUING MY DREAM : YEAR 2003—RACING

For the 2003 training and racing plan, I selected an IRONMAN® full distance triathlon event as the "A" priority race with an ultra-distance trail run being the "B" priority race. Other events in the plan I considered to be "C" priority races.

IRONMAN® Coeur d'Alene Triathlon

IRONMAN® Coeur d'Alene triathlon was held on June 29, 2003, and was a qualifying event located in northern Idaho. This location was special for us, as Idaho was where my wife, Debbie, being an Air Force brat, spent much of her junior and high school years in the community of Mountain Home. She was especially excited about the trip. Keeping with the plan of including the family time at these events, we took the kids and my mother-in-law.

Coeur d'Alene is a spectacularly beautiful area featuring a clear water lake, mountains, and pine forests surrounding the city. The swim venue was in Lake Coeur d'Alene. The lake is a pristine, cold, and clear water lake. This was the inaugural event for this location; athletes were flocking to it.

Our flight from Lubbock to Spokane, Washington took the entire day, with stops and layovers along the way. Debbie and I decided to arrive a week prior to the race to enjoy the sights and activities the area had to offer. We booked a lakefront house across from the event epicenter, thus avoiding all the hustle and bustle of the race site. Our temporary home was a good fifteen to twenty miles from the venue.

Once in Spokane, we rented a car for the thirty-six-mile trip to Coeur d'Alene. It was getting late in the evening with the sunlight quickly fading in this sleepy mountain town.

It seemed that something unexpected had to occur at every major event we attended. This trip was no exception. As you might imagine, the roadway leading to the lake house was full of twists and turns, making it hard to navigate. It was late in the evening, with fading light making navigation even more difficult. We followed the directions provided, with each bend in the road leading to a more remote, less maintained road. The last turn was onto a dirt path, with only tire ruts with tall grass leading the way. Following the ruts we eventually came to a structure. It looked ridiculously small and not that well-constructed or maintained.

Oh my! What had we gotten ourselves into? Honestly, it looked like a shack, not even big enough to house our group. Disappointed, I went to the door, unlocked it, and cautiously went inside. To our surprise and delight, it turned out to be a beautiful lake house with ample room and full-length glass windows lining the living room facing the lake. It was the perfect place. Excellent job, Debbie! We had come in the back entrance, with the main portion of the house out of our sight.

We spent the week leading up to the race enjoying and exploring the quiet and peaceful wooded area around the house. There was a full-size, authentic-looking teepee located close to the lake front. Inside there was a fire pit and cots to sit on. We found out from neighbors that the teepee was originally used on the set for the movie *Dances with Wolves*. The kids loved horseback riding and we toured other interesting sites the area had to offer.

During the week, I met the neighbors, a genuinely nice couple who had seen me on a practice swim. They came down to the dock to visit me, asking questions about the upcoming race. Before parting, they asked if my family and I would join them the night after the race to hear stories of my experience. We agreed to meet at the teepee for an evening campfire and s'mores.

I needed to keep up with my training rides, and the rough dirt roads would not allow me to start my rides from the house. Instead, I had Debbie and the family take me to a paved road then follow me by car so I would not get lost. Inside the city proper, there were stoplights at every intersection with heavy traffic due to the upcoming triathlon event. I somehow lost sight of Debbie in all the congestion. It was not that big of an area, so I stopped in a small parking area to wait for her. She never showed up. I panicked as time ticked by, not sure how I would get back home. I had no way to locate her and no map to get back to the lake house. I had my flip phone with me and hoped I would be able to reach her. Keep in mind this was before the current modern cell phones. The only thing my flip phone could do was call and text.

Debbie answered the phone, but it was a challenge to relay to her where I was and then for her to find me. Finally, we worked it out and were relieved when I finally spotted the car heading towards me. Admittedly, I was annoyed that she had failed to follow me close enough and tensions were high for a bit once I was back in the car. She did not deserve my angry response. She had been the model of a supportive wife, never complaining about anything and always willing to help plan trips, be my shag wagon on long runs, and be there on the racecourse to provide encouragement and congratulate me at the finish line. Thanks to her, the tensions soon dissipated, and we continued on with our trip like nothing had ever happened. I am still ashamed of how I reacted. Whew, I hoped that would be the last unexpected issue before the race.

I checked out the racecourse and got used to the terrain. The swim course was rectangular in shape. The lake water was extremely clear and a chilly fifty-six degrees. Obviously, I wore my full-body wetsuit for the practice swims, with only my face, hands, and feet exposed to the freezing water, making them bright pink after the swim. As I swam, I could see sunken timber logs strewn across the bottom of the lake. I later learned the timber industry once used Lake Coeur d'Alene to float timber to a sawmill. These are the little nuggets of experience that spurred me on in the sport.

The double-loop bike course ran alongside the lake and through beautiful northern Idaho, with sweeping green mountain views full of tall pine and blue spruce trees. The course included about 4,600 feet of climbing. I am a tall man, so climbs were especially difficult, but man could I fly on the descents. The race concluded with a multi-loop run course through McEuen Park to a vibrant finish through downtown on Sherman Avenue.

Race publications indicated the race conditions would be a cold, flat swim, a mountainous bike course, and a mostly flat run course. Temperatures typically reached a high in the mid-eighties, with light winds. Sounded perfect. But on race day, the daytime temperatures rose quickly during the day, reaching the high nineties, with the wind increasing throughout the day. This had a dramatic negative effect on the athletes, including myself.

Before each race I gave Debbie a list of times of when I expected to complete each event. This came in handy, as they could go eat or hit the area shops while I was out on the course but allowed them to be back in time cheer for me as I completed each leg of the event. The times I had given her for the swim and bike events were spot on, but when I arrived late on the first leg of the run I sat down next to my family, telling them I was hot and tired, asking to drink some of Debbie's iced tea. This was a shock to her, as she'd never seen me stop during a race for any reason. It was clear to her I was not having a good run. When I did not arrive at my expected time for the run finish she was concerned. They were hot during the day and had found a spot in the shade trying to stay cool. Debbie said her thoughts were running wild wondering if I had quit the race or was I hurt.

The heat and wind began its brutal assault during the second loop of the bike course. During the run, I could not cool down, causing heat exhaustion and fatigue to set in earlier than expected. I did my best to keep liquids coming in as much as possible to counter the excessive heat. It was a tough day, with my race results reflecting it. Using binoculars, Debbie finally spotted me approaching the finish line area fifty minutes after my predicted finishing time, and I was moving at a much slower pace than was normal. After I finished and met up with them, she could tell that I was disappointed in my overall time. I was completely exhausted and just wanted to head back to the house and lie down.

The following chart provides a comparison of my split times of the 2003 IRONMAN® Coeur d'Alene triathlon race compared with those of the 2002 IRONMAN® Wisconsin triathlon.

	Swim	T-1	Bike	T-2	Run	Total
2003	1:05:08		5:39:22		4:59:43	11:50:27
2002	1:12:59		5:39:54		4:03:58	11:12:43
Change	-0:07:51		-0:00:32		0:55:45	0:37:44

Losing thirty-seven minutes from the previous qualifying competition was not what I had expected. Now that was disappointing. I was heading in the wrong direction. My swim time had improved, I had about the same bike split, but I lost close to an hour on the run. My split time for the first fifty-six miles of the bike was good, averaging over twenty miles per hour, but the heat and wind speed slowed me down on the second loop. I attributed my slow run time to the brutally hot, windy, and humid weather conditions.

Each race is different, with multiple factors that can contribute to a less-than-desirable outcome. High heat and humidity caused my perspiration to increase at a greater rate than normal, raising the risk of dehydration and depletion of salt and electrolytes in my body. Despite my attempts to ward off these conditions I became dehydrated, which reflected my slow run time.

After finishing the race, I was completely spent and gave my bike claim ticket to my wife and asked her and Ashley to retrieve it and take it to our vehicle while I slowly walked with my two younger daughters to the car. We did not get far until I needed to lie down in a grassy area and rest. I felt better after a few minutes, but I was unable to get up. Each time I moved I had severe muscle cramps. The kids were concerned and tried to help me, but I just could not move without intense muscle cramping pain. I did not know what to do but lie there and let it pass.

Luckily, a doctor working at the medical tent was walking by and noticed my condition. He assessed me and suggested that he try massaging my thighs and calf muscles. He worked on me for several minutes but it did not help relieve the cramping when I tried to move. I had experienced cramping muscles before but not to this extent and in every muscle. I was not in any pain until I tried to move and as such was not overly concerned about my general health. I was, however, concerned about how I was going to get to Debbie and our vehicle.

The doctor told me other athletes were suffering from heat exhaustion and that the medical tent was a triage center. There was an emergency vehicle nearby and the first responders lowered a gurney to ground level and rolled me onto it. They then wheeled me to the medical tent, where the staff gave me IV fluids and leg muscle massages until I could move again without cramping.

Meanwhile, my middle daughter Lia ran to our car, telling Debbie what was happening. I am sure that was concerning news. Lia frantically told Debbie that I was in an ambulance and had been taken away, which was confusing, as she had just left me to get my bike and I looked fine. She said her heart stopped and she had to take a deep breath and think! My wife, with Lia in tow, quickly made her way to the med tent, not sure if I was there or on my way to a hospital. She made inquiries about me and my condition. It took a while, but they got back to her, saying I was experiencing severe cramps and they were giving me IV fluids but otherwise I was fine.

This news eased her anxiety a bit, but she still had to wait for them to release me before seeing that I was in fact okay. After spending about an hour in the medical tent and receiving a bag of IV fluids, the cramping dissipated to the point the staff released me from their care, and I gingerly made my way to our vehicle with my arm across Debbie's shoulders to support me. I was no longer in any pain but was extremely exhausted. My poor mother-in-law was stuck at our vehicle waiting and watching the girls during this episode while Debbie came to my side. The girls were relieved and brushed tears from their eyes when we appeared.

My mother-in-law was also happy to see that I was okay but later told Debbie she never understood why I liked this sport but was nonetheless proud of me. Once in the car everyone was hungry, so we stopped for fast food burgers. I was never very hungry after an IRONMAN® full distance triathlon event. My digestive system could only accommodate a small amount of solid food and as such could only eat about half of my food on our return trip. Back at the house I took a hot shower, climbed into bed, and slept soundly.

The next morning my body still felt tired, but I was in no pain. Later that morning we all took off to see more of the sights the area had to offer before packing up and heading home.

Bonking

In later years of racing in long-course triathlon events, I learned a hard lesson about keeping properly hydrated. It was at the 2006 IRONMAN® 70.3® Buffalo Springs Lake triathlon event. I was in peak physical condition and was hoping to place in the top five finishers in my age group and thus make the podium during the awards banquet at my home course event. The weather forecast was for an extremely hot and windy day. This heat was on a whole other level than what was normal. It reached 107 degrees that day. Not the best conditions for a difficult long-course triathlon. I completed the swim in good condition and finished with a respectable finish time. While out on the fifty-six-mile bike course, things began to go south.

The temperature was rising quickly, and as predicted, the wind was strong. If you have never ridden a bicycle against the wind, it becomes exponentially more difficult with the wind. I did my best to stay hydrated by drinking at least one bottle of water, mixed with my nutritional and electrolyte needs, every hour. Pushing hard on the bike, I kept my heart rates near the maximum that I could sustain. In the last ten miles of the ride, I realized I had not taken in enough liquids and was beginning to feel my body forcing me to slow down. I was bonking! Dang! You know what they say about best laid plans. Finishing the bike course, I was already near a full bonk and I still had the entire run to complete.

Racking my bike and donning my running gear, I took off on the run course. The temperature was rising quickly. I knew by the end of the first mile that I was in trouble. I had to start walking to keep my heart rate in check. Each mile was harder and harder. I tried to recover by taking in more water, energy, and electrolyte supplements, but it was not having any effect. I knew from my research that once you have bonked, there is no quick recovery. The body can take hours to recover.

I gutted it out and was thankful to cross the finish line after an agonizing run. Debbie knew that I would never quit a race unless it killed me and that day it darn near did. In retrospect, I should have quit the race at mile three when it was obvious that I had bonked and was unable to run without sending my heart rate into the red zone. The only way to recover was hours of total rest. I was not feeling well at all. I went into the lake to cool my body down. It made me feel a little better, but not much. My wife helped me walk my bike and gear back to our vehicle. At that point I began to empty my stomach. This continued all the way home.

Debbie was volunteering at the race and had to stay, but our good friends, Mark and Gina Carbone, were staying with us. Mark had just finished the race and they were heading home too and took me with them. At home, I showered and got in bed. I was unable to hold anything down and I started shaking like I was freezing but was still overheated.

Later, I was told this is how your body sheds excess heat. I was severely dehydrated, and I needed to get liquids in me but could not keep anything down long enough for it to absorb into my bloodstream. I had been home for two or three hours before Debbie arrived, and I was still having shaking spells and was unable to keep any liquids down. I had been dehydrated before, but never had I had these symptoms, and it was getting worse. I felt terrible, like I had a bad flu. I instinctively knew it was time to go to the ER and get IV fluids. Mark and Gina were concerned as well. Mark was a seasoned, extremely talented triathlete and knew the signs of dehydration. He knew I needed to receive a bag of IV fluids.

Debbie took me to the hospital, where I was admitted to the ER with us both thinking I would get some IV fluids and then be fine. There the medical staff took blood samples and started me on IV fluids. After multiple hours, and about three bags of IV fluids, the shaking stopped, and I began to feel much better and thought I was about to be released and could go home.

This was about the time my general practitioner doctor walked into the room. The doctor was also a friend of mine, and I was surprised to see him. I said, "Hi, doctor, what are you doing here? I'm about to go home."

His first response was, "I heard you did the *dumbassathon* today," and then stated, "You're not going anywhere. Your kidneys are not functioning."

That was the first time I had heard that! The news sucked the breath out of Debbie. I was in shock.

He informed me, "You need to stay here, and the nurses will keep pumping IV fluids into you to flush out your kidneys to get them functioning again." How could this be? I was feeling much better. He was my friend and a very respected doctor, so I had no choice but to trust his judgment.

The news was frightening, and I was not sure how to react to this unexpected turn of events. I am used to being in control of my life and I had no control over this. I had read about the dangers and signs of dehydration, but I did not know this could happen.

He continued, "Once your body has burned through all its energy reserves, it will start burning muscle for fuel. The byproduct of this is a waste molecule that is too large for your kidneys to filter, which can and does clog up your kidneys."

After I was transferred to a room and hooked to another IV, Debbie had to go back home to tend to our kids and take Mark and Gina off to the airport the next morning. I spent the rest of the evening and night lying in a hospital bed watching the IV fluids drip into my arm, wondering what would come next. Would my kidneys begin to work again? If not, what then? How long until I would know one way or the other? That may have been the longest night of my life, waiting and wondering about my future. Was my dream dead because I'd not been careful enough? The nurses came in every hour or so to collect blood and urine samples, so I did not get much sleep. I tried not to overly worry about it, as I had no control over the outcome.

I am tremendously grateful that after about eighteen straight hours my kidneys began to show signs of recovering. My doctor told me had I not come in when I did, it was likely that my kidneys would not have recovered and I would have been on dialysis for the rest of my life. Wow! That was eye-opening. I had no idea that could be the result of a severe bonk. Huge lesson learned.

Rim-to-Rim 50K Trail Run

The Rim-to-Rim 50K Trail Run held on October 18, 2003, was scheduled as an ultra-distance run at an aerobic effort that was perceived as light. It was a long, easy run for the purpose of enhancing my running aerobic base. I decided to compete in the event with one of my old running friends who enjoyed ultra-distance running.

To this point, I had only run the twenty-six miles required in a full distance triathlon event. This trail run was a 50K run. 31.1 miles and unfamiliar territory. I started the race with my friend to help keep my pace noticeably light, which was the plan. The plan was to keep the perceived exertion at a level that was light, but our pace seemed too light. Knowing it was going to be a long run, I decided to just let my friend set the pace. After about five miles, I was not able to take it any longer. I told my friend that I was increasing my pace. He said, "Okay, I'll see you later when you have to start walking." I smiled to myself as I left him behind, knowing there would be no walking for me.

Trail running is very enjoyable, with twists and turns on dirt paths. This event was held in the Palo Duro Canyon State Park located in Northwest Texas. It's the second largest canyon in the country and is 120 miles long, with an average width of six miles, offering spectacular views of rock formations, clear water, spring-fed creeks, and beautiful flora.

As with most ultra-distance training, the perceived exertion tends to increase as the time and miles go by without increasing the pace. By the twenty-mile mark, my light pace was morphing into one that seemed harder. My heart rate was still in the desired zones, so I just kept at the same pace. The trail had lots of short but steep ascents and descents. After hours of running, these tend to wear on your thighs. Mine began to burn after mile twenty-six.

It was about this point where I began to catch and pass other runners who started at a faster pace. Starting with too quick a pace is quite a common mistake among endurance athletes. It's such an easy trap to fall into. Everyone feels strong and fresh in the first few miles but starting too quick usually means you will run out of steam later in the race.

The last quarter mile included a steep decline, with my thighs burning with each step, and I happily crossed the finish line at the bottom of the hill. Afterwards, I met up with Coach Tim and another friend who had placed first overall. Each of us were happy to have completed the event and shared our race day experiences while resting and watching other competitors cross the finish line.

With the 2003 racing season at an end, it was time to start thinking about the 2004 training and racing season. My aerobic base was as strong as it had ever been, and I was racing well. What might 2004 hold in store for me and the pursuit of my dream?

CHAPTER 33

2004, THE FINAL PUSH: PLANNING

My race results in 2003 did little for my confidence. Honestly, I did not dwell too much on the poor IRONMAN® Coeur d'Alene triathlon results. Race day weather conditions were a major factor in my less-than-desirable performance. This journey was full of uncertainties, and bumps in the road were to be expected. It was like traveling to a place you have never been before, with the journey just as fascinating as the destination. All I could do was evaluate my training plan and adjust it accordingly.

> "Success usually comes to those who are too busy to be looking for it."
> –Henry David Thoreau

> "Never give up on a dream just because of the time it will take to accomplish it. The time will pass anyway." –Oprah Winfrey

> "Many of life's failures are people who did not realize how close they were to success when they gave up." –Thomas A. Edison

During the previous four years, I had accumulated a broad base of knowledge and information on training for long-course events. I used all this to develop a computer spreadsheet to plan my annual training goals, map out training periods, identify key races, and define workouts and fitness tests. Coach Tim had been a wonderful asset and mentor in my quest. I would not have come this far without his valuable advice, assistance, and encouragement. It was time to cut the umbilical cord with Coach Tim and become a self-trained triathlete. I have always heard people say not to fix things that are not broken and my coaching relationship with Tim was not broken. So why change now? Having a coach is like having a safety net. I was nervous about removing that sense of security. But I now knew all the training theories and protocols, so designing training programs was not much of a concern. The biggest thing was that with Tim I had someone to rely on and was accountable to. Now it would be all on me. The move was a bit unnerving, but I had the discipline and motivation to make it work. Tim graciously accepted the news and offered to be available should I need him. Tim and I are still the best of friends to this day.

While developing the 2004 training and racing plans, I took a hard look at the race results during the previous four years. I evaluated each major event in the context of location, time of year, local climates, and the overall course difficulty level. I noted my successes and failures. One of the more significant indications of my progress was being awarded All-American status by the USA Triathlon organization in 2003. The cumulative evidence indicated that I was making progress and that all the thoughtful planning and execution of those plans had been effective. I was having the time of my life and competing for the top age group spots at every regional event I attended. Hopefully, I would be able to parlay this success into the national and world arena during the 2004 racing season.

My racing history showed I had always performed well at low altitudes. Noting this, I decided to attempt to earn a slot for the IRONMAN® Triathlon World Championship at the IRONMAN® Florida triathlon event. This was the first qualifying event for the 2005 IRONMAN® Triathlon World Championship, meaning if I earned a slot there, I would have close to an entire year to train for the World Championship race. Following are the key races selected to prepare me for my attempt to earn a qualifying slot at the IRONMAN® Florida triathlon.

Level	Date	Event	Location
C	6/20/2004	IRONMAN® 70.3® Buffalo Springs Lake Triathlon Swim 1.2 miles, bike 56 miles, run 13.1 miles	Lubbock, TX
B	8/29/2004	IRONMAN® Canada Triathlon Swim 2.4 miles, bike 112 miles, run 26.2 miles	Pentiction, BC
A	11/6/2004	IRONMAN® Florida Triathlon Swim 2.4 miles, bike 112 miles, run 26.2 miles	Panama City, FL

As in prior years, I used additional low priority sprint and Olympic distance triathlons to evaluate myself and to improve upon the execution of my race plans for hydration, nutrition, and transitions. I would have to perfectly plan and execute all phases of the IRONMAN® Florida triathlon race if I were to have any chance of qualifying for the IRONMAN® Triathlon World Championship race.

The preparation period plans were the same as in the prior two years, with the base period training focusing on enhancing my muscular endurance abilities in each event. The first "C" priority race on my calendar was the IRONMAN® 70.3® Buffalo Springs Lake triathlon located in my hometown. This was a magnificent event, and it ranks as one of the toughest half distance triathlon events I have ever competed in. It combined a challenging hilly course with harsh winds and hot temperatures. It also drew in top competitors from around the country and world. The ability to place well at this race was a particularly good indicator of how well you might fair in a qualifying distance course. As good of an indicator as it was, it was still only half the distance of a qualifying race. Doubling the distance provided a multitude of opportunities for errors and disrupting even the best formulated race day plans.

I sensed that I was close to realizing my dream. Having a rock-solid race day plan was imperative. My plan included not trying anything new on race day that I had not thoroughly vetted during training sessions. Getting the proper amounts of hydration, calories, and electrolytes, and at the right intervals, was critical to sustaining my performance at an elevated level. In years past I had elected to use products designed to provide all these elements in liquid form. The product was in powder form and was simply mixed in my water bottles that were carried on my bike.

The issue was that the initial three bottles would not be enough for the entire ride. This obstacle was overcome by placing three bottles containing just the powder in my bike special needs bag. The bags were made available to us at the halfway point on the bike course, where I filled the bottles with cool water. All I had to do was drink one-fourth of a bottle every fifteen minutes. Doing so gave me the proper amounts of everything needed. During training rides, drinking this mixture for over five hours straight without including any other food sources was difficult to do. After I tried various solid foods in my training, I landed on fig Newton bars. These gave me a sugar boost and were easily carried in my Bento Bag. Best of all, they put something solid in my stomach and gave me a break from the liquid-only diet.

All this worked great while on the bike, but I needed a different plan for the run event. The run aid stations provided all sorts of liquid and food options. Relying solely on what was available at the aid stations could be very risky because they may be out of what you need, or even worse, what is available is something you have not tried and tested in training. That was a risk I was not willing to take. Most run course aid stations provided water, sports drinks, un-carbonated soda, bananas, and other foods. These aid stations were located at the end of every mile of the running course. The water and sports drinks fit nicely with what I was using during training runs, but not with my calorie and electrolyte needs.

During long training runs, I used energy gel packets. I consumed one every forty-five minutes. It was a bit tricky to keep track of how often I needed to eat. I normally maintained a running pace of 8:45 to 9:00 minutes per mile, so I knew I needed to consume another packet every five to six miles. I could also sense when my energy levels were starting to drop, signaling that it was time for more calories. I consumed electrolyte tablets as needed. This plan required that I carry these products with me during the run. Carrying them was easy enough, as I wore jerseys that had pockets on each side where I stored these supplements. Prior racing experience taught me that at around mile thirteen of the run, my digestive system could no longer take any more gel packets. With up to two hours left in the race, I could not afford to forgo the needed calories.

At this point of the race, I found that drinking un-carbonated cola provided at aid stations gave me the energy boost needed. The issue was that the boost only lasted about ten minutes. I would need to use it at every aid station thereafter.

By mile twenty-two, nothing tasted good, but I would need to keep the liquids and calories coming in or risk bonking late in the race and limiting my overall performance and race experience.

The plan was to practice all this during long training sessions so that I would know what to expect on race day. All that sounded great and was a good plan. However, one single long training day would never be as long as the race itself. As such, anything can happen, and I wanted to be as prepared as possible. Having experienced bonking in a prior race, my plan was to keep these unknowns to a bare minimum.

CHAPTER 34

2004, THE FINAL PUSH: IRONMAN® 70.3® BUFFALO SPRINGS LAKE TRIATHLON

The first major test of my abilities and race day plans came on June 20, 2004, at the IRONMAN® 70.3® Buffalo Springs Lake Triathlon event. The weather conditions were milder than was typical for this event. The high was only eighty-eight degrees, with a morning low of sixty-seven with light winds. This was a welcome relief from the brutal temperatures and high winds I had experienced in prior years.

The morning was cool and stayed that way during the swim and for a good portion of the bike ride. I felt strong on the bike. I passed other riders yet kept my heart rates within the planned ranges. The run course was challenging, but I felt strong throughout. I perfectly executed my race day hydration and nutrition plans. Overall, it was as close to a perfect race day plan execution as I had ever experienced.

I finished the race with a time of five hours and nine minutes. Doubling that time would be ten hours and eighteen minutes. That, my friends, would be good enough to earn an IRONMAN® Triathlon World Championship slot at most qualifying events. I knew there was little chance that I could keep up those paces in a full distance triathlon event, yet my performance was encouraging. I may just be able to qualify this year.

As good as it was, I still missed the awards podium by one spot. Ugh! This race attracted the best athletes, so at least I was right on their heels. It is a completely different thing to place well in a half distance triathlon than repeating that same level of performance when doubling the distance. A full distance triathlon race taxes the mind, body, and soul, each of which had better be prepared and ready on race day.

During the awards banquet, my wife and I sat with a group of our friends. We were all comparing our times and race experiences. A group at our table competed as a team where one did the swim, another did the bike ride, and another the run. Each of them were good athletes. They were surprised that my split times had bettered their team's individual events and combined time. That boosted my confidence and ego a bit.

Below is a comparison of the 2004 race results with that of prior years:

	Swim	T-1	Bike	T-2	Run	Total
2004	0:32:26	0:01:48	2:41:25	0:01:32	1:52:16	5:09:24
2001	0:38:02	0:02:32	2:50:20	0:01:59	1:53:24	5:25:04
2000	0:43:03	0:02:25	2:52:35	0:01:52	2:08:06	5:49:59
1999	0:54:11	0:02:01	2:43:57	0:02:01	2:08:18	5:51:07

CHAPTER 35

2004, THE FINAL PUSH: IRONMAN® CANADA

I selected IRONMAN® Canada full distance triathlon as a "B" priority race, one to use as a final test before attempting to qualify at the IRONMAN® Florida triathlon in November 2004. I planned to use the results at this race to make any last-minute tweaks to my training and racing plans. I'd never been to Canada before and this added a new and exciting element to the race. We did not couple this trip as a family vacation but rather as a quick four-day trip to do the race and return home. We booked it using free flight credits I had earned while flying for my work, which meant that we had numerous stops during our flight from Lubbock to our destination of Spokane, Washington.

Debbie's Memories of Traveling to Canada

After four years of training and racing, Wade decided he wanted to do IRONMAN® Canada triathlon. I loved traveling to all these beautiful places. Had he not been a triathlete, we might not have ever visited them.

We showed up at the Lubbock airport and the ticket agent said our plane had already left. We laughed, and she said, "No, really, you have missed your plane." I had looked at the departure time on the next connecting flight. Talk about stressful! The agent was able to get us rebooked and on our way all on the same day.

After flying most of the day and making multiple connecting flights, our flight ended in Spokane, Washington. We drove from there to Penticton, Canada, arriving at 2:00 a.m. Getting pulled over by a Canadian police officer at 1:00 a.m. did not help Wade's "prerace" stress at all.

New Challenges

The next adventure was finding our hotel. The hotel was a single-story, painted-cinderblock structure with twenty units. Our room had a kitchen, living room, and bedroom area, with the bathroom as the only enclosed space. We quickly unpacked the car and exhaustedly turned in for the night.

I rose the next day to start on assembling my bike and then checking it in to the event organizers. By now I was well acquainted with disassembling and reassembling my bike. I was careful to check that each reassembled component was functioning properly. While attaching the handle bars to the bike frame, the rear cog shifter broke, making shifting gears impossible. This trip was throwing challenges at us! No amount of planning could have foreseen either of these stressful events.

The bike mechanics at the event could not help me, as they did not have the equipment needed to make the repairs. Penticton is a small community of around 30,000. My chances of finding a bike shop with specialized components for a racing bike were slim to none. My good friend, fellow triathlete, and sometimes training partner Shanna Armstrong entered the race as well. She had competed here before and had met some of the locals. She knew the owner of a local bike shop. She contacted him, and we took the broken component to him.

He seemed skeptical that the shop had the necessary part and left us at the front counter while he searched through the shop's parts inventory. I was panicking at this point and saw no workable solution in sight. Had we flown and traveled all this way just to be forced to withdraw from the race due to equipment failures? There was no back-up plan. In my mind, I was going to ask the shop owner if I could rent a race bike or go back to the bike check-in area to ask if the race bike mechanics could loan me a bike. Neither solution sounded very appealing, as I doubted any bike I could use would fit my height and body dimensions. Smiling as he returned with a box in hand, he said, "You are in luck. We had one box of the component." Whew! What a huge relief! Crisis avoided. The good Lord was looking out for me that day. Otherwise, I may have had to drop out of the race.

Bike Shop Rescue

We took the part back to our room and I hastily made the repairs. Once my bike was assembled, I checked and re-checked every moving part, wanting no more surprises. After that near catastrophe, I checked my bike in and could now relax.

My plan was to spend the remainder of the day on the front porch reading and relaxing. My wife and Shanna decided to go check out the town and shop while I stayed off my feet. As I read, a young, tiny Asian woman approached from a nearby room asking if I knew anything about reassembling a bike. She, like other athletes, had her local bike shop disassemble and pack her bike for shipping. Athletes often have their bikes shipped to a bike shop at the event location and hire the shop to reassemble their bike so that it's ready when they arrive. I guess she did not think of doing that, or she could not locate a local bike shop and had the bike shipped directly to the hotel.

Her anxious expression showed her distress. Because I'd just averted a similar crisis myself, I told her that I could help. I could see the stress just melt off her. In a matter of thirty minutes, I had her bike reassembled and ready to go.

She had just returned from taking the bike out to the parking lot for a test ride when Debbie and Shanna arrived, and I introduced the lady to them. Shanna teasingly gave me a little grief about attracting other cute ladies while they were away. I'd had plenty of help along the way, so it was an easy choice. The golden rule is "do unto others as you would have them do unto you." If everyone lived their lives according to this principle, this would be a much different world we live in.

Lending a helping hand

Debbie and Shanna had located a good pasta and seafood restaurant, where we ate dinner that evening. After dinner we returned to our room to prepare for the race and get some much-needed sleep.

Race Day

I rose at dark-thirty the next morning to consume my planned prerace meal of oatmeal, banana, bagel, and coffee then headed out. Our hotel was only a short walk from the race site, and we were able to avoid any traffic issues.

Once there, I turned in my transition and special needs bags then went to my bike to place on it my water bottles, nutrients, and electrolytes. I also loaded the Bento Bag with fig Newton bars and energy gel packets to be used late in the bike race in preparation for the run. After deciding all was ready to go, I returned to my wife for a prerace hug and kiss. I left her in the spectator area to scope out the swim start layout then slipped into my wetsuit and put on my swim cap. Once ready, I entered the water to do a short warm-up swim and to check the seal on my goggles. Satisfied that all was in order, I positioned myself in front of the pack to start the swim. Nothing to do now but wait for the starting cannon to fire.

The swim event was held in Lake Okanagan. It is a clear water mountain lake formed by glaciers, with an average summertime temperature of seventy degrees. After waiting for what seemed like forever with all this pent-up energy, I heard the cannon fire, and the race began.

The start area was broad, so the swim was not as crowded as in other IRONMAN® full distance triathlon events. I seeded myself closer to the front of the pack, as I was now a stronger, more confident swimmer, wanting to waste no time negotiating my way around others. The swim went as planned and I finished it in one hour and seven minutes. That was a great start to the race; hopefully the remainder of the day will go as well.

The wetsuit stripper volunteers helped me remove my wetsuit. I then rushed to retrieve my swim-to-bike transition bag. Once it was in hand, I headed to the transition tent. There was not much to do there, having worn my cycling uniform underneath my wetsuit. Doing so made the first few miles of the swim cold with wet clothing on, but it sure sped up my transition time. When trying to earn a coveted IRONMAN® Triathlon World Championship slot, mere minutes can be the determining factor. After speeding through the transition in one minute and forty-six seconds, I retrieved my bike and headed out onto the course.

Penticton is in the heart of the scenic Okanagan Valley, one of Canada's premier wine regions at an elevation of 1,263 feet above sea level. This worked in my favor, as it was 2,000 feet lower than Lubbock's elevation of 3,202 feet. This was good news, as I historically performed well at lower altitudes. With scenic blue and green mountains on every side of Penticton, it had the look and feel of being in a higher elevation.

I was a bit apprehensive about the weather, having heard stories of how cold and wet the bike course could be. The forecast for race day was for a high in the low eighties with clear, sunny, blue skies and light winds. The bike course was hilly with a cumulative 6,190 feet of climbs. That is a lot of climbing for my tall frame and as a flatlander, and I therefore was not expecting to have a stellar bike split time.

The bike course was divided into multiple segments. Starting at Penticton, it went through Osoyoos, Richter Pass, Keremeos, Yellow Lake, and back to Penticton. The first section began with a gentle four-mile climb out of town. From mile four to nine, the shallow grade continued to Skaha Lake, with sharp climbs requiring a lower gear, then on to a long flat section. The first significant climb came at around the fifteen-mile mark on McClean Creek Road, which caused my heart rate to spike.

The next section of the ride was the historic climb up Richter Pass at mile forty. Richter Pass links the Similkameen Valley with South Okanagan. At its peak, it's 2,130 feet in elevation. The major portion of the climb was around four miles long, with about a 3.5% grade, so it was not as bad as I'd expected. The issue was that Richter Pass is a bit sneaky, as it hides its peak around a couple of corners. Just when I thought I had reached the peak, I turned a corner to find yet another climb.

As I made the ascent up the pass, it was nice to see cheering spectators lining the roadway. I used the Look brand of shoe cleats, which produce a noticeable squeak when under high pressure. I heard one spectator say, "Do you hear that sound? He must be using Look cleats."

Once over the pass, there was a fast four-mile downhill section offering a great but brief time to rest my legs after the climb.

The next section started at mile fifty, dropping the riders into the stunning valley and into rolling hills labeled the home of the 7 Bitches, which skirt the Similkameen River. These rollers are long, with grades of 3% to 4% and sharp downhills afterwards. The scenery at this point was spectacular, with a view of Snowy Mountain and a valley below of farmland. The rollers ended at mile sixty-one, with a very gentle incline for the next six miles. I may have been done with all those rollers, but I still had to keep the pressure on the pedals due to the slight incline.

The next section of the course started at mile seventy-two, with a long five-mile ascent at Yellow Lake. The ascent started slowly then built with short, flat sections offering a little break from all the climbs.

The next climb featured grades peaking at 8.5%. Once reaching the top, I was rewarded with an energy-recuperating coast back into town. This downhill section provided my most vivid memory of the bike course, where I reached speeds of fifty miles per hour on a damp asphalt road. I thought to myself, please, please do not have a tire blow out or another reason to cause a crash, as it will not be pretty.

The last section took the riders back into town to finish the bike race with refreshed legs ready for the 26.2-mile run. This section provided a wonderful opportunity to rehydrate and refuel without having to exert too much energy on the bike. The final few miles were all downhill as we went through town with spectators cheering and enjoying their coffee, baked goods, ice cream, and sunshine. I finished the ride with a time of 5:24:39, averaging 20.5 miles per hour on a hilly course, and I felt relatively fresh to start the run. Everything was going exactly as I planned, keeping my heart rates in check, staying hydrated, and remaining energized by my calorie intake.

Close to the bike finish, I was mentally strong and in high spirits when I passed by my cheering, beautiful wife. Prior to every major race, she always asked me the times I expected to be at certain points in the course. Referring to these expected times, she knew I was a good fifteen minutes ahead of the predicted time at this point in the race and cheered heartily when I passed.

I finished the bike with a personal best time, then rushed to the bike-to-run transition bags. Finding mine, I hurried into the transition tent to ready myself for the run. I was pleased and excited by my good swim and bike times and did not want to spend one second longer than necessary in this transition.

While putting on my socks and running shoes, I opted not to lubricate my toes, heels, and other hot spots, as it had been a long time since I had had any problems with blisters on my feet during a full distance triathlon race. Surely this was being overly cautious. I elected to bypass it in favor of a speedy transition. I did stick with the plan of drinking a half-bottle of my prepared liquids and eating an energy gel packet before starting the run.

Taking four minutes and seventeen precious seconds to exit the transition, I started the marathon run course. Crossing the run timing mat, I knew that if I could just run a four-hour marathon, I would stand a good chance of earning a slot in the IRONMAN® Triathlon World Championship.

The run course was scenic, beginning with an out-and-back section hugging the Okanagan Lake shoreline and taking us through vineyards and orchards. During the first mile or two, I slowly built into my goal run pace and shook off the post-bike course triathlon shuffle. I then settled into a nice running stride. For the first couple of miles, my legs were strong. I felt like I was floating over the roadway.

Those first few miles were through the town streets lined with spectators cheering us on. IRONMAN® triathlon events provide booklets containing the name and race number for each contestant listed in race number order. This allows spectators to quickly find the name of each approaching contestant so they can call out their name, cheering them on as they pass by. Most know one of the athletes and are familiar with how hard those first few miles are to get your legs used to running after being on the bike for five-plus hours. At around the two-mile mark, my running legs were in full ready mode, and I was running smoothly at an 8:40-per-mile pace. I heard a spectator cheering me on, saying, "Wade! Looking strong, nice pace," bringing a smile to my face.

Leaving town and the spectators behind, I settled in for the scenic Lake Okanagan shoreline section of the course. As each mile marker and aid station passed,

I realized that my pace was staying at around 8:45 per mile. If I were able to maintain this pace for the remainder of the race, I would run a sub-four-hour marathon. Perfect, just stay with the plan.

The miles clicked by, and all was going my way. I crossed the thirteen-mile marker with a cumulative time of one hour and forty-nine minutes, thinking I could use two hours and ten minutes to run the final thirteen miles and still break the goal of a sub-four-hour marathon. My legs were beginning to feel the strain of the day but were still strong, and I was running smoothly. My spirits were high, knowing how well I was performing.

I knew the importance of having a solid race plan vetted by years of practice and racing experience. I'd thrown that out the window when I neglected to lubricate my toes and typical hot spots. The result of this deliberate plan deviation started rearing its ugly head at around the fifteen-mile mark. I could feel the outside edges of both little toes start to heat up, and I knew blisters were beginning to form. I told myself, You fool, it would have taken less than a minute to lubricate your toes and now you are paying the price!

I continued to run at a slower pace in hopes that the issue would not get worse. Those hopes soon vanished, as the pain increased significantly in the ensuing next few miles. Each footfall sent searing pain into my little toes. The running shoes I used had breathable fabric around the toe box, allowing ventilation in and moisture out. I glanced down at my feet and noticed on both shoes the area next to my little toes was turning a pink color. The blisters on the outer edges of my toes had ruptured and were bleeding. With each step it felt like my sock had bunched up and knotted over both little toes and felt like sandpaper rubbing against the wounds. The vision of earning a qualifying slot was quickly fading, as I was no longer able to run at the required pace.

At around the seventeen-mile mark, I had to do something to ease the pain in my right little toe. The only thing I could think of doing was to pull off my right sock. I stopped at a boulder to sit on while I took off my shoe and sock. My poor toe looked like a mess. Wrenching in pain, I put my shoe back on and began to run again. Thankfully, taking off my sock did lessen the pain, but make no mistake, it still hurt with each step.

I forced myself to keep as steady of a pace as possible. I continued to run with both feet screaming at me to stop. By mile twenty-two, my left little toe was at the point of stopping or doing something to ease the pain. Once more I stopped and took off my left sock. As with the right foot, this did ease the pain enough to continue to run. I remember thinking that there were only four miles left. Surely I could gut it out for four more miles.

Another runner passed by me noticing my painful gait and the red tent of the toe box area of both shoes, asking if I was okay. I told him of my issue and that I was not sure if I could even walk the remaining four miles. He wished me luck as he passed by.

The final four miles were very painful, but I did not spend the last four years planning and training to give up in the last stretch of the race. I did my best to block the pain out of my mind. As I re-entered town for the final couple of miles, spectators lined the streets, cheering for us as we approached the finish line. There was no greater joy than when rounding a corner and seeing the finish line just one mile away. Nothing could stop me now. The pain in my toes seemed to ease, and I picked up my pace, running the final mile in under eight minutes. I crossed the finish line with a time of 10:46:52. A new personal best, but not likely good enough to earn an IRONMAN® Triathlon World Championship slot. It took me four hours and seventeen minutes to complete the run. I had lost over twenty minutes in the second half of the run due to my failure to properly execute my bike-to-run transition plan. This experience just emphasizes my point that even the smallest error in an full distance triathlon race can have big consequences.

After crossing the finish line, race volunteers met me, congratulating me on my finishing the race. They hung a finisher's medal around my neck and assessed my physical condition, finding that, other than my toes, I was in decent shape and let me go. Then I found the first available spot to stop and take off my shoes. Both little toes looked like they had been through a meat grinder. Limping, I made my way to the massage tent to get a much-needed massage. On my way I met the guy who was asking about my condition during the later parts of the run.

He said, "I'm happy to see you. Seeing the pain you were in, I thought you would DNF (did not finish)."

After the massage I found my wife and retrieved my bike. We then began the very painful mile-long walk back to our room, wearing my post-race sandals. Back at the room, I took a shower then treated my raw, red, and swollen little toes. Afterwards I slipped naked under the bed sheets to cool down and rest.

Not long afterwards someone knocked at the door. Debbie answered the door. It was my friend Shanna and a female friend of hers. Shanna eyed me suspiciously, saying "Why are you in bed?" I stuck my feet out from underneath the bed sheet to show them my damaged toes. Shanna laughed and asked, "Are you naked under there?" I thought she was going to yank the sheet right off me. After visiting for a short while and sharing our race experiences, they left us for the evening. I was happy about having a personal best race time but was angry with myself for what might have been if I'd simply followed the transition plan.

Rising early the next morning, I checked the race results online and found that I had placed tenth out of 226 in my age group and that there were only seven IRONMAN® Triathlon World Championship slots assigned to my age group. It was agonizing to know my dream was so close at hand but lost due to the additional seventeen minutes I wasted from my blistered toes. Had I run the planned four-hour marathon, I would have placed fifth, thus earning a slot.

IRONMAN® Triathlon World Championship slots are awarded the day after a qualifying race. Athletes earning slots must be present at the meeting to claim it. Once their name is announced, they have one minute to claim their slot, or the slot rolls down to the next athlete on the list. Chances were slim to none that at least three athletes would fail to claim their slots. Even so, I could not take that risk. Debbie and I walked to the race site for the meeting, me in socks and loose-fitting sandals with very sore little toes.

We arrived at the meeting early, along with other athletes and their supporters in hopes of claiming one of the sixty available spots allocated to the event. The announcer started the meeting by going over the rules for claiming slots and then began calling out names, starting with the pro men and women and then proceeding to the age group athletes in the order of the youngest to oldest. Most athletes made their claim with little to no roll-down.

After an agonizing and tension-filled wait, the announcer said, "Now for the forty-five to forty-nine age group." He started with the women then moved to the men. As the names for the male athletes were called, two of the seven were not present, meaning that the last slot was awarded to the ninth-place finisher. I was the tenth-place finisher, one agonizing place short of earning a slot. Dang! The finishing time difference between ninth and tenth place was a mere three minutes and eleven seconds. Oh well, I would have to try again in two months at IRONMAN® Florida triathlon. I was fine with that. I had been training this long. What was one more race?

To my surprise, the announcer stated that due to the limited number of contestants in the sixty-five and older age group, two of their slots were re-allocated to the largest attended age group. My hopes rose again. It was my age group, the forty-five to forty-nine men's group. I immediately knew that I had earned a slot, after five years of constant, painstaking planning and racing.

Debbie and I both yelled, "Yes!" in unison when my name was called to claim my spot and register for the 2004 IRONMAN® Triathlon World Championship. Now twenty years later, joyful tears fill my eyes as I write about this climatic moment.

> *"The pyramid of success begins with a dream as its cornerstones, followed by layers of planning and action. The interior is filled with fear, doubt, failure, and hard work. The final, and most important, layer is undying persistence. All are capped by achievement and success." – Wade Wilson*

This was indeed a joyous day. I barely noticed my sore toes on the walk back to the room, where we called the kids. My mom was staying with our daughters at our home. We told them I had earned a slot and that we were all going to Hawaii in two months. They were ecstatic at having the opportunity to travel to the island of Hawaii and to watch me compete on a world stage.

Despite my body type not being ideal for being a top cyclist, my bike split was the fourth fastest in my age group, narrowly missing first place by a mere nine minutes. Never, never let anyone define your limitations. I overcame that one by sheer force of will.

The news spread quickly, and I spent the day talking with friends and family at home. Once home, my friend Shanna arranged a celebration party, inviting all my triathlon family and friends. It was such an honor to share my achievements with them, as they had all been part of my triathlon journey. My uncle and his wife invited us to their home for a small celebration as well. While there, we uncorked the five-year-old bottle of champagne I had purchased in Hawaii after the race in 1999. We toasted the realization of my dream.

After all the fun and excitement was over, it was time to plan my training for the two months left before going to Hawaii to compete in the IRONMAN® Triathlon World Championship race. This was going to be tough, because I needed the first two weeks to rest and recover. My workouts during these weeks were easy, allowing my body time to recover and heal from the effort at IRONMAN® Canada triathlon. My battered little toes needed that time to heal from the damage done at the race. It was at least three weeks before I was able to run without reinjuring my toes. That left only thirty days to prepare for the championship race. It was tough knowing that with each passing day my core fitness level was deteriorating. I spent extra training time on the bike to help maintain my base aerobic fitness level and focused on workouts designed for muscular endurance.

Celebration cake and bottle of champagne from the 1999 race

Chapter 36

2004, Achieving the Impossible Dream—Traveling to Hawaii

The time between the IRONMAN® Canada triathlon and the IRONMAN® Triathlon World Championship was a mere forty-eight days. That was not much time to arrange lodging and travel plans. However, my beautiful travel agent (Debbie) went straight to work putting together all the plans and reservation details.

We elected to stay away from the hub of the race site and avoid all the activity at the host hotel and race epicenter. We booked lodging at the Waikoloa Village, which was thirty miles from the race epicenter at Kailua-Kona. It was a beautiful two-story facility with a swimming pool and within walking distance of a secluded beach. Waikoloa Village is a golf resort, with the golf course being constructed in the middle of ancient lava fields. The contrast of the emerald-green golf course embedded in the jet-black, jagged lava fields was strikingly beautiful. This was not just some other IRONMAN® triathlon race coupled with a family vacation. It was first and foremost a celebration of realizing my long-sought-after dream. The setting could not have been better.

Electing to make this a two-week trip, we arrived a full week before the race. This provided sufficient recovery time from the trip and acclimation to the local environment. Our daughters, ages seventeen, fifteen, and eleven, enjoyed the long plane trip from Lubbock, and their excitement of going to Hawaii was in the air. Our flight was the first one leaving Lubbock International, with one stop in Los Angeles, California, and then on to Hawaii, landing in Honolulu first and then on to Kailua-Kona.

The Kona airport was small, with no gateway from the plane to the terminal. Passengers departed the plane via the stairs. We were greeted at the bottom by lovely Hawaiian ladies dressed in traditional native attire, where they placed leis around our necks. From there we found our way to the outdoor baggage claim area to gather our luggage and most importantly (to me) my bike box. Renting a vehicle, we loaded up and headed to the Waikoloa Village, our home for the next eight days. We stopped briefly along the way to pick up food and supplies for the week.

The thirty-mile shoreline drive from Kailua-Kona to the Waikoloa Village was surreal. It was late in the afternoon, with the sun beginning to set above the vast, deep blue, shining ocean and the sky painted pink and light orange. At our condominium, we unpacked and settled in, having two floors of rooms, with plenty of space. Debbie did a wonderful job finding this place. It was great to have all my family with me to share in this celebration. They deserved this as much as I did after following and supporting me for the last five years of training and racing.

Rising the next morning, we had a nice, relaxing breakfast. Everyone was excited about exploring our new surroundings. We walked around the complex as we checked out the golf course and found the beach. We are all beach lovers, vacationing at South Padre Island, Texas, a week every year since the kids were old enough to walk. The beach was private to the resort, and they provided snorkeling gear for our use. We spent the rest of the day there enjoying the natural beauty of Hawaii and playing in the water. I especially enjoyed snorkeling with all the tropical fish and huge sea turtles swimming close around us.

Condominium Pool

Later that afternoon, I unpacked my bike box and reassembled my bike, not wanting any last-minute surprises. Once assembled, I took it for a test ride and found all systems were operating perfectly. Now I can relax.

Prerace Family Activities

Eight days seemed like an adequate amount of time, but it was not when trying to include family activities with the race itself. I was fitting all these family activities in while continuing to maintain my base level fitness. I rose early every day to have a nice, easy-effort ride or run. Closer to race day, I worked in a practice swim. On one morning after my training routine, we drove out on the bike course to build a good luck symbol, something of a tradition for racers to see while they're on the bike course. We made ours out of pieces of bleached white coral placed on top of the jet-black lava. I built an M shape out of the coral while Lia spelled out her name.

Making bleached coral signs

The helicopter tour was amazing. None of us had ever been in a helicopter before and the views were incredible. The weather for the trip was perfect, with calm winds and clear, blue, sunny skies. The pilot took us all around the island, visiting slightly active lava flows and spectacular, lush, green forests with waterfalls hundreds of feet tall.

Helicopter tour

We spent at least one day in the small town and race epicenter Kailua-Kona, where we shopped and ended the day at a luau party. The main dish at the luau was pork, which had been roasting all day wrapped in tan burlap, buried in a sand pit lined with hot coals and covered with multiple layers of green palm leaves on top to protect it from the coals and sand. We watched them dig it out and prepare it for our feast. The meal included tropical fruits and other tropical side dishes. It was all delightfully delicious.

The dessert selection included poi. Poi is traditionally made by mashing taro corm, a type of plant root that is cooked for hours in an underground oven. It appeared to be delicious, mouthwatering chocolate pudding. We could not wait to try it. The staff told us to try a little before getting a larger portion. We each put a spoonful on our plates along with other desserts. We each taste-tested the poi. The best way to describe the taste is "poi happens." It was awful.

The luau entertainment featured dancers and performers dressed in traditional native attire. We all had a wonderful time soaking in the culture of Hawaii.

Two days before the race, we all went on a four-hour horseback riding trip with all of us enjoying the scenery through beautiful terrain filled with lush tropical forest and flora. We took a break for lunch at a thirty-foot waterfall spilling into a clear, cool natural pool. We had been told to bring our swimsuits. After two hours on horseback, we were all ready to dismount and take a dip into the beautiful blue water.

The waterfall had a wide ledge about fifteen feet above the surface of the pool. We all climbed to the ledge to jump feet-first into the pool. Fifteen feet does not seem that far until you look down, waiting your turn to jump. After the swim, we ate sandwiches and returned to the horses for the two-hour journey back to the stables. I wondered more than once if this excursion was a good idea for me to become bowlegged two days before the race.

Horseback ride

Waterfall

The day before the race, it was time to check in my bike and test out the swim practice area that was set up at the swim course where athletes could swim the entire course or just a portion of it. The swim practice had a start and end time, with race officials providing safety personnel in canoes during the scheduled time span. The course buoys were already set up so swimmers could practice sighting them while swimming eye level to the water's surface in three-foot rolling waves.

The waves were mostly coming directly at us, lifting and lowering us as we swam. I found it best to look up when at the top of these rolling waves to locate the next buoy.

Debbie and I went to the swim practice, leaving the kids to sleep in and hang out at the condo pool for the morning. We were late getting to the swim practice, with most swimmers just finishing. There was still about thirty to forty-five minutes left in the practice window, so I stripped to my swimsuit and entered the water. It was fairly empty, with only a few athletes starting with me. The water temperature was cool but perfect for distance swimming and ultra-clear. I was able to see up to ninety feet and could clearly see the sandy bottom with scattered boulders. Multitudes of tropical fish in every color of the rainbow clustered around each boulder. I stopped several times just to observe them. I moved at an easy pace, enjoying the view and the experience of being there.

While swimming, I tried to get a feel for how the currents flowed and practiced sighting the buoys, trying as much as possible to stay on a direct line with them. At 1,000 yards out, I could no longer see the bottom and decided to rest for a moment. I could see no other swimmers in sight or anyone in canoes. Looking back at the shore off in the distance, a sense of unease overcame me. This was the only open water swim that made me feel that way. I could not see what was beneath me in an ocean full of predators. If anything happened out here, no one would ever find me. I decided to head back, swimming a bit faster, finally relaxing a bit when reaching a point where the bottom was again in my view. Whew, that was unnerving! Slowing down, I again enjoyed the views for the remainder of the swim. Grateful to be back on shore, I dried off and put on dry clothing.

It was now time to check in my transition bags and bike. Afterward, we went to shop for memorabilia. The IRONMAN® village was full of energy, with athletes mingling, shopping, and enjoying a bit of free time before the big event. It was thrilling to be amongst all these ultra-fit athletes representing all corners of the globe. These were the best of the best in my sport, all converged for this one World Championship event. What an honor. I felt very fortunate to be among them. I purchased compressed air canisters for the off chance of having a flat on the bike course.

We also purchased some hats and shirts with the 2004 Hawaii IRON-MAN® triathlon logos. While there, I met with Mr. and Mrs. Webb, both medical doctors and fellow triathletes from my hometown. They were not there to compete but were conducting some kind of study on the athletes. My best recollection is that it had something to do with studying the body measurement norms of the best triathletes in the world. What better place to do that than here at the World Championship? They took and recorded all sorts of measurements from my body.

I never saw the results of their study but did find a study that reported the average male height was 5'9" with the top end being 6'3" (that's me). The average weight for the males was 163 pounds with a high end of 183 pounds (that's me again). I could easily see the differences between most of the other athletes and myself by just mingling with them. This may be what the bike mechanic meant when he said that I did not fit the mold for elite cyclists. This made me feel a little out of place.

With Doctor Webb

Soon we left to head back to our condominium for a delightful early evening of food with our good friends, Mike and Marti Greer, along with other race organizers. Everyone left shortly after our pasta meal, as we all had a big day ahead of us with me racing and them working as volunteers for the event.

Once alone, the significance and enormity of what I was about to undertake began to sink in. I had spent the last five years pouring every ounce of my mind, body, and soul into reaching this point. I was on the verge of realizing my dream of competing with the best triathletes in the world. It was an emotional time. I'd competed in numerous full distance triathlons and knew the challenges that awaited me, but this was different. This was the IRONMAN® Triathlon World Championship, where everyone had made the same sacrifices I had made to be here. I was so honored to be included among them. These feelings and emotions made all that I had invested in reaching this pinnacle worth it. I was equally proud of my dream teammate Debbie and kids (Ashley, Lia, and Amanda) for all their love and support along the way. I could not have realized my dream without them.

At the end of the evening, it was time to lay out everything needed for my prerace meal and race day supplies. We all turned in early to rest for the big day.

Prerace meal with friends

Prerace Thoughts from My Triathlon Sherpas (My Family)

I am fully aware that none of this would have been possible without the love and support of my family. I cannot thank them enough. Their full support and involvement throughout the last five years was priceless.

Triathlon Sherpa team left to right: Ashley, Amanda, Debbie, and Lia

From My Dear Wife Debbie

Our friends and family will never realize how much work went into Wade's dream. He worked full time and traveled three to four days from home each week.

We are immensely proud of him, and we loved watching him compete. We have great memories and had a wonderful family time at these events. For years all our kids volunteered. In the later years of volunteering, I remember our oldest daughter, Ashley, overseeing body marking. I walked up when I heard a six-foot-plus Army guy telling Ashley something about how he thought he knew how body marking should be. I heard our Ashley, who is five foot nothing, telling him to get the cadets in order and mark each triathlete consistently and correctly or they could just leave! After that he would come up to her and say stuff like, "Ma'am, where do you need us now?" It was very funny to watch him cower to her, but she did know her stuff. Ha ha!

We also did "home stays." Pro athletes would come in and stay with us, one of whom was a wonderful man named Animal. He competed in the handicapped division and was a topnotch hand cyclist from Hawaii. He got out in his wheelchair and played basketball in our driveway with the girls, and we enjoyed his visit. A couple of years later he was tragically killed in an accident while out training. Heartbreaking for sure.

There were so many great memories during our triathlon times. Some stressful, but the good times outweighed the bad. I am very proud of Wade and his accomplishments. Never say to him, "You can't do that," because he will do that, and more.

From My Daughter Ashley

My parents started taking us all over the US as my dad competed in more and more full and half distance triathlons in preparation for Hawaii. These vacations are among my most cherished memories of my family. We saw the redwoods tower over us in California and dipped our toes into the freezing Pacific.

I never considered me and my sisters to have particularly strong accents until we made it to Lake Placid, New York. People there would repeatedly ask us to repeat phrases or say the word "y'all" to hear our twang. We stayed in the Olympic Village and purchased my first snowboard amongst the Adirondacks.

Unassuming Idaho ended up being my favorite of the stateside trips. My mom spent her high school years in Idaho, so my grandmother traveled with us. It was late at night when we arrived at the cabin, and the outside looked less than habitable. Once we got inside, though, it became my dream home. It was a three-story cabin with light-pouring windows and an aboveground basement/study that I adored reading in. Down a little way from the house was a lake with a dock. It was the definition of picturesque. We were only there for a week or two, but we have dozens of stories that we still regularly laugh about, like Amanda getting pushed off the dock, me starting a grudge against one of my parents' friends, and

Grandmother and I seeing Lia run into the pristine glass door like a disoriented bird.

The first few days in any of these places would be spent getting my dad prepared for the race. We would go to the course, plot out where we would meet, and look at the transition area. The day after the race, Dad would sleep in and recover. His feet were bruised, and his toenails would begin to fall off. This process taught me that rest was just as much a part of success as planning and practicing.

I do not remember much about his first race in Hawaii, although I do remember how excited we all were for him. On the day of the race, we would check the website to watch his progress and then call to tell him how proud we were once he crossed the finish line. My parents brought home souvenirs and pictures and told us what it was like seeing that many people coming together to compete.

In the fall of 2004, Dad made it back to Hawaii, but this time they took us with them as well. It was the first semester of my freshman year of college, but I was thrilled to go. Like each of the previous triathlons, we got to Kona days before the race to give Dad time to prepare. Mom mapped out where we would stand for each leg of the race so Dad would know where to look for us. The night before the race we met up with Mike, Marti, and others for the athlete's carbohydrate-laden dinner. I did not sleep much that night. The next morning, we armed ourselves with our newly beloved Kona coffee and took Dad to the bike racks. We escorted him to the start, hugged him, and wished him good luck.

Lia, Amanda, and I hopped up on top of the stone wall that overlooked the ocean. We sat in the dark quietly joking about pushing each other in. As the minutes until the start ticked down, the ocean started to ebb and flow in color. What had been inky black was now dark blue with the gold of dawn crashing through the top of the waves. There was soft salt air playing across our cheeks and green sea turtles soaring in the depths. Suddenly, with a joyous bang, the starting gun rang out, and thousands of people jumped into the sea.

My dad's dream was to compete with the best. He did that day and has continued to challenge himself at multiple other races since. We have seen him charge victoriously across the finish line, but we have also witnessed him stop mid-race when his body could not continue. Dad's efforts taught me how to work hard and persevere, Mom's planning showed me what it meant to be a partner, and volunteering alongside my sisters strengthened my abilities to work as a team and as a leader. No matter what goals I strive for in the future, my family has given me the skills to reach for them.

From My Daughter Lia

Dad has always been a dreamer and go-getter.

Growing up in my teens, I remember the start of his journey and was amazed that he was not only training to run, but to bike and swim as well. I enjoyed watching his progress and admired his passion for triathlons. Our family became immersed in the sport. We helped at expos and with swimmers with their wetsuits, marked race numbers with Sharpies, and got to know the families of local triathletes.

Triathlons gave our family the opportunity to travel to multiple states and experience life outside of Lubbock. IRONMAN® USA Lake Placid triathlon was my favorite because of the New Yorkers' accents and perfect weather. The IRONMAN® Triathlon World Championship in Hawaii was the trip of a lifetime. Our dad not only accomplished multiple Ironman events but made it to the IRONMAN® Triathlon World Championship. Watching him complete the swim, the bike, and running through the finish line to be greeted with a lei of flowers—all unforgettable moments.

Dad taught me about setting goals, and with determination and perseverance, you can accomplish whatever you set your mind to. I am very proud and thankful to have him as a father.

From My Daughter Amanda

Hello there, let me begin by introducing myself. My name is Amanda, the youngest daughter of Wade and Debbie Wilson. This is my story about how my father was one of a kind, how I got to see his passion play out through my childhood, and what I learned from this experience.

To begin my story, I can still hear his exercise bike in the living room spinning and spinning while he watched his favorite sitcom as he trained. The sound the bike made was like a ceiling fan's noise as it spins at high speed. I grew quite literally in the realm of a triathlete. I saw first-hand his struggles and successes as a triathlete and as a father of three girls.

When I was born, my dad was beginning to compete. I almost thought of it as his second job, which quite literally was to me—as well as his dream. He was *persistent* at training. He would train along with coaching others to compete in triathlons. I remember the *discipline* and endurance he had in his training before and after work, quite literally every day and weekend. We would go to church, then he was off on his bike that afternoon or a run during the training seasons. The races I got to experience would take place all over, including adventures in North America and the Virgin Islands. I did not have an ordinary childhood like others. If it were not for my dad's hobby as a triathlete, I do not know if I would have experienced the places I saw and or been shaped the way that I am now.

Growing up with an athlete, you would hear my mom say, "Well, your dad is on a diet, so we are too," as she laughed. I remember my dad going on a run or bike as my mom followed him in her minivan. I sometimes tagged along, playing my Game Boy in the front seat on evenings when my dad had to run or bike. It kept my mom company. I remember him exhibiting elevated levels of aerobic fitness from yoga (which I tagged along with at times growing up) to swimming with him, biking, and running. He was always committing to his dream.

A funny memory I have: My dad and I were biking together once. He was on his lighter-than-air bicycle while I was on my mom's road bike, equally light. He was *supporting* me in learning to road bike, so I went on a ride with him. I tried to make my first corner out in the dirt fields of Lubbock, Texas, and completely plowed into a dirt mound and ate dirt. I could hear my dad laughing as he quickly came up to check on me. It was a good moment. One that I will remember forever.

I would wake up many summers bright and early to see my dad race and help with it. I will be honest, there were summers I did not want to go. I had seen my dad training so much, I felt as a child that I was just seeing the same thing. I look back and remember it was worth the mornings waking up because you felt and saw this energy that was around you with athletes ready to compete.

Before these races occur, there is what is called "packet pick-up." I enjoyed these events growing up. I had to help, along with my sisters and mom, pack packets for the athletes. These packets included numbers, race information, etc. It took all day for us to do it in a hotel conference room, but it was fun for us (for me that is). I also met kids my age, their parents, and triathletes.

Our big trips were when my dad was racing. So, a two-in-one trip. Dad races, then we get a vacation at the same time.

A race memory of mine was when we were in St. Croix. If you know a triathlete, you know they like to drive to their race site days before they compete. That said, we were in this rented SUV, and we were driving up a volcanic slope called "the Beast." I remember my mom, dad, my sister, and I being stunned and then laughing it off for how steep this slope was.

Another memorable trip was to Hawaii. My dad just competed in a qualifying race for the championships to go to Hawaii and my parents called me and my sisters, telling us we were going to Hawaii! I remember me and my sisters jumping with excitement.

Before all these trips, he had to wake up early, swim, then go to work, then work out after he got home. I would go up to the university's pool with my dad sometimes before I could drive, to sit there and watch him do laps because Mom had obligations that day.

As I grew older, after school, I would meet him in the living room or in my parents' bedroom on his bike to say hello. I would sit on the floor and chat with my dad as he cycled and tell him about my day.

As years of training went on for him, he took me and my family to places like Idaho, Wisconsin, Hawaii, and St. Croix. I remember one con of traveling with an athlete is their gear is expensive, and they need it to perform for the race. If it is lost, all hell breaks loose. I remember the airline lost my dad's bike box once with his bike inside and he did not get it until the day before his race. That was not a good time, but we just had to support him in any way that we could. Can you imagine training all year, if not longer, and then your gear is lost? A series of unfortunate events.

When my dad raced, he was happy. You could see it every time, which made it worth the absence of his training and traveling, and the experiences that came along with it. As an athlete's daughter, I was encouraged to do a sport along with my sisters growing up. He was teaching us to be good competitors. We were a sports family. I think seeing him doing this held me and my sisters to a higher standard in our sports. I did not want to fail him and neither did my sisters. When I was thirteen or so, I was encouraged by my father to do a kid's triathlon in Lubbock. It was fun, but I remember saying to my dad that he was crazy for doing this all day long during races and that I was never doing that again. He laughed.

Being an athlete's daughter is marching to a different drum. I am proud. It inspires me as an adult. Proud of you, Dad! I learned many things through the lens of watching him compete and train. It taught me to be *humble* in the moment. I learned how to be committed to what I want. I did not learn to become a triathlete, though I learned how to be a supporter in the end, seeing his passion play out through my childhood. Love you, Dad!

Chapter 37

Race Day

I woke at 3:30 a.m., consumed my prerace meal, then catnapped for another hour. Rustling three sleepy young ladies from their sleep at 4:30 a.m. was not an easy task. After everyone dressed and loaded in the car, we left for the thirty-minute trip to Kailua-Kona. While loading everything in the car, I noted that the wind was stronger than it had been since we arrived. In the back of my mind, I was anxiously thinking, this is not what I wanted for my race. The drive was on the bike course, and volunteers were busy setting up their aid stations as we passed by.

After arriving at the race site, we found a parking spot, and I then went to the bike racks to check the pressure in my bike tires, load the Bento Bag with food items, and put fresh bottles of liquids in the bottle holders. The brightly lit bike transition area was buzzing with activity and pent-up energy of the athletes all nervously scurrying around carrying air pumps, water bottles, and their nutritional needs to load onto their bike. The anticipation of the day's event was clearly evident in their eyes and facial expressions. I have always loved being part of this excitement, but this had the added significance of being the World Championship. Nerves were on edge as we all awaited the day of competition we were about to embark on. We wanted everything to be perfect before starting the race.

This is a time when athletes have time to speak with those whose bikes are racked close by. The conversations were wishing each other luck, finding out where they were from, what brand of bike they had, and anything else to help settle our nerves. I did not know any of the other competitors, many of whom were from foreign countries speaking languages I did not understand. Remember this was the World Championship, with athletes coming from eighteen different nations. All competitors were the best of the best in their age groups. That was an extremely small pool of individuals who likely did not know each other. It was evident that nerves were on edge when viewing the long lines at the port-a-potties. Yes, I was in line as well! Before leaving the transition area, I took a moment to look back at all the sights and sounds, which emphasized how special this was and how fortunate I felt to be here. Few people would ever be able to experience something like this.

Satisfied that all was in order, I headed back to be with my family before going to the swim start area. It was wonderful having my family there with me, getting hugs, kisses, and well wishes from them before the announcer called all competitors to the swim start area. I could see the pride and concern in each of their faces. Lia always got sick to her stomach with concern for me before each major event. I reassured them that I would be okay and loved them and said "This is it! Time to get this party started!"

We were directed to cross the timing mat, registering our computer chip and race number in the timing computer. Then I walked out onto the pier amongst all the competitors. Here I was standing among legendry pros like Noman Stadler, Peter Reid, muti-year champion Natascha Badmann, and Heather Fuhr. I had only read about the accomplishments of these people, yet here I was in the same championship event with them. It was very crowded, with everyone waiting until the last possible moment before jumping feet first off the pier into the ocean. Tensions were high as the soft yellow sun began to rise above the horizon of the ocean. I could not believe this was happening. I was here about to take my place with the fortunate few who would know the thrill and excitement of competing in the World Championship of their chosen sport. I could not stop smiling while thinking about it.

I knew from past racing experiences the challenges I would face today. All the things that might go wrong. I just kept telling myself that I earned the right to be here, and no matter what happens, I was going to give it my best and enjoy every moment of it. My biggest fear was of bonking and DNF (did not finish) in the race that I worked so hard for the past five years to be a part of. I would do everything in my power to avoid that. This race had all the hallmarks of a difficult course. The open ocean swim had rolling waves with currents to deal with. The bike course was notorious for its high winds and rolling hills. Hot, humid conditions were a norm for the run course. All these taken individually would make for difficult racing conditions, but combined was a reality I had to contend with.

When it was announced that there were ten minutes before the swim started, I sucked in that final pre-race breath and jumped off the pier into a sea of 1,728 people and found my way to the middle of the pack. The top swimmers would finish in approximately one hour. I had the ability to complete the swim in around an hour and five minutes. I was racing with the best in the world, so the middle of the pack seemed a very appropriate place for me to start. We were shoulder to shoulder with swimmers only feet away on each side. I anxiously treaded water while checking the seal of my goggles and waiting for the start cannon to fire.

Five years of meticulous training, planning, and scores of races later, I was mere minutes from starting the adventure and experience of a lifetime. Just an ordinary guy about to experience an extraordinary dream. All the prerace anxiety and jitters immediately disappeared the moment the cannon fired as the competitors started swimming.

Swim start

When the race started all my nervous tension and anxiety vanished as I started to swim on the epic adventure. It was crowded for the first ten minutes as everyone settled into their pace. Imagine driving on a crowded freeway with hundreds of cars all moving in unison and not far apart. I did my best to swim at my planned pace and slightly lifted my head every twenty or so strokes to look for the next buoy. The water conditions were three-foot rolling waves moving directly against us but not significantly slowing our progress. The fish that were around the boulders during my practice swim had mysteriously vanished. This was no time to be sightseeing anyway.

I did my best to take long, steady strokes and stay face down to keep my body parallel to the surface of the water. I felt strong and comfortable throughout the swim course. Just like my 1999 race, the final hundred yards seemed to take forever, as the backwash of the waves hitting the shore slowed our progress. Remembering this, I swam harder until I was on the downhill side of a swell and used the power of the wave to propel me forward.

I finished the swim in 1:11:21, which was a little slow but close to my expectations and ranked 941 out of 1,782. Again, I was competing with the best in the world and expected to be in the middle of the pack of such accomplished elite athletes.

Athletes all around me grabbed their transition bags and hurried to the changing tent. Pumped about having a decent swim, I followed them to prepare myself for the bike ride. I made sure to put on ample amounts of sunscreen, as it would be a sunny day. It took five minutes and forty-nine seconds to make the transition, mount my bike, and head out onto the bike course. Volunteers helped to quickly locate and retrieve my bike. I made a quick check with both the front and rear wheels to make sure they spun freely then headed to the bike mounting line.

I especially remember mounting my bike amongst thirty to forty athletes trying to do the same thing and get moving. We had to dodge other riders during this chaotic transition. At this point I felt strong, confident, and excited to see how the bike course would unfold. The start was like many other long-course triathlons I had competed in. It was different in that the athletes seemed more eager to make a fast transition and get on their bikes. I was trying to stay focused and not make any mistakes in this Super Bowl of triathlons. I took time to build into my average heart rate goal of 145 beats per minute, not worrying about my speed. My prior experience to this point gave me confidence to trust my training. If I just managed my heart rate, the speed would take care of itself.

The winds were light and against us at five miles per hour at around seventy-five degrees. Not bad starting conditions, but my average speed was below my expectations. This was concerning and it felt like my brake pads were rubbing against the tire rim. I did not want to ride 112 miles like that, so I stopped for a moment to make sure that was not the case. The tires were spinning freely so I remounted my bike and continued.

Kailua-Kona is on the dry side of the big island with little vegetation, providing a sharp contrast to the lava fields. The Kohola Coast hugs the Queen K Highway we were on, and Mount Mauna Loa towered over the terrain towards the central part of the island. The bike course was not likely what most think of Hawaiian roadways. I'd expected lush island forests and beautiful tropical plants and flowers normally only seen in nurseries or botanical gardens. Instead, I was surrounded by vast, dry, jet-black lava fields full of sharp, jagged lava stones.

The bike course was out and back on the same road with the turnaround point at the town of Hawi. As the miles passed, I realized my speed was slower than I had wanted. Wind and temperatures were ramping up, slowing me down, not boding well for a fast bike split. Unexpectedly, my heart rate monitor began to malfunction and would discontinue reading my heart rate about every twenty minutes. This was very irritating, and I was constantly resetting it. Without it I would have no idea if my heart rate was in the planned zones. Thankfully, I was able to keep it functioning. Miles forty-six to the turnaround at mile fifty-six were nearly a constant climb against an ever-increasing wind speed. I finally reached Hawi and made the turn. I was immensely relieved to be on the downside of the hill, with the wind at my back giving my legs a much-needed rest.

The wind direction and force tend to change during the day as the cooler morning air at the higher elevations of the volcano rushes down towards the ocean, then reverses direction as the sun heats the ground, causing the hot air to rise and rush off the ocean onto land. Facing south now, the winds were a problem, and the rising temperatures took a toll on me. Eventually I reached a notorious section of the course known for extraordinarily fierce winds coming down Mount Mauna Loa. Officials strongly discouraged the use of flat full disc rear wheels, as these winds could blow a rider completely off the road. The winds were not that strong today, but we had to battle the wind on the first leg of the course and were now facing it again on the return trip. Living in the Northwest Texas panhandle, I was accustomed to riding in hot, dry, windy conditions, but the wind normally only blew in one direction. This was wearing on my legs and was holding down my speed.

With fifteen miles left, another rider slowly passed me. I slowed just long enough to let him pull ahead to the required three bicycle width between us, then I reapplied the power to maintain my speed. When about fifty yards in front of me, he slowed, and I caught up and passed him. I was merely trying to maintain my speed and was surprised when he again passed me, forcing me to change my pace to adjust the spacing again. Frustratingly, the rider repeated this process multiple times, forcing me to vary my speed to accommodate his moves. I only wanted to stay in a zone and grind out the final miles, and not be pestered by the game he was playing.

One final time, he passed and immediately slowed. I caught up again when an umpire riding on the back of a motorcycle came alongside of me, telling me to stop because I had violated the drafting rules. When I stopped, he told me he was going to issue me a five-minute time penalty. At the time, the rule was that you could be no closer than three bicycle lengths behind the lead rider. When passing a slower rider, you had fifteen seconds to enter the draft zone and for your front tire to pass theirs. Riding closer allows the chasing rider to put forth less effort to go at the same speed. You see this when watching the Tour de France as the competitors ride mere inches from each other. Such a group of riders is called a peloton, and it is a group effort. Triathlon is an individual effort sport, and no one is allowed to receive assistance in any form during the race. I had just entered the draft zone and was in the process of passing the other rider. I did not use a stopwatch to time it, but I may have been in the zone for five seconds when the umpire came alongside of me. I was shocked when he put a red slash mark through my race number signifying the time penalty.

I told him, "I had no intention to break the drafting rules. There was no drafting benefit since I was riding to the left of the rider while making my pass and was not directly behind him. Any rider knows that there is no drafting benefit unless you are directly behind the lead rider." I was furious. I would never intentionally break the rules. In my view doing so would taint my race results. This was the first time in my racing career to have received a penalty. Making it worse, it happened in my dream race, the World Championship. Truth be told, I suspected the other rider was drafting off me when he was behind me. He had none of it and issued the penalty regardless of what I said. Well, this day was not shaping up in my favor!

Now tired, hot, and angry, I slowed enough to give this guy a wide berth as I completed the final miles of the ride. I crossed the dismount line with a bike split time of 6:12:57, forty-eight minutes slower than my bike split in Canada just two months prior. I was discouraged and upset and even more so with the undeserved drafting penalty.

After dismounting, I located my bike-to-run transition bag then headed to the transition tent to prepare for the marathon portion of the race. Not wanting a repeat of my mistake at the IRONMAN® Canada triathlon, I took time to lubricate my toes and other hot spots. I could not find my electrolyte tablets in the transition bag. Wow, nothing was going according to plan today! I later found them on the countertop at our condominium. This was particularly concerning, as the aid stations typically do not provide electrolyte tablets, and it was a hot day. My only option was to use the sports drinks provided at the aid stations that contain electrolytes. What else was going to go wrong today?

Leaving out on the run, I first stopped at the penalty tent to serve my five-minute drafting time penalty. The only consolation was that my friends, Mike and Marti Greer, were there staffing the penalty tent. I told them the story of how I received the penalty while serving my time. Mike tried to comfort me, saying, "You had a good swim," while Marti noted how tough the winds were on the bike and every rider finishing the bike looked beat up, hot, and exhausted.

They both pointed out I had worked too long and hard to be at this place and time to let these mishaps ruin my experience. They encouraged me to just enjoy the rest of my race. If I had to be in the penalty tent, I was happy the time was spent with them. Truthfully, I needed that five-minute rest before starting the run.

I started the run discouraged and not feeling strong or fresh. This was not how I pictured my day at the World Championship race. I had not come this far to give up. I forced myself to settle into a run pace but struggled to keep my heart rate in the desired zone. When I saw Debbie and the girls shortly into the run, it sparked my energy, and I did my best to feed off their positivity and encouragement. This was a long, sweltering day for my family as well. Following is a photo of them sitting in the shade on a bench in front of a jewelry store.

Hot and sleepy Sherpas on race day

Debbie felt bad about them sitting in front of the shop for hours and made a purchase as compensation for allowing them to spend time there. Following is a picture of her purchase of a bicycle ornament that we put next to our finisher's family photo in one of our display cabinets.

Jewelry shop purchase

Leaving town, I ran along the coast for three miles then looped back towards town. This leg of the course had us running parallel to the churning ocean. I could see and hear the waves crashing into the rocky shoreline and could smell the salty ocean air. Swaying palm trees and brightly colored tropical plants and bushes lined the roadway. These sights, sounds, and smells provided a distraction from my aching lower back and tight leg muscles and reminded me of why I was here and what I was doing. I was living out my dream.

I rarely experience lower back pain during a race but today it was there. I believe it was from pushing against the wind for 112 miles on the bike ride. It was now the hottest part of the day. My perspiration rate was high, and I quickly depleted my body's store of electrolytes. Forced to use the sports drinks provided at the aid stations was not in my race plan, and I was concerned how my body might react to it. Using these drinks slowed the electrolyte loss but caused mild nausea. At each station I drank sport drinks then diluted them with a serving of water. Seven miles into the course we headed out of Kona, going north towards the energy lab, notorious for its oven-like temperatures with no wind to help cool your body.

Twelve miles into the run

The sun was setting, and I'd been racing for nine and half hours. The air was finally starting to cool down. My back was no longer aching, and my thighs and hamstrings had loosened up. My spirits were higher now and I was enjoying being there with all the other athletes close to me. We all encouraged each other and briefly exchanged where home was, shared our experiences in the swim, and noted how windy and tough the bike course had been. I soaked in the beautiful view of a reddish-orange sky reflecting off the ocean as we entered the leg of the race known as the natural energy lab.

It derives its name from the small office park in the area that provides space for environmentally focused companies. The sun bakes this completely isolated, exposed area, which has the ugly distinction of being the worst thing at the worst time for the competitors. I have previously described hitting the wall in long-course running and triathlon events. The wall often comes at around the eighteen-mile point where no drink, energy gel packet, or positive mental attitude is going to save you. It is the point where your only thoughts are to finish the race before it finishes you.

After 132 miles of racing, we hit this wall while in this bowl of heat and stagnant air. Aid station volunteers say athletes exiting this three-mile section are rarely in the same physical and mental condition as they were when entering it. While in the lab area, I experienced all of this and gratefully made it through. Beaten and battered I exited the energy lab and turned back to the south for the final seven miles back to Kailua-Kona and the finish line. Darkness came with the final five miles remaining. The only light was now from the glow sticks provided to us by the volunteers, the floodlights at the next aid station, and the glow of a full moon.

The glow sticks are about five inches long and half an inch wide with a plastic hook on the top end. Lanyards were provided so that we could hang the glow sticks around our necks. After shaking the sticks for a few seconds, they emit a soft green light. Some competitors carried them in their hands, others put them in their jersey's side pockets, while others hung them around their neck. I elected to put it in my jersey side pocket, as I did not want it bouncing off my chest while running. I kept mine as a memento and a reminder of my experiences.

After racing for twelve straight hours, I reached the top of the final hill with three miles left, where the lights of Kailua-Kona came into view. This was a very special moment, as this epic day and race were nearing an end. I was grateful to God for allowing me to have this experience, and for the love I felt for my wife and children with their encouragement and support. The beauty of God's creation was before me, and I was proud of myself for realizing my dream, overcoming so many obstacles and challenges along the way.

I stopped for a moment to let it all soak in and reflect on all that I had sacrificed and worked for just to be at this place and time. I might never again have an experience like this and did not want to cut it short. Every part of my body was exhausted, begging me to stop moving, but I could not allow it until I crossed the finish line and began running and was ready to put this race into the history books.

While rounding the hot corner I spotted my family. They too had been up since 4:00 a.m. and in the hot sun all day. Still they were all smiling and yelling "Go, Dad, you've got this, you're almost done."

That brought a huge smile to my face. I called out, "Thanks. I love you! Meet me at the finish line area."

Not performing as expected was discouraging, but here I was fulfilling my wildest dream with the best triathletes in the world at the Super Bowl of triathlons. These thoughts and the cheering spectators comforted me as I ran the final mile. I made the turn for the final 300 yards and saw the finish line banner ahead. The stands were still completely full of cheering spectators, as there were still over 700 competitors out on the racecourse. I could hear them calling my name with congratulatory comments. My body's endorphins kicked in and I was feeling fresh with no pain as I entered the brightly lit finish line area and practically sprinted to the finish line banner. I wish everyone could experience the thrill and excitement of this moment. There is nothing in life, apart from marrying my wife and the birth of my children, that equals being at the climax of a multi-year journey ending with the fulfillment of a dream. Though hot, exhausted, and discouraged, I wore a huge smile as I crossed the finish line, hearing the announcer calling my name. "Wade Wilson from Lubbock, Texas, you are an Ironman."

I finished the run with a split time of 4:37:52 and a total race time of 12:17:28. The tough day was mostly due to the windy conditions on the bike, which also reduced my energy and strength for the run.

My wife Debbie's thoughts about the race.

> The girls and I were exhausted and hot. It had been a long day. When we spotted Wade coming towards the finish line lights, exhaustion turned to joy. We were jumping up and down cheering as he approached and passed by us. I was so proud of him. All of his years of hard work paid off when the announcer said, "Wade Wilson from Lubbock, Texas, you are an Ironman!" This brought

tears to my eyes. I could not wait to get my finisher's hug. There were so many spectators around the finishing area that it took around thirty minutes to find Wade after he crossed the finishing line. Once we found him, we all went to have the finisher's photos taken then headed to our car to hear all about his race experience on our trip back to the condominium. Unless you have raced in a full distance triathlon event or are close to one that has, you cannot truly understand the physical and mental strength of a full distance triathlete. Proud is a weak word to describe how the girls and I felt unless proud means: Wow, he did it! Our dad is the greatest! We were more than just proud and still are all these years later.

Looking back, I do not think forty-eight days was enough to fully recover from the IRONMAN® Canada triathlon and train for the IRONMAN® Triathlon World Championship. Especially considering the extra downtime required to let the skin heal on both my little toes. If I'd had more control over the situation, I'd have spread this out longer. But I am happy with how it all went.

It was surreal as this epic journey and race came to an end. Even though my race results were not what I was hoping for, I had persevered through all the challenges the race threw at me. Not unlike the journey of the last five years. I finished ahead of over 700 of the finest triathletes in the world and felt extremely blessed and honored to be counted among these awesome athletes, from the winner down to the last person crossing the finish line. I would not trade my experience for anything in this world.

It was hard to believe that the past five years spent dreaming of and pursuing this one goal, the constant planning, training, and racing, had come and gone so quickly. I relished this time pushing myself to the limit to find out what I was capable of with my investment of time and energy toward this lofty goal. God is intentional with the talents he gives us. That is what Psalm 139:14 tells us: "I will praise You, for I am fearfully and wonderfully made." James 1:17 says, "Every good gift and every perfect gift is from above, and comes down from the father of lights, with whom there is no variation or shadow of turning." Each of us should reflect on these divinely inspired words and do our best to use our talents and gifts to bring glory to his name. It is my sincere hope and prayer that my story will inspire others to identify their gifts and talents then pursue their wildest dreams.

I now have a firm belief that anyone can accomplish seemingly impossible goals using their God-given talents and gifts and through the sheer will of the human spirit. Even if you do not achieve your wildest dream, you will grow immensely through the process of trying. A dream becomes a goal when you act towards its achievement. The only thing that can stop you from fulfilling your dreams is you. Chasing after your dream does not have to be as demanding as mine to be just as rewarding. We are all wonderfully and purposely made, each having our own talents, goals, and desires. What makes pursuing your dream uniquely special to you is the sacrifices made and overcoming the inevitable challenges during the journey. Chasing a dream is not for the timid or weak-minded. It will take all your mind, body, and soul, and even then, the goal or dreams may not be fully realized if the dream is lofty enough. Set your dreams as high as you dare. Doing so will liberate your energy and inspire your self-confidence. By shooting for the stars, you may only reach the moon, but oh what a ride it will be!

Finisher photo with my family

We elected not to attend the post-race banquet in lieu of flying to Maui early the next day where we took surfing lessons and toured the moonlike crater of Haleakala, the largest dormant volcano on Earth. Once back home in Lubbock, I enjoyed reliving my race experiences with all my friends and family. Coach Tim wrote to me saying he was sorry my race did not go according to plan. He encouraged me to focus on the positives such as having qualified for the race, persevering under tough conditions and circumstances, and most importantly having my family there to share the experience with. The most significant and memorable thing he said to me was, "I am very proud of you as a person and athlete. It means a lot to me to be able to work with someone who puts so much effort into all aspects of their life."

I continued to compete in full and shorter distance triathlons for many years, even placing eleventh in my fifty-to fifty-four-year-old age group in the 2008 IRONMAN® Arizona full distance triathlon event. Having attained my dream in 2004, I never again was sufficiently motivated to train and race at the effort it takes to compete in the IRONMAN® Triathlon World Championship. I still enjoyed participating in the sport but in a less focused way and retired from twenty years of racing at the age of fifty-eight.

References

The Triathlete's Training Bible by Joe Friel

Precision Heart Rate Training by Edmund A. Burke, PhD

Going Long: Training for Triathlon's Ultimate Challenge by Joe Friel and Gordon Byrn

Total Immersion: *The Revolutionary Way To Swim Better, Faster, and Easier* by Terry Laughlin

ABOUT THE AUTHOR

Wade Wilson has a passion for pursuing his dreams and interests, some of which he has talents for and some not so much. He loves to challenge himself, and the bigger the dream the better. His goal is when God calls him home that he will have nothing left on his bucket list that he is healthy enough to pursue.

Wade's other interests include studying and teaching God's word, playing and performing classical guitar music, and traveling with his wife. He has provided motivational and inspirational speeches on his experiences in the sport of triathlon and of having the opportunity to compete on a world stage at the age of forty-six.

Authoring this book was a huge challenge and required all the skills and lessons previously learned about setting and pursuing lofty goals.